Robert de Smet

BERNARD SHAW

DICTIONARY

to the

PLAYS AND NOVELS

of

BERNARD SHAW

with

BIBLIOGRAPHY OF HIS WORKS

and of

THE LITERATURE CONCERNING HIM

with a record of the

PRINCIPAL SHAVIAN PLAY PRODUCTIONS

by

C. LEWIS BROAD

and

VIOLET M. BROAD

Republished 1972
Scholarly Press, Inc., 22929 Industrial Drive East
St. Clair Shores, Michigan 48080

First Published 1929

L.C. 76-131645
ISBN 0-403-00532-9

TO MAN
SUPERMAN
AND
BERNARD SHAW
WE DEDICATE THIS BOOK

PREFACE

Good wine needs no bush and a dictionary no preface. To this salutary rule a Shavian dictionary must rank an inevitable exception. For a book on the greatest of preface writers to appear lacking in so essential a particular would be a reflection on Shaw's own art.

Setting out to follow his example, we ought next to explain how our book came into being, we having failed in other branches of literary endeavour; but what G. B. S. can carry off with dignity would be reckoned impudence in us, so we will content ourselves with making a few modest claims, in the Shavian fashion, for our work.

We would say that it has been reserved to ourselves to place the final mark of public approval on the career of Bernard Shaw. Many authors have won the renown and rewards of best sellers, but only the very few and privileged have been reckoned worthy of a dictionary of their works. Of novelists there are not a score all told, and of dramatists (qua dramatists) Shaw is, we believe, the first since Shakespear. Thus, then, after public appreciation has been growing for over four decades, spreading from England to the confines of the civilised world, do we stamp the ultimate hall-mark of the gold of literature upon Shavian wares.

Personal experience of the need for a Who's Who to Shaw's literary progeny prompted the beginning of this compilation. We had not advanced far before we found that Shaw himself would once have welcomed an index to his works. In the preface to the Irrational Knot he refers to his hero as "Whatshisname", explaining "I have sent my only copy of the novel

to the printer and cannot remember the name of my hero".
If the author forgets sometimes, the reader does so ofttimes.
There are, also, those forgetful ones who, like the professor,
could never remember whether Mr. Collins appears in
"Emma" or "Sense and Sensibility".

Similarly some record is plainly needed of the writings which
Shaw has scattered with a fine promiscuity in the periodicals
of England and America. For a bibliographer he has been a
tantalizing author. Our net has been a wide one, but we cannot
hope to have enmeshed all the fish from the vast Shavian seas,
though it will only be Shavian shrimps that have escaped.

We have few acknowledgments to make. We found useful
clues in Henderson's official life; but, for the rest, books about
Shaw are critical rather than informative and would not repay
milking. We have to acknowledge the assistance of a co-
adjutor who gave up much of his annual leave to forward
the tedious compilation of the last section of this work and to
con over the rest, and we have also to thank Mr. Ernest Rann
for wading through the proofs.

Last of all, we would record our indebtedness to those
officials who serve the cause of research among the books of
the British Museum. Their good offices conduce to the diver-
sion as well as the instruction of the reading public in ways
little imagined. Was it not, indeed, beneath the dome in
Bloomsbury that Shaw penned those obscure shorthand notes
that were the germ of his first play and the foundation of his
fame and fortune? We too, beneath the dome, have written
notes of rare obscurity.

We have had one regret in our compilation : that it implies
that the bulk of Shaw's work has been written. It is not
so much that we feel that Shaw's activities will be circum-
scribed by the normal courses of senectitude—no doubt he
will set Nature's Golden Rule at defiance—but that he seems
to have become infected by the taciturnity of the Ancients of
his own creation. During the past ten years his output in
books marks a decline in the prolificity of the two pre-

vious decades. He is now verging, doubtless, to the vortex of pure thought, the ultimate Judith-envisaged goal of the sons of Eve. We, the shortlivers, are no longer, alas, to be enlivened and enriched by the wit and wisdom of his younger and more loquacious years.

C. LEWIS BROAD
VIOLET M. BROAD

WHETSTONE, MIDDLESEX,
November, 1928

CONTENTS

Note.—The synopses of novels and plays and the record of play
productions appear in alphabetical order.

HIS LIFE AND HIS WORKS

HIS LIFE

1856–July 26—George Bernard Shaw, born at Dublin, third and last child and only son of George Carr Shaw, for many years an old-style civil servant, and of Lucinda Elizabeth, daughter of Walter Bagnal Gurly, country gentleman of Carlow. Educated when quite a small boy by his clerical uncle, the Rev. William George Carroll, Vicar of St Brides, Dublin, the first Protestant Parson in Ireland to declare for Home Rule; later sent to a Wesleyan Connexional School (afterwards Wesley College), Stephen's Green.

1871—Entered Land Agency office as clerk, in the employ of Mr Charles Uniacke Townshend.

1879—Employed in London by City firm to exploit Edison's telephone, his "last sin against nature".

1879—Joined Zetetical Debating Society.

1884—Joined Fabian Society and elected to Executive.

1885—Appointed through agency of William Archer to the reviewing staff of the *Pall Mall Gazette*.

1886–87—Art critic to the *World* under Edmund Yates.

1888—Lectured to the Economic section of the British Association at Bath.

1888–90—Music critic to the *Star* as "Corno di Bassetto".

1890–94—Music critic to the *World* in succession to Louis Engel.

1895–98—Dramatic critic to the *Saturday Review*.

1897–1903—Vestryman and Borough Councillor, St Pancras.

1898—Married Miss Charlotte Frances Payne Townshend.

1904—Progressive candidate L.C.C., St Pancras; defeated.

1909—Gave evidence before Select Committee on licensing of plays.

1911—Elected Academic Committee, Royal Society of Literature.

1926—Awarded Nobel prize for literature; made arrangements for money to be funded and the annual proceeds used to encourage intercourse and understanding in literature and art, between Sweden and the British Isles, through a Society to be known as the Anglo-Swedish Literary Foundation.

HIS WORKS

PLAYS—*continued*

COMPOSED.		PUBLISHED.	PRODUCED.
1912	Overruled	1916	1912
1913	Great Catherine	1919	1913
1917	Heartbreak House	1919	1920 (New York)
1921	Back to Methuselah (Cycle of Five Plays)	1921	1922 (New York)
1923	St. Joan	1924	1923 (New York)

PLAYLETS OF THE WAR (Published 1919)

O'Flaherty, V.C.; The Inca of Perusalem; Augustus Does His Bit; Annajanska.

THE TOMFOOLERIES (Published 1926)

The Admirable Bashville; Press Cuttings; The Glimpse of Reality; Passion, Poison and Petrifaction; The Fascinating Foundling; The Music Cure.

TRANSLATION (Published 1926)

Jitta's Atonement, from the German of Siegfried Trebitsch.

SYNOPSES

THE NOVELS

CASHEL BYRON'S PROFESSION

"On its prizefighting side it is an attempt to take the reader behind the scenes without unfairly confusing professional pugilism with the blackguardly environment which is no more essential to it than to professional cricket." (Preface.)

Cashel Byron, son of an actress, is unhappy at school and decides to run away. By night he takes flight and knocks down one of the masters who attempts to stop him. In his travels he reaches Melbourne, where he takes employment with a "professor" of pugilism, Ned Skene, formerly prizefighting champion of England. Cashel shows himself to be an adept as a boxer, and, when Skene backs him, he founds his reputation by breaking the jaw of his first opponent—Sam Ducket. Seven years pass, Cashel has fought his way to fame and is champion of Australia and of the United States. He returns to England and goes into training for a new fight, taking as his quarters a lodge in Wiltstoken Park, Dorset. As prizefighting is illegal, he is represented as being a young man desirous of recruiting his health in solitude. During his training he is seen by the young mistress of Wiltstoken, Lydia Carew, who imagines him to be a sylvan god. Lydia, whom her father left one of the richest and best educated women in Europe, secures, through his backer, Lord Worthington, an introduction to Cashel. Although she regards him as something of a ruffian, Lydia finds that her emotions have been stirred by the young sylvan god, and Cashel falls deeply in love with her. He becomes apprehensive lest she should discover that he is one of the despised class of prizefighters and terminate their acquaintance. In Lydia's service is a footman, Bashville, who also is devoted to Lydia, and he discloses Cashel's secret to Lucian Webber, a Cabinet Minister's secretary, cousin of Lydia, and her ardent suitor. At a society gathering Cashel had employed Lucian as an object on which to illustrate his argument that more effort does not necessarily mean more force, knocking him down with a deft blow, and Lucian informs Lydia of Cashel's occupation. Lydia orders that Cashel is no longer to enter her home. When Bashville refuses him admittance, Cashel forces his way in. By a wrestling trick Bashville throws Cashel and runs off to warn his mistress. Lydia receives Cashel with the intention of breaking with him, but he declares his love for her, defends his profession against its detractors, and adds, in support of his suit, that shortly he will leave the ring with a fortune of £10,000. He is dejected on learning the smallness of his wealth compared with the riches of Lydia.

Cashel's final opponent is William Paradise, whom he first meets, with the gloves on, at an exhibition given in London for the entertainment of an African King. Paradise gets the worst of it and tears off the gloves in order that his blows may have more effect, and Cashel throws him, employing the wrestling trick he had learned from Bashville. The pugilists meet again at an illicit prizefight, and Paradise is being badly battered, when the police interrupt the proceedings. Paradise is taken into custody, but Cashel runs off and seeks refuge in the lodge, where Lydia happens to be working. She is very angry at finding that he has again entered the ring, but she assists in concealing him from the police, who bring in Paradise, bearing terrible evidence of the recent conflict. When the police have gone, Lydia, who is more disgusted than ever with prizefighting, tells Cashel that he must never see her again. In despair he surrenders to the police. Mrs Skene, the wife of his first patron, who has "mothered" him throughout his career, pleads his cause with Lydia. Cashel is again summoned to Wiltstoken, to be reunited, through the agency of Lydia, with his mother. From her Cashel learns that he is the heir to Bingley Byron, a miser, from whom he can expect £5000 a year. With this knowledge he hastens to renew his suit of Lydia, who had already decided to accept him. The marriage of the philosopher wife and the unsophisticated husband—who obtains a seat in Parliament—proves to be a happy one.

THE IRRATIONAL KNOT

"I HAVE found with some access of respect for my youth that this is a fiction in the first order; by this I do not mean that it is a masterpiece in that order, but simply that it is one of

8

those fictions in which the morality is original and not ready made. It may be regarded as an early attempt on the part of the Life Force to write a Doll's House in English by the instrumentality of a very immature writer aged twenty-four." (Preface.)

At an amateur concert, organized by the Dowager Countess of Carbury for the benefit of working men of Wandsworth, Edward Conolly meets Marian Lind, who is attended by Sholto Douglas, her devoted and jealous lover. Marian's father is a grand-nephew of the late Earl of Carbury; Conolly is an electrical engineer in the employ of the Earl, a scientific amateur. After the concert Conolly accompanies Marian's cousin, Marmaduke Lind, to the Bijou Theatre to see Lalage Virtue. Marmaduke, who is in love with the actress, is surprised to find that Conolly is acquainted with her—she is his sister Susannah. From her brother, Susannah learns that Marmaduke has deceived her over his name, and that his family regard him as the future husband of Lady Constance Carbury. The following day she has a stormy interview with Marmaduke, at the conclusion of which he offers to marry her in secret, for it would ruin him to do so openly; she declines, scorning matrimony, but she is prepared to live with him, and they set up an establishment at Twickenham. Marmaduke's relations try to rescue him from the misalliance. The Rev. George Lind, who is sent to interview Susannah, finds that she regards her position as being no less moral than that of a regularly married wife, while as to buying her off, it is she who is keeping the expensive home going, rather than Marmaduke. Douglas Sholto proposes to Marian, and his vanity is sorely wounded on finding himself rejected. Marian takes instruction in electricity from Conolly. She is ignorant of his relationship with Marmaduke's mistress, and asks Conolly to take a message to Marmaduke that his liaison is causing anxiety to the family of Lady Constance. Conolly leaves the employ of Lord Jasper to develop his electro-motor invention, and after becoming rich and a celebrity he proposes, by letter, to Marian, who, by keeping tryst with him at the Academy, signifies that she accepts him, but she insists that their engagement must be kept secret because of her father. Sholto returns from travels abroad and through the gossip of Mrs Leith Fairfax is induced to renew his suit of Marian. He is again rejected, and he accuses Marian of acting in concert with Mrs Leith Fairfax to make him ridiculous. Marian is forced to disclose her engagement, and her father at first forbids her to entertain it, but finding that his daughter is regarded as having made a good match he soon becomes reconciled to her union with a man he had looked down on as an artisan. Some months after her marriage Marian again meets Sholto. Conolly has been a model husband, but he has not made his wife happy—he has been too inhumanly rational, never subject to human weaknesses. Sholto again pays court to Marian, who elopes with him, and they travel to America. Marian finds Sholto to be selfish and petulant, and when he taunts her with being dependent upon him and threatens that unless she makes herself agreeable to him he will not marry her after the divorce, she resolves to leave him. Sholto returns to England and is bitterly reviled by Mr Lind when he declines, even when a pecuniary inducement is offered, to marry Marian. Abandoned by Sholto, Marian is obliged to move into poor lodgings in New York, and she encounters Susannah Conolly, from whom Marmaduke has parted because of her drinking habits; drink has ruined Susannah as an actress. Conolly, learning that his wife has been abandoned, crosses to America and arrives to find his sister dead, the victim of drink. He offers to take Marian back, but, sensible of disgrace and with the knowledge that she is shortly to become the mother of another man's child, she considers it wiser to decline. He does not contest her decision to end the irrational knot.

IMMATURITY

The first of the nonage novels, it has never been published. Referring to it, in the preface to Cashel Byron, Mr Shaw relates how the four other novels found serial publication, and says "This left me with only one unprinted masterpiece on my hands, my Opus I, which had cost me an unconscionable quantity of paper and was called, with merciless fitness, 'Immaturity'. Part of it had by this time been devoured by mice, though even they had not been able to finish it. To this day it has never escaped from its old brown paper travelling suit, and

I only mention it because some of its characters appear, Trollope fashion, in the later novels."

LOVE AMONG THE ARTISTS

"It is what is called a novel with a purpose. I had a notion of illustrating the difference between enthusiasm for the fine arts, which people gather by reading about them, and the genuine artistic faculty which cannot help creating, interpreting or at least unaffectedly enjoying, music and pictures." (Preface.)

While seated in Kensington Gardens, Mr Sutherland discusses with his daughter Mary and her lover Adrian Herbert, an artist, the appointment of a tutor for his son Charlie. An unkempt individual who overhears the conversation, and introduces himself as Owen Jack, proposes himself as a suitable candidate, and, largely through the advocacy of Mary, is appointed. After a short period of tutorship at Windsor, Jack is discovered by Adrian playing in extraordinary fashion on Mary Sutherland's piano, assisted by a drunken clarionetist, and Adrian, who had been antagonized, like several of the tutor's patrons, by Jack's brusqueness of manner, secures his dismissal. On his return journey to London, Jack quarrels violently with a fellow traveller, Mr Brailsford, who is escorting home Magdalen, his daughter. Madge had disgraced the family by running away to go on the stage, and at Waterloo Jack assists her to evade her father, giving her all the money in his possession. Shortly after the encounter in the train Madge again meets Jack, from whom she has been recommended to take lessons in elocution, in furtherance of her theatrical ambitions. In due course Madge again runs from home, and this time she is not recaptured, but obtains a part in a provincial pantomime, and then in a stock company, gaining, after a long novitiate, a considerable reputation. She is disowned by her family, but her father gives her a yearly allowance. Owen Jack is an indigent musical composer, forced by lack of recognition into making a living by taking pupils and acting as tutor. Fame comes to him at last with the production of his fantasia by the Antient Orpheus Society. In the production, the piano part is taken by Mademoiselle Aurelie Szczymplica, a Polish lady, with whom Adrian Herbert falls madly in love. Adrian, in spite of his mother's wishes, had adopted painting as a profession, encouraged thereto by Mary Sutherland, who had kept up his spirits in his early days. He was engaged to Mary, but he breaks off the engagement in order to marry the pianist. On learning Mary to be free, Jack proposes to her. She had never thought of him as a suitor, but is making up her mind to accept him, rather than cause him the pain of a refusal, when he divines from her face that she has no love for him, and he declares music to be the only mistress for whom he is fitted. After a fortnight's seclusion he produces a new masterpiece.

Mary Sutherland meets John Hoskyn, a man of business, engaged in the Conolly electricity undertaking, who does not share Mary's artistic tastes. After a three weeks' acquaintance John proposes to Mary, who refuses him, but he does not despair, and, in a letter, urges upon her the financial advantages she would gain by becoming his wife. Lady Geraldine Porter advises Mary to accept him, arguing that community of tastes are not essential for happiness in marriage; that John, being an ordinary man, is calculated to make her a better husband than Adrian Herbert or Owen Jack, genius being somewhat of a disqualification for mating. Lady Geraldine is supported by Edward Conolly (see Irrational Knot), who, from his own matrimonial experience, advises Mary to marry a man who begs for her and will never cease to need her. Mary writes an acceptance, and after its despatch would recall her letter, having discovered that her real mind about Mr Hoskyn is that she detests him. Adrian finds married life very difficult with his Aurelie, who subordinates everything to her profession and frequently leaves her husband for long periods to undertake engagements abroad. While in Paris, Aurelie encounters Charlie Sutherland, Owen Jack's old pupil, picking him up in the street, drunk and injured after a scuffle. Charlie falls in love with Aurelie and, while she is ministering to him, attempts to kiss her, whereat she admonishes him severely. Adrian learns that Charlie had passed a night in Aurelie's rooms, and, becoming furiously jealous, questions his wife's fidelity. At this the fury of her anger exceeds his jealousy, and he is made to apologize in the humblest of terms for having doubted her. Despite lack of community of tastes the marriage of Mary and John Hoskyn is a happy one, and Mary resumes her former friendship with Adrian, which causes no jealousy to Aurelie. Madge attempts to induce Jack to become her husband, but he declares himself to be wedded to his art. Charlie again declares his love for Aurelie, who again reproaches him for acting dishonourably towards his friend, her husband. At this point the story ceases.

THE UNSOCIAL SOCIALIST

"PEOPLE who will read the Unsocial Socialist will read anything." (Preface, Cashel Byron.)

Sidney Trefusis, who had inherited the fortune of his father, a Manchester cotton merchant, and who is an ardent socialist, has married Henrietta Jansenius, but finds, within six weeks, that in the company of his beautiful wife he is unable to devote himself to his Socialist purposes—to help liberate the Manchester labourers who were his father's slaves, and to bring them and their fellow slaves into a vast international association of men pledged to share the world's work justly. He runs away from Henrietta and their pretty London home. Masquerading as a labourer, under the name of Jeff Smilash, he seeks a retreat in a chalet near Lyvern. Not far away is Alton College, a girls' school, and he makes the acquaintance of some of the older pupils, including Agatha Wylie. In the character of Smilash, Trefusis does odd jobs at the College, and while he is so employed he is recognized by his wife. Henrietta's father, the guardian (unbeknown to Trefusis) of Agatha, has been summoned to the College—which is conducted on the principle of "moral force" without physical coercion—because of the unruliness of his ward, and Henrietta accompanied him. She had been broken-hearted at the flight of her husband, and she attempts to induce Sidney to resume life with her, but he is obdurate; in her presence, he declares, he is unable to carry on his work, and, after haranguing her on the subject of Socialism and the iniquities of capitalists, he induces her to return to London. Trefusis develops his acquaintance with Agatha, who is unaware of his identity, and who comes to believe that he is in love with her. She writes to this effect to Henrietta, little thinking her to be the wife of "Smilash". Henrietta, in a fit of jealousy, hurries down to Lyvern to reproach Sidney, who again succeeds in talking her round. After

his wife's departure Sidney discloses to Agatha the embarrassing situation she had unwittingly caused, and Agatha regards
him as having trifled with her affections. It had been a bitterly
cold night on which Henrietta made her sudden journey to
Lyvern, and Sidney is recalled to town, to find her dead. He does
not show the conventional symptoms of sorrow at his bereave-
ment, protesting against the "trumpery set of social observ-
ances" connected with funerals. After a lapse of some years
Trefusis meets three of his former acquaintances from Alton
College. While leading a party of men to demolish a wall which
Sir Charles Brandon, Bt., had illegally erected, blocking a
right-of-way across his estate, Trefusis recognizes the girl who
was Jane Carpenter—now Lady Brandon. For old times' sake
she asks him to lunch, and he meets Agatha Wylie, who has
not forgiven him, and Gertrude Lindsay. Gertrude, a beautiful
young woman of aristocratic birth, is a financial burden to her
father, a retired admiral, who considers it time that she was
married and off his hands, but she has rejected all her rich
suitors. She is a proud girl, always insisting on her social standing, and Trefusis resolves to humanize her—or "tame her", as
he calls it. He cannot help playing the gallant to any pretty
woman with whom he comes in contact, but does not realize
that, in the course of the taming, Gertrude is falling in love
with him, mistaking his interest for a deeper feeling. Chichester Erskine, an art critic and author of the Patriot Martyrs, a
tragedy in verse, is in love with Gertrude, and he becomes very
jealous of Trefusis. Erskine and Sir Charles Brandon are invited by Trefusis to see his collection of photographs, formed
to illustrate the arguments of Socialism. After haranguing
them at length on the evils of the Capitalist system, he induces
them to sign a petition praying that the holding back from the
labourer of any portion of the net value produced by his labour
be declared a felony. The decisive argument in overcoming
the reluctance of Sir Charles to sign is the fact that Donovan
Brown, a well-known artist, was one of the former signatories.
The baronet and Erskine are greatly annoyed, a few days later,
to find an announcement in the papers that they have joined
"an infernal socialist league", their names having been used
by Trefusis, as he had used the name of Donovan Brown to
them, to draw others to the cause of Socialism. While talking

one day with Trefusis, Agatha remarks that to avoid mis-understandings arising out of his friendships with women he should get married. This is a point of view which makes a sudden appeal to Trefusis, and when she jokingly suggests "Do marry me", he takes her humour seriously and in a short space has talked her into agreeing to marry him. Gertrude is heartbroken at the announcement, but Trefusis, to console her, promises to keep a special sanctuary in his heart for her, and persuades her to agree to accept Erskine.

THE PLAYS

THE ADMIRABLE BASHVILLE ; OR, CONSTANCY UNREWARDED

BEING the novel of Cashel Byron's Profession done into a stage play in three acts and in blank verse.

The plot of the play deviates only slightly from that of the novel (*q.v.*). It was written for protection under the copyright law against unauthorised performances of dramatized versions of Cashel Byron. An American stage version was actually played in New York, with the boxing scenes under the management of the eminent pugilist Mr. James Corbett.

ACT I, A glade in Wiltstoken Park.—Meeting of Lydia Carew and Cashel Byron. When his second, Mellish, protests against his infatuation, Cashel knocks him out.

ACT II, Scene I, In Lydia's house.—Cashel, who tries to force his way in, despite Lydia's orders that he is not to be admitted, is thrown by the footman, Bashville. Cashel defends his profession to Lydia. Before leaving he asks Bashville how so deft a wrestler can stoop to be a flunkey, and receives, in reply, a blow on the nose. Bashville bemoans the fact that, while for love of Lydia he blacks her boots, she appears as if she will stoop below him and condescend upon this "hero of the pothouse".

Scene II, A boxing ring in the Agricultural Hall, Islington. —In the presence of Cetewayo, Cashel engages in a bout with Paradise. Cetewayo and his chiefs, their emotions aroused by the fighting, run amok in the crowd, and Cashel earns the admiration of Lydia by the manner in which he sets about them.

ACT III, Wiltstoken, a room in Warren Lodge.—Cashel seeks sanctuary after his fight with Paradise has been interrupted by the police. Lydia conceals him, but when his mother, Adelaide Gisborne, the actress, comes to seek her son, Cashel, to escape her, surrenders to the police. Adelaide declares him to be the son and heir of Bingley Bumpkin FitzAlgernon de Courcy Cashel Byron, who, after three months of marriage, poisoned himself. The police are about to bear Cashel off, when Lucian Webber enters with an amnesty for Cashel's past, proclaiming him Deputy Lieutenant of Dorset, and conferring on him the hand of Miss Carew. Lord Worthington offers his hand to Adelaide, who accepts him. All leave for church.

ANDROCLES AND THE LION

"IN this play I have represented one of the Roman persecutions of the early Christians, not as the conflict of a false theology with the true, but, as what all such persecutions essentially are, an attempt to suppress the propaganda that seemed to threaten the interests involved in the established law and order, organized and maintained in the name of religion and justice by politicians." (Preface.)

PROLOGUE, A jungle path.—A lion, with a thorn in its paw, lies down to sleep, and is not perceived by Megaera and her henpecked husband, Androcles, who is being rebuked for having embraced Christianity. Megaera nearly falls over the lion, and Androcles, stepping forward to protect her, perceives the thorn in the paw. He extracts it.

ACT I, Roads converging on Rome.—Two parties of Christians are being conveyed to the Coliseum for martyrdom. In addition to Androcles they include Ferrovius the strong man, Spintho the debauchee, and Lavinia, handsome, clever and fearless. The Captain urges them, particularly Lavinia, to save themselves by paying the simple tribute of incense. Two young Roman nobles enter with the intention of baiting the Christians and are rebuked by Lavinia. Ferrovius, who first accepts a blow on one cheek and then turns the other, puts the fear of the Lord into his persecutor. Ferrovius is in perpetual dread that he will betray his religion by giving rein to his anger and offering violence to his persecutors.

ACT II, Behind the Emperor's box at the Coliseum.—The Christians are assembled for martyrdom. Spintho at the last moment finds that he is not yet ready for a martyr's death. He dashes away to make the necessary sacrifice, but, taking the wrong turning, runs headlong into a cage and is devoured by the lion. The Emperor offers Ferrovius the opportunity of entering the Pretorian Guard, but Ferrovius declines. Taking with him a sword, Ferrovius enters the arena, where he is to be despatched by the gladiators, but at the last his anger overcomes his religion, and he turns on the gladiators, killing six of them. The Emperor is wildly pleased by the feat of the superb fighter, whom he again presses to enter the Guard. This time Ferrovius agrees. The Emperor also orders that the

2

other Christians shall be spared, but the Editor protests that
the audience are expecting to see the new lion, and to save
them from disappointment Androcles offers himself as a victim. In the arena he falls on his knees to make his last prayer
as the lion gathers himself for a spring. At the sight of Androcles' face the lion checks itself, investigates his intended
victim and purrs like a cat. Finally he limps on three paws,
holding up the other as if wounded—it is Androcles' old friend,
and the two waltz around the arena. After having been chased
by the lion and saved by Androcles, the Emperor takes leave of
the Christians. Ferrovius says that, because the Christian God
forsook him and Mars has taken him back, he will serve the
gods that are and not those that will be. Lavinia declares that
she will strive for the coming of the God yet to come, but she
gives her admirer, the handsome Captain, permission to come
and hold debate with her. Androcles, threatened with the fate
of becoming a slave to tend the beasts in the arena, marches
off, protected by the lion.

ANNAJANSKA; or THE BOLSHEVIK EMPRESS
A REVOLUTIONARY ROMANCELET

"It is frankly a bravura piece. The modern variety theatre demands for its 'turns' little plays called sketches to enable some
favourite performer to make a brief but dazzling appearance.
Miss Lillah McCarthy, and I and Mr Charles Ricketts un-
bent to devise a 'turn' for the Coliseum."

General's Office in a military station on the Eastern front in
Beotia.—General Strammfest, whose family has served the
Panjandrums of Beotia for seven centuries, sad at now having
to serve the revolution, declares his loyalty to the old régime,
which he lives only to restore. He is informed that the beautiful Annajanska, the Grand Duchess, daughter of the Panjandrum, has joined the revolution, and what is even worse, has
eloped with a young officer; the officer has escaped, but the
Grand Duchess has been captured. Annajanska is brought in,
or rather drags her guards into the room. Under examination
by the General, she denies the elopement, and she asks leave to
speak to him in private; when he refuses, she chases all the
others out of the room at the revolver point. She then seeks to

dissuade the General from his attachment to the
again she says shall a Panjandrum reign; royal
and feeble that it has come at last to will its own ~~~~ ~~
to do otherwise would be to keep the people in their hopeless
misery, to thrust the rising sun of liberty back into the sea of
blood from which it has risen. Strammfest protests that under
the revolution there is no more liberty, and just as much hanging, shooting and imprisoning as under the old régime. The
Duchess replies that if the people cannot govern themselves,
if they will not do their duty without being half forced and
half humbugged, then some energetic and capable men must
always be in power; and she is on the side of the energetic
minority with whose principles she agrees—the Revolution.
As to the officer with whom she was supposed to have eloped
—she throws back her cloak and reveals herself to be in the
uniform of a Hussar—the Bolshevik Empress.

ARMS AND THE MAN

"IN 1894 I, having nothing but unpleasant plays in my desk,
hastily completed a first attempt at a pleasant one and called it
'Arms and the Man'. It passed for a success." (Preface.)

The action takes place at the house, in Bulgaria, of the Petkoffs, an ancient family. ACT I, Bedchamber.—Raina Petkoff
retires for the night, after kissing the portrait of her fiancé,
Sergius Saranoff, officer of the Bulgarian Army, now at war
with the Servians. A fugitive officer from the Servian Army
bursts in through the window, hotly pursued, he tells Raina,
and, at the pistol point, he appeals for assistance. He touches
the heart of the romantic Raina, who conceals him, and when
the search party have retired she feeds him with chocolate
creams. The fugitive, who explains that he is a professional
soldier, Swiss by nationality, who only joined the Servians because their country came first on his road from Switzerland,
shatters some of Raina's ideals and romanticism regarding
war. Mrs Petkoff is induced by her daughter to assist in getting the fugitive away.

ACT II, The garden.—Major Petkoff returns, the wars over,
and his wife and daughter are embarrassed to learn that the
fugitive, who got safely back to his army, has been indiscreet
enough to tell the story of his escape; fortunately the Major is

unaware of the exact identity of those who helped the fugitive. Sergius also returns, and, after a "higher love"-making scene with Raina, he is relieved to indulge in a more natural flirtation with Louka, the peasant servant girl. Madame Petkoff and Raina are embarrassed by a third arrival from the wars—the fugitive officer, who has come to return the civilian coat in which he made his escape, and before he can be hurried out of the place by the anxious women, Major Petkoff claims him as an old war-time acquaintance and enemy no longer—Captain Bluntschli.

Act III, The library.—Bluntschli, the professional soldier, is drawing up for the amateur Bulgarians plans for the foraging of three cavalry regiments. He is left alone with Raina, and refuses to play up to her romantic posturings, winning her admiration by declining to believe that in her whole life she has only told two lies—when concealing him. Discovering the truth of the concealment story, Sergius challenges Bluntschli to a duel, but the Swiss evades a meeting. Notwithstanding his engagement to Raina, Sergius declares his intention of marrying the servant girl, Louka. Bluntschli then announces himself as the suitor for Raina's hand. The parents demur; their daughter is the child of one of the richest families in Bulgaria, accustomed to very comfortable establishments. To satisfy them on this score Bluntschli reads an inventory of the property to which he has just succeeded under his father's will—200 horses, seventy carriages, 9600 pairs of sheets and blankets, ten thousand knives and forks, six palatial establishments and much more besides. The Petkoffs offer no further opposition to their daughter's choice of her chocolate cream soldier.

The comic opera "The Chocolate Soldier" is the musical version of this play. Shaw insisted that the programme at the first production (Berlin, 1909) should contain a frank apology for "this unauthorized parody of one of Mr Bernard Shaw's comedies".

AUGUSTUS DOES HIS BIT

A TRUE TO LIFE FARCE

"THE shewing up of Augustus scandalized one or two innocent and patriotic critics, who regarded the prowess of the

British Army as inextricably bound up with Highcastle prestige, but our Government Departments knew better. Their problem was how to win the war with Augustus on their backs, well meaning, brave, patriotic, but obstructively fussy, self-important and imbecile."

Mayor's parlour in the Town Hall of Little Pifflington.—Lord Augustus Highcastle, a distinguished member of the governing class, reveals to his secretary Beamish his acute sense of the seriousness of the war and of his own important relation to the winning thereof. He receives information that a woman spy is seeking to obtain possession of a state paper which is in his custody. A lady visitor, very attractive and brilliantly dressed is ushered in and is received by Augustus with an air of pompous condescension. After playing on his vanity, she explains that the spy against whom Augustus has been warned is her sister-in-law, her bitterest enemy. With Augustus' brother, "Blueloo", the spy has had a wager that she will secure possession of the document, a list of gun emplacements, and bring it to "Blueloo" at the War Office. Augustus is confident that he will frustrate the intentions of the siren. During the conversation Beamish enters with the document, which Augustus had left in the coffee room of the hotel. On the pretext of assisting him in concealing the document, the lady obtains possession of it and gives him a sham document in an envelope. She then takes her leave. Having, before witnesses, got into the street with the document, the lady returns, obtains permission to ring up the War Office, and informs "Blueloo" that the bet is won and that she had no difficulty in imposing on Lord Augustus. Only then does Augustus discover that he had lost possession of the document.

BACK TO METHUSELAH

A METABIOLOGICAL PENTATEUCH

"In 1901 I took the legend of Don Juan in the Mozartian form and made a dramatic parable of creative evolution. . . . I now find myself inspired to make a second legend of creative evolution, without distractions and embellishments. . . . I abandon the legend of Don Juan, and go back to the Garden of Eden. I exploit the eternal interest of the philosopher's stone which enables men to live for ever." (Preface.)

PART I—IN THE BEGINNING

"When Adam and Eve were immortal it was necessary that they should make the earth an extremely comfortable place to live in. . . . But the moment Adam invented death and became a tenant for life only, the place was no longer worth the trouble. It was then he let the thistles grow. Life was so short that it was no longer worth his while to do anything thoroughly well. . . . That is only the first step of the fall. Adam did not fall down that step only, he fell down a whole flight. For instance, before he invented birth he dared not have lost his temper, for if he had killed Eve he would have been lonely and barren to all eternity. But when he invented birth, and any one who was killed could be replaced, he could afford to let himself go. He undoubtedly invented wife-beating. One of his son's invented meat eating. The other was horrified at the innovation. With the ferocity characteristic of bulls and other vegetarians he slew his beefsteak-eating brother, and thus invented murder. It was so exciting that all the others began to kill one another for sport, and this invented war. They even took to killing animals, as a means of killing time, and then of course ate them to save the long and difficult job of agriculture. . . . So our fathers came crashing down all the steps of Jacob's ladder from paradise to a hell on earth in which they had multiplied the chances of death and disease until they could hardly count on the three score years and ten of life, much less the thousand that Adam had been ready to face." (Franklyn Barnabas.)

ACT I, The Garden of Eden, 4004 B.C.—Adam and Eve discover a dead fawn, their first experience of death. Adam cannot bear the knowledge that like the fawn they may cease to be. The Serpent tells Eve that there is a way to conquer death; it is by birth. Lilith, like Adam, saw death, knew that she must renew herself, willed and strove and gave birth to Adam and Eve; Adam must share with Eve the labour of renewing life. The Serpent, very Subtle, teaches Adam and Eve many new words and thoughts—of to-morrow, love and jealousy, of fear and hope. Adam is oppressed by the sense of the uncertainty of the future; he cannot endure fear, and the Serpent counsels him to bind the future by making a vow—to choose a day for his death and to love Eve until that time; then life and love will no longer be uncertain. Adam decides to live a thousand years, and says that he will love Eve all that time and no other woman; on which Eve undertakes to love no other man. The Serpent tells them that they are husband and wife, and they have invented marriage. Adam leaves Eve with the Serpent, who imparts to her the secret of creation.

ACT II, A few centuries later.—Adam is digging in a garden in Mesopotamia. Eve is spinning flax. Cain enters, in pose and dress insistently warlike, and he reproaches his father for sticking to the same old furrow and for lack of advanced ideas. He proudly proclaims that he is the first murderer; to be the first man is as easy as to be a cabbage, to be the first murderer one must be a man of spirit. Abel, he says, a true progressive, invented fire and killing and kept himself alive by taking meat, thereby reducing drudgery. After killing Abel, Cain forsook his former mode of living, took to Abel's way of life and became happier, stronger and freer. He has found that there is no joy like fighting. Eve is dissatisfied with the life of Adam the digger, and of Cain the killer; it was not for these cheap ways of life that Lilith set them free. Eve has better hopes of life; there are others of her sons, more useless, perhaps, weaklings and cowards to whom is given what they want because they tell beautiful lies in beautiful words, or weave lovely patterns of sound in the air; there is Tubal who has made the distaff, and Enoch who walks the hills and hears the Voice; they are always creating things or wisdom; Cain's boasting that nothing but the dread of death makes life worth while is stupid. Cain has an instinct that death plays a part in life; who, he asks, invented it? Adam replies that he must be thankful to his parents for inventing death for man and enabling him to hand on the burden of life to new and better men, and to enjoy eternal rest. Cain leaves them to return to his warriors. Through him and his like, reflects his mother, death is gaining on life; already most of her grandchildren die before they have sense enough to know how to live.

PART II—GOSPEL OF THE BROTHERS BARNABAS

A study overlooking Hampstead Heath about the year A.D. 1920.—The Brothers Barnabas—Conrad the biologist and

GEORGE BERNARD SHAW

Franklyn, once of the Church—have reached a common point in their researches—that the term of human life must be extended to at least three centuries; life is too short for men to take it seriously. Haslam, the rector (who is engaged to Franklyn's daughter Savvy), lends support to their theory by remarking that if he thought he was to live as long as Methuselah he would not stay in the Church; the parlourmaid, too, who wishes to marry, says she has only "one life to live and may not get a second chance", she does not think her intended husband would take her for better or worse if it were to be for a thousand years. Joyce Burge, Prime Minister in the war-time Coalition Government, and Lubin his predecessor in the premiership and rival for the leadership of the Liberal Party, seek to secure the support politically of Franklyn. Savvy urges the brothers to teach the politicians the long-life theory, not to let them continue talking as if the world only existed for their "silly Parliamentary game"; the electioneering cry of the brothers Barnabas, she declares, is "Back to Methuselah". The Brothers comply. Burge and Lubin, they declare, will go down to posterity as members of a group of immature statesmen who, doing the best for their respective countries, succeeded in all but wrecking the civilization of Europe; the political and social problems raised by civilization cannot be solved by such mere human mushrooms who decay and die when they are just beginning to have a glimmer of wisdom. Mankind must come to live for centuries. The force behind evolution is determined to solve the problem of civilization, and if it cannot do so through men, will find more capable agents; God proceeds by way of trial and error, and if man turns out to be one of the errors, he will go the way of mastodon, megatherium and other scrapped experiments. The politicians, impressed at first, are "completely let down" when they discover that there is no specific for longevity; that the Brothers cannot make longevity happen, but can only put it into men's heads that there is nothing to prevent it happening but men's will to die. To Lubin the Brothers appear to be the mildest of all cranks, if the most interesting. Burge promises to work this "stunt" after he has "adapted it", and he visualizes an election fought on the death rate and Adam and Eve as scientific facts. The brothers are much discomforted at the reception of their theory. Even Has-

24

lam is unconvinced, and Savvy, too, when she realizes that the parlourmaid might be one of those living three hundred years, sees how absurd it is.

PART III—THE THING HAPPENS

The year A.D. 2170; the official parlour of the President of the British Isles.—Mankind is shown to have advanced to the invention of a device for communication whereby people may see as well as talk with each other by telephone. By means of his switchboard, the President, Burge Lubin (who looks like a composite picture of Burge and Lubin), holds communication with the Accountant General, who looks like Conrad Barnabas. The Accountant General protests against having to receive an American visitor, but is persuaded to do so when it appears that the American may upset the calculations for the estimate of the average duration of human life, under which the people are by law required to go on working until they are forty-three years of age. The President next converses with Confucius, the chief secretary, a Chinaman; the British having realized that Government is an art of which they are congenitally incapable, have imported educated negresses and Chinese to do the work of government. By means of his switchboard Burge Lubin also has an interview with the Minister of Health a negress, whom he surprises at her toilet. She has inspired him with an infatuation. The Accountant General returns with the surprising information that an exhibition of films of eminent persons who lost their lives by drowning, revealed that the Archbishop of York is the same person as his fourth predecessor in office; the same also as Archbishop Stickit, as President Dickenson and General Bullyboy, all of whom died by drowning. The Archbishop enters. He is older than the Rev. William Haslam was when he wooed Savvy 250 years before, but is recognizably the same man, looking not a day over fifty. The Accountant General charges him with being a thief—a person who has lived longer than the statutory expectation of life entitles him to, and has gone on drawing a public pension when, if he were an honest man, he would be dead. The Archbishop does not deny his identification with the men who were supposed to be drowned; he has had, he explains, several careers under different identities, and the drownings had to be arranged in order to avoid the complexities of long-evity among a nation of short-livers. Mrs Lutestring, the Domestic Minister, enters. She recognizes the Archbishop and he her; she was parlourmaid to the Brothers Barnabas, and is another to have experienced getting back to Methuselah, being 274 years of age. She and the Archbishop turn critics of the white race. In devising brainless amusements and pursuing them with enormous vigour the English, they say, are the wonder of the world, but the maturity that should make them the greatest of all nations lies beyond the grave. "Mr Archbishop", says Mrs Lutestring, "if the white race is to be saved our destiny is apparent", and they leave to discuss the matter. Seeing that they contemplate marriage, the Accountant General urges that they should be killed as monsters, but he is overruled. Confucius points out that any of them may become long-livers. Burge Lubin, on realizing this, tells the negress that, infatuated though he be, he is no longer prepared, in order to meet her, to take the risks he might have run when he was still under the impression that his life was so short that it was not worth while bothering about.

PART IV—TRAGEDY OF AN ELDERLY GENTLEMAN

AcT I, Burrin pier on the south shore of Galway Bay, Ireland, in the year A.D. 30,000.—An elderly gentleman, sitting sobbing on a bollard, is found by a woman whose hat bears the number 2 (signifying that she is in the second century of her life). He explains that he has come from the capital of the British Commonwealth, at Baghdad, in a pious pilgrimage to the land of his fathers, the centre of the British Commonwealth during the period of antiquity now known as the "Exile". Under the strain of conversation with the woman (Fusima) the elderly gentleman becomes hysterical, a symptom, she tells him, of the dangerous disease of "discouragement" which afflicts short-lived people who converse with persons of her age. Zozim, a younger person of ninety or so, arrives to take charge of the stranger—Joseph Popham Bolge Bluebin Barlow, O.M. who is promptly called "Daddy" for short. The intellectual strain of talking with a man who is almost in his second century again results in discouragement for "Daddy," and Zozim summons Zoo, "a young thing of fifty", to take charge. "Daddy" still finds conversation trying with the native of a country where things are so entirely different from his own—where morality seems to be unknown and "improper female" is reckoned a contradiction in terms—and he resents the patronage which Zoo, as a long-liver, adopts towards him, "an ephemeral little thing". In a moment of extreme vexation "Daddy" accuses Zoo of being a "primary flapper playing at being an oracle", which causes her to experience feelings of anger she has never felt before; she warns him that he is doing something so evil in throwing words as if they were stones, intending to hurt her, that if he does not cease at once she will kill him. Never before, she says, has her nature thus been aroused, and it has altered her entire political outlook; hitherto she had been a Conservative, holding that the race of long-livers should remain apart in those islands, wrapt in majesty and wisdom; henceforth she will be of the Colonization party, who believe that the race should increase its numbers, colonize and exterminate the short-livers.

Act II, Courtyard before the columned portico of a temple. —A man, very like Napoleon I., places himself before a veiled woman of majestic carriage. As he is of the race of short-livers, she is surprised at his audacity. He explains that he wishes to have a personal interview with the Oracle; the prescribed ritual does not impose on him, and he wishes to speak with the Oracle face to face. Finding him an unusually sensible person, the woman explains that she is the Oracle on duty for the day. When Napoleon goes further to declare his disbelief in the "fable of discouragement", she unveils, and Napoleon, shrieking and staggering at the sight of her countenance, implores her to resume the veil. Having recovered his self-control, he explains that he is a man whose particular talent is to organize the slaughter of war, which is the only means whereby he can maintain his popularity; but if it goes on, he foresees that he will be execrated, imprisoned, perhaps executed. His question for the Oracle is how is he to satisfy his genius by fighting until he dies. The way out of his difficulty, she replies, is simply to die before the tide of glory turns, and she fires at him with the pistol he has given her. He falls with a shriek; but after the Oracle has gone haughtily into the temple he scrambles to his feet; she had missed her aim. Napoleon makes

27

GEORGE BERNARD SHAW

off, but is restrained by electrical isolation. The British Envoy, accompanied by his wife and daughter and "Daddy" Barlow, is ushered in by Zoo. Having learned of the intentions of the Colonization party, the Envoy diplomatically suggests a friendly arrangement between his own nation and the long-livers.

ACT III, Inside the temple, a gallery overhanging an abyss. —Violet rays flicker in the gloom, and the solemnity is enhanced by the playing of impressive organ music. Despite their previous assurance, the Envoy and his party are over-awed, and something supernatural about the Oracle terrifies them. The Envoy is so overcome that "Daddy" thinks it advisable to give him a stimulant. Under the influence of half-a-pint of neat brandy the Envoy harangues the Oracle after the manner of a politician. The question he ultimately submits is —shall his party decide on a general election immediately, or wait for the spring; and he appeals to the Oracle to repeat the signal favour conferred on his illustrious predecessor (who consulted the Oracle fifteen years before) and to "answer exactly as he was answered". The Oracle replies, "go home poor fool", and vanishes. The Envoy realizes that his words have been taken literally, and that his illustrious predecessor must have invented the sonorous phrases with which he returned; in order to obviate bringing contempt upon himself by repeating the words of the Oracle, or telling a lie, the Envoy decides to tell the British electorate the literal truth—that the Oracle repeated word for word what was said to his illustrious predecessor. "Daddy" finds himself unable to connive at this deception, and invokes the Oracle; he asks to be allowed to remain in her country. She warns him that he will die of discouragement, but he prefers that to going back to die of disgust and despair. "Be it so then," says the Oracle, looking steadily into his face. He stiffens and falls back, dead. "Poor short-lived thing," muses the Oracle, "what else could I do for you?"

PART V—AS FAR AS THOUGHT CAN REACH

In the year A.D. 31,920, a sunlit glade with an altar, in the form of a marble table.—A dance of youths and maidens is in progress. There are no children, but none of the dancers seems younger than a normal person of eighteen years of age. A strange figure appears, deep in thought, naked except for a sort of linen kilt. In physical hardihood and uprightness he seems to be in the prime of life, but his face bears a network of lines, as if time had worked over every inch of it through whole geologic periods. One of the youths reproaches him with being an Ancient and leading a dull life, never dancing, laughing, singing or getting anything out of life. To this he replies that one moment of the ecstasy of life as the Ancients live it would strike the young folk dead. The young people participate in the birth of a child, conducted by a She-Ancient. The birth takes place from a huge egg, which is sawn open and reveals the newly born child to be a pretty girl, whose age in the twentieth century would be guessed at seventeen. The newly born in the course of two years' growth in the egg, it is explained, has recapitulated the life history of creatures that preceded mankind and passed in fifteen months through a development that once cost human beings twenty awkward stumbling years of immaturity after they were born; the newly born will not need to die until her accident comes, perhaps not until many centuries.

It is Festival day and the artists are exhibiting their works in the temple. Martellus informs the party that he and Pygmalion have produced the two most wonderful works of art in the world—artificial but living human beings. After much research in the laboratory, he succeeded in producing the tissues and protoplasms (which Martellus moulded in human shape) which would "fix the high potential life-force". His human creatures are all reflexes and nothing else, automata that only respond to stimuli from without. Two figures, a man and a woman of noble appearance, emerge from the temple; they are specimens of normal mankind of the twentieth century. The woman claims to be Cleopatra-Semiramis; the man announces himself as Ozymandias "King of Kings". The woman, in a fit of temper, bites Pygmalion, causing him to die. The Ancients are consulted regarding the fate of the figures, and cause them to die of discouragement. The Ancients lecture the young people on the folly of such vanities as art. The Ancients have come to realize that their only true creative powers are over themselves, the final reality where they can shape and create at will. At first they made themselves into all sorts of fantastic monsters with three heads, ten arms, twenty hands and a hundred fingers, but then came the realization that this monstrous machinery of heads and limbs was only an automaton. The day will come, they prophesy, when there will be no people, only thought, and that will be life eternal. The trouble of the Ancient is that he wants to be a vortex, of pure mind, freed from the unnecessary machinery of flesh and blood that imprison man on this petty planet and forbid him to range through the stars.

The light fades. The Ancients go their several ways, the young people enter the temple. Out of the dark appears a vague radiance which shapes itself into the ghost of Adam. It is followed by the ghosts of Eve, Cain and of the Serpent. They pass their judgment upon their ultimate successors. The Serpent declares itself justified for having chosen wisdom, the knowledge of good and evil; Cain says that the earth is now no place for him; Eve finds that the diggers and fighters have all dug themselves in with the worms, the clever ones, her favourites have inherited the earth; Adam can make nothing of it, "foolishness" he calls it. Finally Lilith, first mother of creation, gives her judgment. Mankind, she says, have accepted the burden of eternal life, have taken the agony from birth, and their life does not fail even in the hour of their destruction. Is this enough, or shall she again go through the labour of birth? Her patience with mankind was sorely tried for many ages. They did terrible things, embraced death and said that eternal life was a fable. The pangs of another birth were already upon her when one man repented and lived 300 years. And so men redeemed themselves from their vileness and turned away from their sins. Best of all, they are still not satisfied, which is well, for of all things let them dread stagnation; in the moment that Lilith loses faith in them they are doomed. Because they are still not satisfied, but, after passing a million goals, they press on to the goal of redemption from the flesh, to the vortex freed from matter, to the whirlpool in pure intelligence, so she will have patience still, though she knows that when they attain that goal they will become one with her, and Lilith will be only a lay that has lost its meaning. Of life only is there no end.

CAESAR AND CLEOPATRA

"AN offer to my public of my Caesar as an improvement on Shakespear's. Whoever expects to find Cleopatra a Circe and Caesar a hog, will be disappointed. . . . I wrote it for Forbes Robertson because he is the classic actor of our day and had a right to require such a service from me." (Preface.)

ACT I, Scene I, Outside an Egyptian palace on the Syrian border of Egypt in the year 48 B.C.—Bel Affris brings tidings of the near approach of Caesar and his legionaries, who have defeated the Egyptian troops. It is proposed that Cleopatra should be sold to Ptolemy, but Ftatateeta, the chief nurse of the girl Queen, announces that Cleopatra has disappeared.

ACT I, Scene II, The desert.—Cleopatra is disclosed lying asleep between the paws of her favourite Sphinx. Caesar enters and, ignorant of her presence, apostrophizes the Sphinx. Cleopatra, who is awakened by him, hails him as "Old Gentleman", and says he had better come up on to the Sphinx or he will be eaten by the Romans, of whom she is in dread. On learning her identity, Caesar, who does not disclose his own, says that if she ceases to be a silly, terrified girl and plays the brave Queen, Caesar will not eat her. He leads her back to the Palace.

ACT I, Scene III, The Palace interior.—Caesar gives Cleopatra an illustration of royal authority by making the arrogant Ftatateeta (the power behind Cleopatra's throne) yield him obedience. Roman soldiers arrive and hail Cleopatra's new acquaintance as Caesar.

ACT II, Palace in Alexandria.—The young boy King Ptolemy Dionysus, rival for the throne of his sister, Cleopatra, recites to his court (in a set speech, much prompted by his guardian Pothinus) how Marc Antony established his father on his throne; that, with the aid of the witch Ftatateeta, Cleopatra has cast a spell on Julius Caesar to uphold her rule, but that this the gods will not maintain. Caesar enters and bluntly demands 1600 talents; his secretary Britannus, with more formality, declares this sum to be a debt due to Rome. The Egyptians demur and threaten to take captive Caesar and Cleopatra, a step forestalled by the summoning of the Roman Guard. Rufio, Caesar's "shield" and chief of staff, is indignant that Caesar, in his clemency, forbears to capture the Egyptians. Caesar debates how he may secure his return to Rome, as he is besieged by the Egyptians and the Roman Army of Occupation under Achillas. He orders the capture of the Island of Pharos.

ACT III, The edge of the quay of Alexandria near the mole leading to the lighthouse. — Apollodorus, the patrician, brings some carpets for the Queen's inspection. Cleopatra wishes to go by boat to the Pharos to join Caesar, but is stopped by the Roman sentinels. Apollodorus is permitted to take, by boat, a carpet which Cleopatra selects as a present for Caesar.

ACT III, Scene II, Beneath the lighthouse.—Caesar is apprehensive regarding the outcome of the Egyptian expedition. Apollodorus arrives with the carpet, which is hauled up by the crane, and when it is unrolled Cleopatra steps out. The Roman party find that their escape by way of the mole is cut off, and they decide to swim to safety. Caesar dives into the sea and Cleopatra is thrown in to him.

ACT IV, The Palace six months later.—Cleopatra has developed in dignity and wisdom through contact with Caesar, whose greatness has impressed her. Pothinus arrives in the hope of being able to plot with her for the overthrow of Caesar, but is rebuffed, and to Ftatateeta he expresses the hope that the Queen may perish. On Caesar's arrival he declares that Cleopatra is using Caesar as a catspaw, and that her throne gained, Caesar, for all she cares, may return to Rome or depart through the gate of death. Cleopatra indignantly protests, but Caesar says that he has already credited her with this "quite natural" attitude. Pothinus is allowed to go, but Cleopatra tells Ftatateeta to kill him. The nurse returns, indicating that she has done the deed, and the Queen piles jewels upon her. Caesar is furious when he learns that the man he had liberated had been stabbed. The populace are soon rising in the street to avenge their murdered leader, and Caesar, who has only two legions at his command, threatens to abandon Cleopatra. Lucius Septimius brings tidings that the army of relief is at hand, and Caesar is soon oblivious of all else as he makes his dispositions for an engagement with Achillas. He departs, almost ignoring Cleopatra, who becomes speechless with rage. Rufio learns that it is Ftatateeta who assassinated Pothinus, and Cleopatra bids him, like all her enemies, beware of the nurse. With a grim jest that he will "look to it" Rufio goes behind the curtains. He slays Ftatateeta.

ACT V, Esplanade before the Palace.—Caesar, on the point of departure for Rome, appoints Rufio as Roman Governor. He had forgotten to say good-bye to Cleopatra, who enters, attired in mourning for Ftatateeta. At first she refuses to say farewell, but when Caesar promises to send Marc Antony to her, she throws herself into his arms.

CANDIDA
A MYSTERY

THE action throughout takes place in the work-drawing room of the Rev. James Mavor Morell, the Christian-Socialist, hard-working vicar of St Dominic's, Victoria Park, E.

ACT I.—Mrs Candida Morell returns from a holiday to find that her father, Mr Burgess, and her husband have agreed to end their long-standing quarrel. Burgess was a sweating em-ployer, and through Morell's influence his tenders had been rejected by the local Board of Guardians. Candida returned, attended by Eugene Marchbanks, a youthful poet, whom her husband has befriended. He tells Morell that he is in love with Candida, whose life, he declares, is being blindly sacrificed to the parson's self-sufficiency; a woman with a noble soul, she is being fed on metaphors, sermons, stale perorations and rhetoric. Eugene claims that Candida really belongs to him. Morell threatens to put him out of the house, but is driven to wonder whether there may not be some truth in what Eugene is saying.

ACT II, Later in the day.—Candida tells her husband that part of his success as a preacher is due to the fact that his women hearers have all got Prossy's complaint—Prossy being Miss Proserpine Garnett, Morell's typist, who is in love with her employer—that really he is in love with preaching because he does it so beautifully, although, like his hearers, he believes it is all enthusiasm for the kingdom of heaven on earth. Morell's uneasiness is increased by this "cynicism" of his wife, and he becomes alarmed when she declares that Eugene needs more love; that the poet, "although he does not know it", is ready to fall in love with her; and she wonders whether Eugene, in after years, will forgive her for not herself teaching him what love is, for abandoning him "for the sake of my goodness, my purity", to the bad women; but for her love for her husband she would give both to Eugene willingly, for she cares little for her husband's sermons, mere phrases with which he cheats himself and others every day. Morell is driven to think that perhaps Candida may prefer the poet to himself, and to put the matter to the test, he arranges that she and the poet shall be left alone together in the house that evening.

ACT III.—Candida and Eugene are alone, sitting by the fire, the poet continuing to read his own and other people's poetry, although she has long since withdrawn her attention, the reading being Eugene's device to stall off the dangers of conversation. When she interrupts his reading he kneels beside her chair and asks if he may say some "wicked" things to her, to which she assents, providing it is what he really and truly feels, and is no gallant, wicked or poetic attitude. Morell finds them thus. He is disappointed to learn that the poet only "got to the gate of Heaven", without being either repulsed or admitted; Candida's preference is "still unsettled". Their discussions are interrupted, when Morell's curate (Lexy Mill), the secretary Prossy Garnett, and father-in-law return from the meeting at which Morell scored a rhetorical triumph; since then they have had a champagne supper, and Prossy's sobriety is none the better for it. On their departure Morell and Eugene agree that Candida shall herself decide between them. On learning of the contention and of the decision before her, Candida asks her "lords and masters" what they have to offer for her choice. Morell offers "My strength for your defence, my honesty of purpose for your surety, my ability and industry for your livelihood and my authority and position for your dignity". The poet bids "my weakness, desolation and heart's need". That, says Candida, is a good bid, whereupon Morell, from the depths of his anguish, breathes her name in a suffocated voice of appeal. Candida announces her decision for "the weaker of the two". Morell takes this to be against himself, but the poet understands that her choice is for Morell. The poet, "with a secret in his heart", leaves husband and wife embracing.

34

CAPTAIN BRASSBOUND'S CONVERSION

"ONE of the evils of the pretence that our institutions represent abstract principles of justice, instead of being mere social scaffolding, is that persons of a certain temperament take the pretence seriously; and when the law is on the side of injustice, will not accept the situation, and are driven mad by their vain struggle against it." (Preface.)

ACT I, In the seaport of Mogador, Morocco, the house of the Presbyterian missionary Rankin.—Sir Howard Hallam, a Judge of the High Court, and his sister-in-law, Lady Cicely Waynflete, a celebrated traveller, become the guests of Rankin, who recognizes in Sir Howard the brother of his old friend Miles Hallam, who emigrated to Brazil. Sir Howard explains how Miles married a native woman and, following his death shortly afterwards, his estate was seized by a trick by an agent, from whom Sir Howard succeeded in recovering it by means of the trick reversed. Lady Cicely wishes to make a trip into the Moroccan interior, and is prevailed upon to accept an escort. The business of providing escorts is carried out, in between smuggling operations, by Captain Brassbound, master of the schooner Thanksgiving, and his crew. Before undertaking to provide the escort, Brassbound warns Sir Howard that "in the mountains there is a justice that is not the justice of the courts in England", and that if he has wronged a man he may meet him there. Sir Howard has no qualms on that score.

ACT II, Room in a Moorish castle.—There has been an encounter with the Beni Siras, in which Marzo, an Italian member of Brassbound's gang, has been wounded; Lady Cicely, acting as nurse, completely disorganizes the arrangements of Brassbound, who angrily protests to Sir Howard, but his annoyance quickly melts before Lady Cicely's charm of manner. Sir Howard complains that he is not being treated with the civility due to a guest, to which Brassbound replies that he is no guest, but a prisoner; Brassbound explains that he is the nephew of Sir Howard, being the son of Miles Hallam, and he declares his intention of wreaking vengeance on Sir Howard, charging him with having caused the death of his mother and with the theft of his own inheritance; his intention is to hand

Sir Howard over to the Sheikh Sidi el Assif, an anti-Christian fanatic. Sir Howard, declares Brassbound, has brought to many a poor man in the dock the vengeance of society disguised by its passions as justice; now the justice he has outraged will meet him disguised as vengeance. Sir Howard is led out a prisoner. Lady Cicely undertakes Brassbound's conversion. If Sir Howard, she argues, failed in doing his duty as a brother, Brassbound is failing in his duty as a nephew; the time for Brassbound to have done his duty as a son was when his mother was alive; his idea of teaching other scoundrels to respect widows and orphans is the same justice for administering which Sir Howard gets £5000 a year. Before her arguments Brassbound finds his life's purpose failing, and he agrees to try to save her brother, but fears that it is too late. The Sheikh and his followers arrive. Brassbound offers to buy back Sir Howard from the Sheikh, who is willing to agree if he is given Lady Cicely in exchange, a proposition with which Lady Cicely declares herself to be delighted. The Sheikh's superior, the Cadi of Kintafi, marches in. He has acted, he explains, on the receipt of information from the American warship Santiago. He admonishes the Sheikh for having offered violence to the Europeans, and takes Brassbound and his men into custody. Before being led away, Brassbound turns to Lady Cicely, saying, "You have persuaded me to spare my uncle, will you be able to persuade him to spare me?"

Act III, Rankin's house.—Commander Kearney, of the Santiago, is about to preside at a court of inquiry on Brassbound and his men. Sir Howard is quite resigned to letting affairs take their course against his nephew; he can, he declares, be no party to concealment, but Lady Cicely has little difficulty in wheedling her brother-in-law into allowing her to give the account of what happened on the trip. Lady Cicely also has no difficulty in giving a version of the incidents which satisfies Commander Kearney, who orders the discharge of Brassbound and his gang. Brassbound, finding his life's purpose destroyed, appeals to Lady Cicely to let him "take service under" her by marrying her. For the first time in her life Lady Cicely learns what terror is, as she finds that he is unconsciously mesmerizing her, but as she is on the point of accepting him, a gun-shot is heard. It is the signal that the Thanksgiving and her crew are ready for their captain, who turns and flies. "What an escape," reflects Lady Cicely as he goes.

In the notes following the play Mr Shaw explains that he stole the scenery and atmosphere from the book of travel written by Cunninghame Graham, Mogreb-el-Acksa (Morocco the Most Holy)—"without which Captain Brassbound's Conversion would never have been written". The West Indian estate story, it is further explained, is derived from Mr Frederick Jackson, of Hindhead.

When Ellen Terry's son, Gordon Craig, became a father, Ellen Terry said that now no one would ever write plays for her, a grandmother. Shaw immediately wrote Captain Brassbound's Conversion to prove the contrary. The character of Lady Cicely was drawn from letters Ellen Terry wrote to Shaw.

THE DARK LADY OF THE SONNETS

"This little *pièce d'occasion* was written for a performance in aid of the funds of the project for establishing a National Theatre as a memorial to Shakespear. The play was not to have been written by me at all, but by Mrs Alfred Lyttelton, and it was she who suggested a scene of jealousy between Queen Elizabeth and the unfortunate bard." (Preface.)

Midsummer night, *fin de siècle*, 1500–1600; the terrace of the Palace of Whitehall.—William Shakespear, challenged by a Beefeater, explains that he has come to keep tryst with his mistress. He supplements the bribe of four tickets for the Globe Theatre, which he had previously given to the Dark Lady for presentation to the Beefeater (who only received two of them) with a piece of gold, and is allowed to remain. From the Beefeater the bard learns that the Dark Lady has similarly met other gallants, and, as a snapper of unconsidered verbal trifles, he obtains from the lips of the Beefeater several jewels of speech for his tablets, such as "frailty thy name is woman" and "angels and ministers of grace defend us". A cloaked lady, whom Shakespear takes to be his Dark Lady, enters from the Palace, and wanders along the terrace, walking in her sleep, muttering "Out damned spot, all the perfumes of Arabia will not whiten this Tudor hand". She wakes when the bard accosts her as his Mary. He discovers she is some other lady, and makes love to her, charmed by the music from lips which, he declares, he will kiss. As he embraces his new enamorata, the Dark Lady enters and, seeing her gallant philandering with another woman, gives each of them a vigorous cuff. The cloaked lady then discloses herself to be Queen Elizabeth. The Dark Lady is aghast that she should have struck the Queen, but the poet admonishes her for having dared to strike William Shakespear. The Queen's displeasure at such presumption melts before the bard's flatteries, and he craves a boon from her—that she will endow a great playhouse, or if he may make bold to coin a scholarly name for it, a National Theatre for the better instruction of her subjects. While professing sympathy with the poet's aims, the Queen says she is unable to gratify him, and she ventures on prophecy—"That until every other country in the Christian world have its own playhouse at the public charge England will not adventure". When Shakespear asks her to remember the theatre in her prayers, Elizabeth concludes, "That is my prayer to posterity".

THE DEVIL'S DISCIPLE

"DICK DUDGEON, the devil's disciple, is a Puritan of the Puritans. He is brought up in a household where the Puritan religion has died, and become, in its corruption, an excuse for his mother's master passion of hatred in all its phases. The young puritan finds himself starved of religion, pities the devil and champions him, like a true Covenanter, against the world. He thus becomes, like all genuinely religious men, a reprobate and an outcast." (Preface.)

The action takes place in the town of Websterbridge, New Hampshire, in the year 1777, during the American War of Independence.

ACT I, Kitchen of the farmhouse.—Mrs Dudgeon, whose brother-in-law, Peter Dudgeon, has been hanged by the British troops as an example to the rebel Americans, has to mourn the further loss of her husband Timothy, who succumbed to the shock. Mrs Dudgeon is always prating of her religion, and has among her neighbours a great reputation for piety, the result of being exceedingly disagreeable. The Presbyterian divine, Anthony Anderson, who comes to console the widow, brings her the disquieting news that on his deathbed Timothy softened towards his elder and prodigal son Richard, the Devil's Disciple, who has lived with smugglers and other scum of the earth, intelligence which the widow foresees may result in the passing of the family farm to Richard. To hear the reading of his father's will Dick arrives with other members of the family. In contrast with his mother, who prates of religion and is uncharitable, Dick is always boasting of serving the devil and behaving with charity. He is regarded with scorn by the respectable members of the family, and particularly by Mrs Judith Anderson. As his mother feared, Dick is, by the will, made heir to his father's estate. He warns the family that the soldiers of King George will shortly arrive in the town, and that they are likely to make another example, this time of the most respectable man in it, probably the Minister.

ACT II, The Minister's house.—Richard has been summoned to be warned that he is in danger of sharing his uncle's fate. Having given the warning, the Minister is suddenly called away, and his wife, to her great embarrassment, and Richard are left alone together, *en famille*, drinking tea. A sergeant of the British Army arrests Richard in the name of Anthony Anderson, "a rebel". Richard accepts the identity, checking Judith when she would correct the mistake; he tells her that while he goes to his death she must get her husband safely away. After Richard has been marched off, Anderson returns. He learns what has happened, calls for pistols and money and rides off post haste into the night.

ACT III, Scene I, British headquarters in the Town Hall. —Judith meets Richard before the court-martial, and implores him to allow her to tell the truth of how he has been arrested in mistake; she loves him, she says, and is ready to go to the end of the world with him. Richard replies that he did not do what he did for love of her—he cared not half so much for her husband or her as he did for himself; he could not take his own neck out of the noose at the price of putting another man's neck in.

ACT III, Scene II, The Council Chamber arranged for the court-martial.—General Burgoyne, the British commander, discusses with Major Swindon the seriousness of the military position, now that Springtown is in the hands of the rebels.

He does not receive much assistance from his subordinate, a man distinguished by his loyalty and devotion to duty rather than by brains, at whose expense the General indulges his satirical humour. Richard is placed on trial. He wins the admiration of Burgoyne by his verbal duel with Major Swindon, and for "taking the very disagreeable business so thoroughly in the spirit of a gentleman". Richard speaks enough treason to secure his being hanged ten times over, thus obviating the calling of witnesses, who might disclose his secret. Mrs Anderson, unable to stand the strain, blurts out the truth, but it is of no avail. It is a "political necessity" that an example should be made, and Richard will be hung at noon, unless in the meantime the real Anderson surrenders. Burgoyne receives a despatch telling him that some gentleman in London, leaving for a holiday, forgot to send out important orders. As a result General Howe, with whom Burgoyne was to have joined forces, has not left New York, and 5000 British will have to face 18,000 rebels in an impregnable position. The rebels ask for a safe-conduct, which is granted, for one of their officers to arrange terms for Burgoyne's surrender.

Act III, Scene III, The market-place, with gallows erected.—Richard maintains to the end the pose of the Devil's Disciple, refusing to accept the ministrations of the Chaplain. He is pinioned, mounts the cart; the noose is placed around his neck, and the clock begins to strike twelve, when Anderson rushes in. Swindon orders his arrest, but the Minister produces Burgoyne's safe-conduct; he is now a commander of the militia, and has come to arrange the terms of surrender. He asks for the release of Richard, to which Burgoyne accedes, "humane enough to be glad of defeat". When Burgoyne asks him how he, as a clergyman, is in the militia, Anderson replies that in the hour of trial a man finds his true profession; as the Devil's Disciple found that it was his destiny to suffer and be faithful to death, so he, who thought himself a decent minister of the Gospel of Peace, found that his destiny was to be a man of action. Before he is carried off by the enthusiastic townsfolk, Richard promises to Judith that the secret of her love shall never be disclosed.

The outcome of a suggestion made to Shaw by William Terriss (the actor who was murdered), the play was written for Richard Mansfield, on whom Dudgeon was modelled. (Henderson.)

THE DOCTOR'S DILEMMA

"It will be evident to all experts that my play could not have been written but for the work done by Sir Almoth Wright on the theory and practice of securing immunization from bacterial diseases by the inoculation of vaccines made of their own bacteria." (Preface.)

Act I, Consulting room in Harley-street.—Professional friends of Sir Colenso Ridgeon call to offer their congratulations on the knighthood conferred on him as discoverer of a consumption "cure" by the employment of vaccines. Mrs Dubedat implores him to save her husband, a consumption victim, but the doctor can undertake no more work; to cure Dubedat would mean abandoning another victim. Dubedat is an artist, and on being shown his brilliant work Ridgeon, who becomes infatuated with Mrs Dubedat, tells her that if she can convince his colleagues that her husband's life is more important than the worst life now being saved by the cure, then Dubedat shall be treated.

Act II, Terrace of the Star and Garter, Richmond.—Dubedat has been on trial among the doctors, who, charmed by him and his wife, give their verdict that he is "worth saving". Thereafter the doctors discover that the artist, with all his charm of manner, is in financial matters quite unscrupulous. From each of the five doctors he sought to raise a loan, from half a crown to £50, and one he has relieved of his cigarette case. The doctors are further disconcerted by a waitress at the hotel, who asks to be given the address of the departed guest, as he is her husband. They are distressed to think that the charming Mrs Dubedat should be the victim of a bigamist. The moral issues become involved, when Blenkinsop, an impecunious general practitioner, without medical skill or knowledge but of unimpeachable integrity, appeals to Ridgeon to save him from consumption. The doctor's dilemma—is he to save the honest, decent man Blenkinsop, of no particular use, or the rotten blackguard of an artist, a genuine source of pretty, pleasant and good things? There is for Ridgeon the further complication that if the charming Mrs Dubedat were a widow he might woo her.

Act III, Dubedat's studio.—The artist gives the doctors further revelations of his entire lack of honesty and morals. He tries to borrow £150 from Ridgeon, proposing that the doctor should get back the money by blackmailing Mrs Dubedat; he further suggests that the doctor should blackmail his patients into sitting for their portraits. He has no remorse for having married the waitress (a case of double bigamy) for the sake of three weeks' honeymoon on her money. He proclaims that all the doctors' moralizings have no value for him; he does not believe in morality; he is a disciple of Bernard Shaw. Ridgeon finally declares that he will "not lift a finger to save this reptile", and decides to treat Blenkinsop. Walpole at first consents to operate, but when Dubedat suggests that, instead of paying, he should be paid a fee as the subject of an experiment, the surgeon too throws up the case. The bland Sir Bloomfield Bonington ("B. B.") protests against the moralizings of his colleagues; they will be driven to the conclusion, he says, that the majority of their patients will really be "better dead", and he undertakes to treat Dubedat.

Act IV, The studio.—The artist is dying, "B. B." 's treatment having stimulated instead of arrested his disease. The artist commands his wife not to mourn for him or to remain a widow, "because people who have found marriage happy always marry again".

Act V, Bond-street Picture Gallery.—Just before the opening of the exhibition of the works of the dead Dubedat, Ridgeon discusses the artist with his widow, and he tells her that one of the reasons he declined to go on with the cure of her husband was that he was in love with her. The widow expresses surprise that he, an elderly man, twenty years her senior, should be thus infatuated; in any case, there is no hope for him, as she has already remarried. "Then", declares Ridgeon, "I have committed a purely disinterested murder."

"I myself have had to introduce into one of my plays a scene in which a young man defends his vices on the ground that he is one of my disciples. I did so because the incident actually occurred in a criminal court where a young prisoner gave the same reason and was sentenced to six months' imprisonment, less I fear for the offence than the attempt to justify it." (Preface to Plays by Brieux.)

FANNY'S FIRST PLAY

"BEING a potboiler it needs no preface. Its lesson is not, I am sorry to say, unneeded—that in an age when custom has been substituted for conscience, and the middle class are as dead as mutton, the young had better get into trouble to have their souls awakened by disgrace."

PROLOGUE: Saloon in an old-fashioned country house.—As a birthday present from her father, Count O'Dowda, Fanny decides to have a private presentation in her own home of the play she has written, professional actors to take the parts, professional critics, to whom the authorship is a secret, to be present. Her father is a man who finds England ugly, and who, refusing to recognize the vulgar nineteenth century, has passed most of his life in Venice. Fanny, who has been two years at Cambridge, fears that her play will be an artistic offence to him.

The Play: ACT I, Denmark Hill dining room.—Mr and Mrs Gilbey, persons of eminent respectability, are apprehensive regarding the fate of their son Bobby, whose fourteen days' unexplained absence from home is detracting, they fear, from that respectability. They are shocked to learn from Miss Delaney ("Darling Dora" to friends), a girl of the streets, that Bobby was sent to prison with her for being drunk and disorderly and assaulting the police. The eminently respectable parents cannot imagine how, if their disgrace becomes known, they will be able to meet Mr Knox (Gilbey's partner), his wife, and the rest of their eminently respectable acquaintances.

ACT II, Drawing room in Denmark Hill.—Mr and Mrs Knox, of similar respectability, are similarly distressed to find that their daughter Margaret has served a sentence of fourteen days. On Boatrace night she and a young Frenchman, she had picked up, were involved in a fracas with the police. She rid one officer of two of his teeth, while the Frenchman, Duvallet, felled his constable with a "magnificent moulinet". Margaret, far from being penitent, declares that the incident has enlightened her, "set her free from her silly little hole of a home and its pretences". Worse still, from the point of view of the anxious parents, she does not intend to conceal her experience.

ACT III, Gilbeys' dining room.—Bobby is discussing with the footman, Juggins, how he can break with his fiancée, Margaret, without "being a cad"—that is, incurring the odium of jilting her. Margaret arrives with similar intentions regarding their engagement, which dates from the cradle. They surprise each other with accounts of their recent police court experiences, and Bobby, though an offender, is scandalized that Margaret should have offended. "It's not the same for a girl", he tells her, and he does not think she can "hold him to the match now". They come to blows over Darling Dora, Margaret, who had Dora as a companion in prison, being disgusted with the snobbish way in which Bobby treats her. On the arrival of the parents, the three, joined by Duvallet, run off to hide in the pantry, to be entertained by Juggins. Unsettled by their children's sins, the fathers, finding that life will still go on even if they are not so eminently respectable, are beginning to kick over the traces. The religious Mrs Knox pronounces judgment upon them—that people brought up in the conventional way to be just the same as their parents were, had better stick to their conventions; if they don't they will find out that with all their respectability and piety they have no real religion and no way of telling right from wrong—nothing but their habits. The play ends with Margaret becoming engaged to Juggins, the footman, who is disclosed to be the son of a Duke, and to have entered domestic service as a form of penance.

EPILOGUE: Fanny's fears regarding her father are realized. The Count denounces the play as one which "amazes, outrages and revolts his deepest, holiest feelings". The critics are not so decided in their views; so much depends on the identity of the author. Flawner Bannal, who speaks for the men in the street, believes that Shaw is the author; Gilbert Gunn, one of the intellectuals, has no doubt that it is by Granville Barker; Vaughan is equally confident that it is Pinero. Trotter has solved the mystery of authorship and reveals Fanny's secret. All join in congratulating her. Trotter also divines that the "bit about the police" was founded on first-hand experience, and her father (like Knox) has to face the fact that his daughter has been to prison; Fanny was a militant suffraget.

THE FASCINATING FOUNDLING

"A DISGRACE to the author." Office of the Lord Chancellor, Sir Cardonius Boshington.—Horace Brabazon, a foundling, ward of the Court, approaches the Lord Chancellor, gaining an interview after a scuffle with his faithful clerk Mercer. As the father of all orphans in Chancery, his Lordship is besought to provide Horace with an engagement on the stage and a wife. Shortly after Horace's departure, Miss Anastasia Vulliamy, another foundling, beseeches his Lordship to provide her with a husband whom she can bully. Horace, returning to find his walking-stick, appeals to Anastasia as the very thing she wants. Horace is at first reluctant to become her lover, but when he learns that she too is a foundling, he embraces her as his own.

GETTING MARRIED

A LONG one-act comedy presenting a series of dramatic situations for the discussion of marriage and divorce. The action takes place in the year 1908, in the Norman kitchen of the Bishop of Chelsea.—It is the wedding morning of Edith, youngest daughter of Alfred Bridgenorth, the Bishop. Her uncle, Boxer, the General, has come to give her away, having fulfilled the same office in turn for her elder sisters, and, as at the previous ceremonies, he renews his suit of Miss Lesbia Grantham, aunt of the bride, who refuses him for the "tenth and last" time. Lesbia is not prepared to rear a family (which she wants) at the price of having a pipe-smoking, untidy man about the house. The General is horrified to learn that his brother Reginald, who has just been divorced (by his wife Leo, whom he knocked down before going off with a woman of the streets), intends to be present at the wedding. The uneasiness of the company is increased by the arrival, shortly after Reginald, of Leo herself. She does not evince the expected embarrassment; the knocking down and woman of the streets were only necessary ends for a collusive divorce, arranged for the benefit of Leo, who wishes to marry Sinjon Hotchkiss. When the time arrives for the departure for the church, the party learn that the bride has locked herself in her room and will not emerge until she has finished reading a pamphlet, and hard

45

upon this surprise follows a second, that the bridegroom, Cecil Sykes, is similarly engaged, the tidings being brought by Hotchkiss. The pamphlets finished, the bride and bridegroom arrive to express doubts whether they can proceed with the ceremony, because of the legal responsibilities attaching to marriage, of which they were previously unaware. Her objection is that she may be tied for a lifetime to a criminal lunatic; his that he may be made to pay damages for his wife's torts. The parties seek the advice of the Bishop, who is writing a history of marriage, and has reached the period when the Romans were abandoning a religious ceremony in favour of a civil contract; he suggests that Edith and Cecil should be the pioneers of marriage by contract. Soames, the Bishop's chaplain, formerly a solicitor, is called in to assist in drawing up the contract, the task proving very difficult. From their varied matrimonial experiences all have suggestions to make, and there is little they are able to agree upon—duration of the contract, custody of children, and vaccination and baptism being all subjects for dissension. They realize that the Bishop was in the right when he said that a contract would be worse than marriage, and he urges that the solution of all their marriage difficulties may be found in easier divorce. Ultimately Cecil and Edith go off on their own and return to say that they are man and wife (as the result of a ceremony at which the Beadle gave away the bride), an insurance corporation having solved the difficulty of the wife's torts, and the husband having undertaken that, if he ever commits a crime, he will furnish the necessary facilities for divorce. The play concludes with a scene in which Hotchkiss (who has been the victim, not the pursuer, of Leo) falls in love with Mrs George Collins, a siren, and Leo orders that her divorce from Rejjy is to be reversed.

THE GLIMPSE OF REALITY

A TRAGEDIETTA

IN the fifteenth century A.D.: An inn on the edge of an Italian lake.—A girl, Giulia, implores an aged friar to absolve her from a very great sin which she is about to commit in order to earn the dowry of thirty crowns, without which she cannot marry her fisherman lover, Sandro. When she mentions the name of Count Ferruccio, the friar remarks that she could not sin with a more excellent young man; but she explains that it is his life not his love she is to take; she is to lure him to the inn where her father, Squarcio, a professional assassin, will do the rest. "Will he, by thunder!" exclaims the aged friar, who, throwing off his cloak, reveals himself to be the young Count in disguise. He challenges Squarcio to fight him, but Squarcio says that it is useless, as he is too experienced with the sword. After trying to buy the girl from her father, the Count offers to marry Giulia if she will help him outwit her father and lover. When she refuses he nearly breaks down; is he, a nobleman, to die by such filthy hands? Giulia replies that he has lived by such hands, and poor people bring death as well as life; she will help the others to kill him, for he has a wicked soul. By her callousness the Count is inspired to rise superior to his fears of death; he has at last, he declares, after a life of make-believe, come up against reality; having tasted the water of life from the cup of death, it may be that his real life will now begin; he shouts defiance to the "dog of a bandit", and, when Squarcio appears, strikes him in the chest, but his dagger merely breaks on the under coat of mail. Sandro casts his fishing net over the Count. Instead of killing him—it is unlucky to kill a madman, and from what he has said about the soul they fear him to be one—they announce that they will take him to a place safe from the Cardinal, whom he has offended, for which they hope they will be rewarded—say with a wedding present for Giulia.

GREAT CATHERINE
WHOM GLORY STILL ADORES

"I MUST not pretend that historical portraiture was the motive of the play. The truth is it grew out of the relations which inevitably exist between authors and actors. Those who have seen Miss Gertrude Kingston play the part of Catherine will have no difficulty in believing that it was her talent, rather than mine, that brought the play into existence." (Preface.)

Scene I, Bureau in the Winter Palace, St Petersburg, in the year 1776.—Captain Edstaston, of the English Army, a handsome young officer of the Light Dragoons, is seeking an audience of the Empress. When the gigantic Patiomkin, favourite of the Empress, who is drunk and has just kicked a

47

general downstairs, suggests that the Empress will fall at the feet of so handsome a young officer, Edstaston rebukes him for his lack of chivalry, and Patiomkin in a fury rushes at him, only to be thrown by a wrestling trick. Patiomkin summons the guard, but Edstaston keeps them off with his pistols. Sobering himself with a great draught of vinegar, Patiomkin causes his men to bring some diamonds for the English officer, who indignantly rejects the offered gift. Having told Edstaston that, while enjoying the favour of Catherine, he may receive wealth and titles, but that he must not aspire to be Tzar or he will be murdered, Patiomkin offers to take Edstaston forth with into the presence of the Empress. The Englishman demurs; he is not dressed for the occasion. Patiomkin, assisted by his niece Varinka, thereupon picks him up under his arm and carries him off.

Scene II, Petit Lever of the Empress.—Catherine, who is attended by her court, has just risen, when Edstaston, still protesting against the indignity, is borne in. At the entrance of a stranger Catherine plunges back into bed, at the foot of which Patiomkin dumps the Englishman. Rebuked by the Empress, Patiomkin falls like a log to the floor, apparently dead drunk, and Catherine kicks him in disgust. She then turns to Edstaston, who, after somewhat undiplomatically denying that he shares Europe's admiration of her Majesty's policy and her eminence in literature and philosophy, pleases the Empress by his explanation that "it was rather natural for a man to admire your Majesty without being a philosopher". When Catherine withdraws, the courtiers pay deference to the man who, they imagine, is likely to become favourite and lover of the Empress; but when Patiomkin, recovering from his "diplomatic" drunkenness, says that Edstaston's fortune is made, as Catherine likes him, the Englishman does not manifest any delight; he is, he explains, engaged to be married to a girl who has just arrived in St Petersburg. Princess Dashkoff bears the command of the Empress for Edstaston to attend her. The Englishman hurries off, telling the Princess to say that he had gone before the command arrived.

Scene III, Terrace garden overlooking the Neva.—Edstaston explains the situation to his fiancée, Claire, and urges that, if they are to escape Siberia and the knout, they had better fly.

While they are talking, servants of the Empress take Edstaston into custody and bear him off to the Palace. Claire follows.

Scene IV, Triangular recess, communicating by a heavily curtained arch to the huge ballroom of the Palace.—Edstaston, trussed to a pole, is brought in. When the Empress enters he is thrown roughly at her feet, but the torture he was led to expect proves nothing worse than tickling in his ribs from her toe, administered to make him agree that Voltaire is a philosopher and philanthropist, which, as a Briton, he had emphatically denied. His shrieks are heard by Claire, who, despite the warnings of the courtiers that she will be sent to Siberia, bursts in. She starts to unloosen the straps binding her lover, but as she grasps the situation, that he has been merely tickled, she turns sick with jealousy. The Empress, "to show how much kinder a Russian savage can be than an English one", stoops to loosen the straps, at which Claire in her jealousy also pounces on them. Between them they set Edstaston free. The lovers are made to embrace before the courtiers, who are much amused by their embarrassment. Catherine, on the point of departure, wishes the Captain every happiness that his little angel can bring him, adding for his ear alone, "I could have brought you more". Edstaston feels her Majesty's kindness so much that he cannot leave without offering her a word of plain wholesome English advice: to set an example to Europe by marrying some good man, who will be a strength and support to her old age.

HEARTBREAK HOUSE

"A FANTASIA in the Russian manner on British themes."— "Heartbreak House is not merely the name of the play which follows this preface. It is cultured, leisured Europe before the war."

The action of Act I and Act II takes place in a room (of a villa in Sussex) built so as to resemble the after part of an old-fashioned high-pooped ship. It is the home of the ancient and eccentric Captain Shotover, who has retired from the sea and lives with his daughter Hesione and her husband. He is an inventor and is trying to find a psychic ray which will explode dynamite. Hesione has invited her friend Ellie Dunn to visit her, but is not there to receive her, and Ellie is discovered by the Captain. Hesione hopes to dissuade Ellie from the marriage she contemplates with Boss Mangan, the financier who rescued her father, Mazzini Dunn, from bankruptcy. Hesione divines that Ellie has a real love affair. It is with a man she met at the National Gallery, who tells her the most fascinating stories of his life. A stranger enters—Ellie recognizes him as her lover, and Hesione introduces him as her husband, Hector. Hesione is not jealous; very few women, she explains, can resist her husband. Hector is soon engaged in a flirtation with his sister-in-law Ariadne (wife of Sir Hastings Utterword, a Colonial Governor), whom he finds a most "accursedly attract ive woman". Hesione complains to her father that money is running short; cannot he invent something destructive? The money from his last invention has all gone—£500 for a lifeboat; living at the rate they do, they cannot afford life-saving inventions, cannot he make something that will destroy half Europe?

ACT II.—Mangan finds that Ellie, who had previously avoided him, is eager for an interview; he no longer has to press his suit, as she regards herself as engaged to him. Before this change of attitude his ardour gives way to reluctance; he explains that it was not kindness of heart that impelled him first to secure a financial advance for her father, and then take over his business; he, as a financier, could in that way acquire at least risk a business founded by someone who only lacked the financier's instinct to make it pay. This does not make Ellie alter her view about the marriage; her mother married a very good, but poor man, and Ellie is not going to do the same. When Mangan confesses that he is in love with Hesione, she retorts that she is in love with Hector. Mangan is reduced to hysterics by the ways of the "crazy house"; Ellie calms him and sends him into a hypnotic trance, and while thus semiconscious Mangan overhears the true opinions entertained of him by Ellie, by Hesione, who had pretended to flirt with him, and by Mazzini Dunn, who declares that as a captain of industry he is a fraud. A burglar alarm is raised. Hector marches in a villainous-looking man, the skin of whose ear has been taken off with a pistol shot by Mazzini. Most of the party are reluctant to prosecute, and the intruder threatens to give himself up unless they make it worth his while not to do so. Ellie asks the Captain's advice about marrying Mangan; she explains that it is a matter of money; young people nowadays know that a soul is a very expensive thing to keep, and she will pretend to sell herself to Boss Mangan to save her soul from the poverty that is damning her by inches. The Captain says that he sees his daughters and their men are living foolish lives of romance and sentiment and snobbery; the younger generation, as he sees it in Ellie, is turning from romance and sentiment and snobbery to money, comfort and hard common sense; she is going to let the fear of poverty govern her life, and her reward will be that she will eat but will not live. Ellie is sorry that the Captain, old as he is, may still have a wife alive, a black one; she feels so happy again, although when she broke her heart over Hector she thought she never would be.

ACT III, The party assembled in the garden.—Lady Utterword has a ready solution for putting the crazy house aright. All that is needed, she says, to make it sensible, healthy and pleasant is horses; wherever in England there are natural, wholesome and contented people, there the stables are the real centre of the household. Mangan, to the merriment of the party, declares that, as a practical man of business, he is joining the Government as a dictator of a great Government department. Ellie astounds the party by announcing that she has no intention of marrying Mangan, it would be bigamy—she has already become Captain Shotover's white wife; she has given the Captain her broken heart and strong soul, he being her soul's natural captain, her spiritual husband, and a second father. Hector is anxious for the future of the country "left to chance and Mangan, and his mutual admiration gang". Captain Shotover prophesies that with the Captain on his back drinking, and the crew gambling in the forecastle, the ship of England will strike and sink; the laws of God will not be suspended in favour of England because they were born in it. A distant explosion is heard and the lights in the house go out; an air raid is threatened. Hector, to shew his bravery, turns the lights on full and a bomb falls at the bottom of the garden, on the dynamite pit, killing Boss Mangan and the burglar. The survivors find the world tedious and dull once the danger has passed.

HOW HE LIED TO HER HUSBAND

"Nothing in the theatre is staler than the situation of the husband, wife and lover, or the fun of knockabout farce. I have taken both and got an original play out of them, as anybody else can if he will only look about him for his material instead of plagiarizing Othello and the thousand plays that have proceeded on Othello's romantic assumptions and false point of honour." (Preface.)

A flat in Cromwell-road.—Mrs Aurora Bompas is greatly distressed because the love poems Henry Apjohn, the boy poet, has addressed to her are lost, stolen perhaps by a sister-in-law, and she fears they will reach her husband. The poet wishes her to take the straightforward course, and fly with him, after explaining matters to the husband. Aurora has no intention either of facing a scandal or leaving her husband, and implores him to take the "honourable course of a gentleman". The poet is chagrined to find how shallow are the feelings of his enamorata. To save her honour he pretends to the husband that the poems were not inspired by Aurora Bompas, but Aurora of the dawn; for Mrs Bompas his feelings are cold, and it is absurd to suggest that he should have written the poems to her. At this Bompas is furious; his wife, he declares, has been admired by much better men than "you soapy-headed little puppy". Aurora has to separate her husband and her lover, who meet in conflict. The poet, losing self-control in his anger at having banged his head, blurts out the truth that the poems were written for Mrs Bompas, whom he adored. On hearing this, Bompas passes from rage to jubilation, gratified that his Aurora has secured another admirer, and he seeks permission to publish the poems, suggesting "To Aurora" as the title of the book. The poet speaks the last line of the play—"I should call it 'How he lied to her husband'".

Written in 1905 to eke out Mr Arnold Daly's bill in New York. Daly had asked for a play about Cromwell.

THE INCA OF PERUSALEM

"I must remind the reader that this playlet was written when its principal character, far from being a fallen foe and virtually a prisoner in our victorious hands, was still the Caesar whose legions we were resisting with our hearts in our mouths."

A brief prologue before the curtain.—Ermyntrude, widow of a millionaire, now reduced to poverty, announces that as her father, the Archdeacon, cannot allow her more than £150 a year she will take service with a Princess.

Hotel sitting room.—A self-effasive Princess is ushered in by a manager, who imposes upon her graciousness. Ermyntrude, who now presents a plain appearance in a long straight waterproof, has no difficulty in getting herself appointed as lady's maid. An officer of the Inca of Perusalem is announced. He has come to arrange a marriage between one of the Inca's sons and the Princess. When Ermyntrude declares that it is the Inca travelling incognito, the Princess is alarmed, and Ermyntrude offers to see the visitor and arrange matters. She receives the self-styled captain with the utmost haughtiness and, as Princess, is presented with a jewel as token of the regard of the Allerhöchst. The visitor is impressed by the snubs and flattery he alternately receives, and divulges his identity as Inca. He begs Ermyntrude, whom he has recognized as the Archdeacon's daughter, to marry him, offering to turn Mahometan to facilitate matters. Ermyntrude refuses him because he is too poor, bankrupted by the war he is waging. Regarding the war—which will result, he says, in the loss of his throne, but, he hopes, in his ultimate election as super-president of the republic—the Inca expresses amazement that his subjects tolerate it; for years he gave them art, literature and science, and they ridiculed him; now he gives them death in its frightfullest forms and they are devoted. Before leaving (without bothering to see the Princess), the Inca offers to take Ermyntrude for a drive round the town. She is delighted to accept, promising to "refuse any incorrect proposals" from him.

JOHN BULL'S OTHER ISLAND

"It was written in 1904 at the request of Mr William Butler Yeats as a patriotic contribution to the Repertory of the Irish Literary Theatre. Like most people who have asked me to write plays Mr Yeats got rather more than he bargained for. ... The play was at that time beyond the resources of the New

Abbey Theatre. . . . There was another reason for changing the destination of John Bull's Other Island. It was uncongenial to the whole spirit of the neo-Gaelic movement, which is bent on creating a new Ireland after its own ideal, whereas my play is a very uncompromising presentment of the real old Ireland." (Preface.)

ACT I, Office in London.—Tom Broadbent is preparing to visit Rosscullen, where the syndicate of which he is chief have a mortgage interest. Although a captain of industry, he is sufficiently under the influence of his romantic conceptions of an Irish brogue and Celticism to advance £5 to a worthless Irishman, Tim Haffigan. Broadbent is anxious to persuade his partner, Larry Doyle, to accompany him to Rosscullen, but Larry is not inclined to visit his birthplace, which he has never seen since he left it to seek his fortune in America. This reluctance, Broadbent discovers, is partly inspired by the presence in Rosscullen of Nora Reilly, who for eighteen years has been waiting to marry Larry. Realizing the extent to which the sentimental Broadbent is under the influence of Irish romance, Larry agrees to go, in the hope that his partner may become a "chance" for Nora (as a husband) and for himself (for freedom).

ACT II, Hillside at Rosscullen.—On the first night of his arrival Broadbent, inspired by a romantic moonlit scene and two glasses of potcheen, proposes to Nora Reilly. Nora, as yet unaware of the feelings of Larry, bids him behave himself, and though he protests his earnestness, she induces him to believe that the potcheen has unbalanced him.

ACT III, Garden in Rosscullen.—Larry is invited by a deputation to become Parliamentary candidate for the division, but shews that his views regarding Ireland's future would not be acceptable to those seeking to honour him. Broadbent addresses the gathering and is adopted in Larry's stead. As a first step towards propitiating the electorate he arranges to drive home Matthew Haffigan with the pig he has bought.

ACT IV, A parlour in Rosscullen.—The deputation are enjoying the joke of the pig in the car of the prospective candidate: the car wrecked a crockery stall and the pound in Rosscullen market, after killing the pig. Larry and Nora meet alone for the first time, and Nora is shewn that though she has waited eighteen years she is not likely to become Mrs Larry, and when Larry walks off she breaks down. Broadbent finds her sobbing, consoles her, and eventually she agrees to marry him. Larry returns and tells Nora that he has at last discovered what he ought to say to her; she replies that he has thought of that too late, she is engaged to Broadbent. "That", says Larry, "is the very thing I was going to advise you to do." The play ends in a further debating scene, a discussion of Broadbent's plans for constructing at Rosscullen a hotel and golf links for the entertainment of plutocratic week-enders from England.

MAJOR BARBARA

"In the millionaire, Undershaft, I have represented a man who has become intellectually and spiritually, as well as practically, conscious of the irresistible natural truth, which we all abhor and repudiate; to wit, that the greatest of evils and worst of crimes is poverty, and that our first duty—a duty to which every other consideration should be sacrificed—is not to be poor." (Preface.)

Act I, Lady Britomart Undershaft's house, Wilton-crescent.—Lady Britomart, in family council with her son Stephen, reveals that she separated from her husband several years before because he proposed to follow the Undershaft tradition and appoint a foundling, rather than his own son, to succeed to the inheritance of the Undershaft and Lazarus explosives factory. She has invited her husband to meet her to secure increased allowances for her daughters—Sarah, engaged to a man who will ultimately be a millionaire, and Barbara, Major in the Salvation Army, engaged to Cusins, a Greek Professor. Undershaft has to be introduced to his own children. As a maker of canons he causes surprise by taking an interest in the affairs of the Salvation Army, and he explains that he has a religion, a morality, in the same manner as the others who condemn the explosives business, only it is not the same religion. Barbara invites her father to come and risk conversion to her religion at her shelter in Canning Town, and he accepts on condition that she will visit him at his works at Perivale St Andrews, warning her that the visit may induce her to give up the Salvation Army.

Act II, Salvation shelter, Canning Town.—Bread and

treacle is being shared by a number of down-and-outs who are ministered to by Jenny Hill. Bill Walker, a rough customer, comes in threatening violence against members of the organization which has robbed him of his "girl", and he executes his threats on Jenny Hill and an old woman, Rummy Mitchens. Major Barbara reasons with Bill, whose conscience responds to the expert touch of Salvationist wooing his soul. Undershaft, discussing with Cusins the religion of the Salvation Army, makes a profession of his own faith—that there are only two things necessary to salvation, money and gunpowder; honour, justice, love and so forth are the graces and luxuries of a strong and rich life. He declares his intention of converting Major Barbara to his religion of freedom and power by buying the Salvation Army. Bill Walker tries to buy forgiveness for having broken the jaw of Jenny, but is told by Barbara that the Army is not to be bought. Commissioner Baines announces that Bodger, the whisky distiller, has promised £5000 for the Army's funds if a second £5000 can be collected. Undershaft offers to subscribe that sum, and Mrs Baines has no scruples in accepting, for the purposes of the Army, the profits of war, as of drink. Barbara demurs; she finds that her faith in the Army is lost, and she takes off her badge in token of resignation. Bill Walker also declaims against an organization which will not afford him forgiveness for a pound, but will accept the capitalists' thousands.

Act III, Scene I, Wilton-crescent.—Stephen discusses his future with both his parents, declining, quite apart from the foundling custom, to have anything to do with his father's business. Undershaft advises him that, as he does not know enough to qualify for any of the professions, he had better try politics. The family leave to inspect the factory.

Scene II, Explosives factory, Perivale St Andrews.—The family are amazed at the factory, which does not accord with their evil expectations. To Cusins, the Greek sceptic, it is "frightfully, immorally, unanswerably perfect", while the supercilious Stephen is impressed by the "triumph of organization". Cusins discloses a possible solution of the inheritance problem: he is the son of a marriage between a man and his deceased wife's sister, valid in Australia, where it took place, but not in England, where, consequently, he is a foundling.

Undershaft offers to take him into partnership, and, after moralizing on the ethics of ammunition-making, Cusins decides to accept the offer, to sell his soul for power, that, unlike his spiritual Greek, can be "wielded" by all men. Barbara tells him that if he had not accepted she would have given him up for the man who did; she has recovered her faith, as a result of her visit to the factory, where there are so many souls waiting to be saved, not weak souls in starved bodies, but full-fed, quarrelsome, snobbish creatures. "There", she proclaims, "is Salvation needed and Major Barbara will die with the colours." Barbara makes arrangements to take a house in the village for herself and Cusins.

Shaw made the acquaintance, at Ayot St Lawrence, of a young man and neighbour, Mr Charles McEvoy, whose father fought on the side of the confederacy in the American Civil War. He was a most gentle and humane man and established a factory for the manufacture of high explosives. There is the germ idea of Andrew Undershaft. (Henderson.)

MAN AND SUPERMAN

EPISTLE dedicatory to Arthur Bingham Walkley—"You once asked me why I did not write a Don Juan play. The day of reckoning has arrived. Your Don Juan has come to birth as a stage projection of the tragi-comic love chase of the man by the woman; and my Don Juan is the quarry instead of the huntsman. Yet he is the true Don Juan, defying to the last the fate which finally overtakes him."

ACT I, A study in Portland Place.—Roebuck Ramsden, an elderly man of business, condoles with Octavius Robinson, the young poet, on the death of his friend Whitefield. Ramsden expects to be appointed guardian of Whitefield's daughter Ann, and he hopes that she and Octavius will marry; he also warns the poet against his friend John Tanner, author of the Revolutionist's Handbook, a Socialist whom he regards as an immoral person. Tanner arrives with the information that he has been appointed by the will to act with Ramsden as the guardian of Ann. Ramsden declares that he will refuse to act with such a man, and Tanner would gladly withdraw, but he prophesies that it will be of no use their proposing anything;

Ann will dispose of herself as she thinks fit, a forecast Ann soon justifies. She is a masterful, fascinating young woman, whom Tanner regards as an unscrupulous siren, and Octavius, who is devoted to her, as an ideal among womankind. "Terrible news" is brought by Octavius' sister Violet, who, Ramsden fears, is about to become an unmarried mother. Tanner congratulates Violet on what she has dared to do, on the assumption that she is not married. Violet, flushing with indignation, repudiates his compliments, forced to declare that she is a married woman, under the necessity of keeping her marriage secret for the sake of her husband.

ACT II, A carriage drive in the park of the house near Richmond of Mrs Whitefield.—Tanner is watching his chauffeur, Henry Straker, repair his motor car. Octavius claims his sympathy; Ann has rejected his suit. Tanner declares that that is only because she has not finished playing with him; he need not worry, he is the marked-out victim, not Ann's pursuer, but pursued by her. Octavius gives Tanner a note from Rhoda Whitefield, who writes that Ann (her elder sister) has forbidden her to go for a motor trip with Tanner or "to be alone with him on any occasion". Ignorant of the note, Ann informs Tanner that Rhoda has a headache and cannot motor with him, and when Tanner accuses her of being an "incorrigible liar" she implies, falsely, that she was acting under instruction from her mother. Tanner, having declaimed against the tyranny of mothers, challenges Ann to show her independence by coming with him on a Continental motor trip; he is chagrined to find her accepting. Hector Malone, a young American, reveals his devotion to Violet, and is warned by the others that she is a married woman. Left alone together, Hector and Violet exchange kisses—he is the secret husband; his father, a millionaire, has threatened to cut him off without a penny if he marries anyone less than the daughter of a duchess. Ashamed of having to deceive his English friends, Hector wishes to avow his marriage and work for his wife, but Violet will "not have her marriage spoiled". Tanner consults his chauffeur regarding his Continental trip. Straker tells him that he is the man Ann is really bent on capturing, "the bee, the spider, the marked-down victim". Fearful of such a destiny, Tanner calls upon Straker to set up a new motoring record to get him away across the Continent out of the reach of Ann.

ACT III, Evening in the Sierra Nevada.—Mendoza and his gang of brigands resume their evening debates on Anarchists and Social Democrats, and are interrupted by the approach of a motor. It is successfully held up, and Tanner, with his chauffeur, is brought in a prisoner. He accepts his capture in good part and Mendoza confides to him his life story—of how he, once a successful waiter, was driven to become a brigand by disappointment in love. His enamorata is Louisa, sister of Straker.

DON JUAN IN HELL

The bandits and their captives sleep. The darkness deepens. The Sierra scenes give way to omnipresent nothing. To the accompaniment of ghostly music a man, incorporeal but visible, is revealed in the void; a Spanish nobleman of the fifteenth to sixteenth century, Don Juan, with a curious suggestion of Tanner: Juan Tenorio—John Tanner. An old crone wanders into the void. She is a new-comer, having died that morning, and she is distressed to learn that she is in Hell. She expected to go to Heaven, and she laments wasted opportunities for wickedness and wasted, too, her good deeds. She declines to believe it is Hell; she feels no pain, at which Juan declares there can have been no mistake; she was intentionally damned, because as Hell is the place for the wicked, the wicked are comfortable in it. Hell, he declares, is the reward of duty; it is the home of honour, duty and justice and the rest of the seven deadly virtues in whose name all the wickedness on earth is done. From Juan the old woman learns that in Hell she may assume what age she desires, and, electing to be twenty-seven, she becomes a handsome young woman, who would be mistaken for Ann Whitefield. Juan greets her as Dona Ana de Ulloa, with whom he had one of his affairs; she summoned her father, with whom Juan had to fight a duel, running him through. Ana, who erected a statue to her father, is pleased to learn that he is in Heaven. The father, the Commander of Calatrava, enters as a statue closely resembling Ramsden in appearance; he has retained the form the sculptor gave him, because he was so much more admired in marble than he was in his own person. He announces his intention of leaving

Heaven, where existence has bored him. The Devil (who is not unlike Mendoza) bids him welcome to Hell. Don Juan is also bored—with his existence in Hell—and declares his intention of proceeding to Heaven. The Devil seeks to dissuade him, emphasizing the attractions of his kingdom—its warmth of heart, love and joy. Juan wishes to escape the tedious, vulgar pursuit of happiness, to spend his eons in contemplation; he also wishes to assist in the work of helping life in its struggle upwards, and he eulogizes man, the highest pinnacle of organization yet attained by life. The Devil decries man as a creature whose heart is in his weapons; in the arts of life, he declares, man has invented nothing, but in the arts of death he outdoes nature herself; the marvellous force of life of which Juan boasts is a force of death. To this Juan rejoins that the Devil is rating man at his own valuation; man loves to think of himself as bold and bad, whereas he is only a coward, whose civilization is founded on cowardice. Juan, in long dissertations on the destiny of man, declares that the darling object of the Life Force is intellect—the philosophic man.

From his experiences with women Don Juan reached the conclusion that it is impossible to impose such conditions as virtue, honour and chastity on the Life Force, which respects marriage only because it is a contrivance of its own to secure the greatest number of children; marriage is the most licentious of the human institutions, that being the secret of its popularity.

When Ana, in defence of marriage, urges that it is an institution that populates the world, whereas debauchery does not, Juan declares that the day is coming when the prudent, the selfish, the worshippers of success, art and love will all oppose to the Force of Life the device of sterility. He prophesies, however, that long before that process of sterilization becomes more than a clearly foreseen possibility, the reaction will begin, and the great central purpose of breeding the race to heights now deemed superhuman—a purpose now hidden in the mephitic cloud of love, romance and prudery—will break through into clear sunlight as a purpose no longer to be confused with the gratification of personal fancies, the impossible realization of young dreams of bliss, or the need of the older people for companionship or money.

When the Devil speaks of love and beauty, Don Juan evinces disgust, and on ascertaining from the statue that in Heaven there are no artistic folk, he is impatient to begone. He asks directions to the way to Heaven, to which the Commander replies, "The frontier between Heaven and Hell is only the difference between two ways of looking at things; any road will take you across". Don Juan departs.

The Devil gives the Commander a warning against the pursuit of the Superman as being dangerous, in that it leads to "an indiscriminate contempt for the human". "Where", asks Ana, "can I find the Superman?" The Devil replies that he is not yet created. "Then", declares Ana, "my work is not yet done. I believe in the life to come. A father (she cries to the universe), a father for the Superman." She vanishes into the void. The scene reverts to the Sierra.

The morning after.—The brigands are awakened by the announcement of the approach of another motor. It contains Ann and the others. The brigands are threatened with capture by soldiers from two armoured cars, but Tanner saves them; the brigands, he declares to the soldiers, are not his captors but his escort.

ACT IV, Garden of a villa in Granada.—Straker enters with an Irishman, who explains to Violet that he also is named Hector Malone. From a note she has written, which has been delivered to him as bearer of the same name, he has learned that she must be on terms of considerable intimacy with his son; if he marries her, adds the father, Hector "will not have a rap". Violet treats the millionaire with decided coolness, and impresses him as being a "pretty straightforward, downright sort of young woman". Hector is indignant with his father for having opened the letter, and Tanner complicates matters by informing the father that his son's infatuation is for a woman already married. Hector has no alternative but to avow his marriage to Violet. "Then", says his father, "she has married a beggar." Violet has little difficulty in wheedling round the millionaire on the subject of finance, and he confides to Tanner that she will make a grand wife and that he would not change her for ten duchesses. Ann once again rejects Octavius, and makes it clear that her intention is to marry Tanner, who protests against this matrimonial destiny. Ann, declares Tanner, is a liar, a bully, a coquette and so forth, for which he does not blame her, as these are womanly attributes; but while insisting on her own right to do what she likes she also insists on the conventional code for everybody else—in fact she is an arch hypocrite. Ann, without dissimulation, woos the reluctant Tanner, who makes his last resistance; from their childhood, she declares, the Life Force had laid a trap for them. Tanner at length capitulates, declaring his love for her.

In the first production Mr G. Barker, as Tanner, was made up as Shaw, but Shaw states that in Tanner, with all his headlong loquacity, is satirized Mr H. M. Hyndman. (Henderson.)

THE MAN OF DESTINY

"NAPOLEON is not L'Empereur yet; he has only just been dubbed 'Le Petit Caporal'. The world has already begun to manufacture L'Empereur, and thus to make it difficult for the romanticists of a hundred years later to credit the hitherto unrecorded little scene now in question at Tavazzano."

The action takes place on May 12, 1796 (Napoleon then being twenty-seven years of age), at an inn at Tavazzano, on the road from Lodi to Milan, being timed two days after Napoleon's victory at Lodi.—Napoleon is impatiently awaiting the arrival of his despatches, and passes the time in finishing his evening meal, working out his dispositions with the aid of a map, and chatting with mine host, Giuseppe Grandi. A chuckle-headed lieutenant arrives to say that the despatches entrusted to his care have been stolen by a youth who imposed on his good nature—that is, played off the confidence trick; he is placed under arrest. The lieutenant hears a voice which he declares to be that of the villain who robbed him. The owner of the voice enters—it is a woman, whom the lieutenant declares to be the Austrian spy in disguise, but he accepts the lady's explanation that he who duped him is her brother. Napoleon is not so credulous, and he demands the despatches, which he quickly divines to be concealed next the lady's heart, and he makes it plain that he will not hesitate to take them. A person of beauty, charm and ready wit, the lady tries to make Napoleon, who is by no means unimpressed by her looks, fall the victim of the confidence trick in more subtle form. Eventually she has to surrender the papers, but she continues her efforts to keep Napoleon from examining their contents. She suggests that he would do well not to read one of the enclosures, a letter from a woman which compromises Napoleon's wife and the Director Barras: once he is known to have received the information, she says, a duel must be the result. The sequel is a *volte-face* on the part of Napoleon, who takes steps to prove that he has never received the despatches, and he summons the lieutenant, bidding him set out to find the lost documents, or he will be degraded in the presence of the regiment. To defeat Napoleon's new intention and save the lieutenant from the threatened disgrace, the lady quickly alters her tactics. Within a few moments she reappears in man's attire and is recognized by the simple lieutenant as the "brother" who robbed him. Pretending that witchcraft inspires her, the lady produces the documents from Napoleon's coat. The play closes with a dissertation from Napoleon on the character of the English nation.

Written for Ellen Terry and Richard Mansfield.

MISALLIANCE

A LONG one-act comedy concerning parents and children. The action takes place in the hall of the Surrey home of John Tarleton, who has made a fortune by making underwear. A series of conversations introduces the characters—the two fathers—Lord Summerhays, the courtly, retired Colonial Governor, and Tarleton, man of superabundant vitality and intellectual inquisitiveness; the amiable Mrs Tarleton, and the children—Johnny Tarleton, a conventional young man of business, and his sister "Patsy" (Hypatia), a "glorious brute" of a young woman, engaged to Bentley (Bunny) Summerhays, whom she terms a "squit of a thing" because his brains have developed at the expense of his body. Patsy has chosen Bunny because he is intellectually the "best of the bunch" of her suitors. Before he learns of their engagement Lord Summerhays, a widower, proposes to Patsy, who laughs unfeelingly at the middle-aged man's infatuation. The glass house is wrecked by an aeroplane, from which the occupants alight unhurt. One is Joey Percival, an undergraduate friend of Bunny's, and the other, to the surprise of the company, a woman, Lina Szcze-panowska. She is a professional acrobat, who went up in the aeroplane to maintain the family tradition that no day must pass without the life of one of its members being risked in some hazardous undertaking. Patsy, learning from Bentley that Joey is a fascinating young man, who has had the advantage of having been brought up by three fathers, sets her cap at him, and in a mood of most unmaidenly modesty dares him to chase her through the heather, with a kiss as the prize for catching her. Joey runs from the temptress, who gives pursuit. The escapade has been watched by a young man hidden in a Turk-ish bath (awaiting installation). He emerges to threaten Tarle-ton senior with a revolver. He is, he explains, a city clerk, and he has come to avenge his mother, Lucy Titmus, with whom, in his younger days, Tarleton had an amour. The gunner is on the point of taking the revenge when Lina intervenes, and he is disarmed. As the gunner begins to speak of the "goings on", of which he was an unsuspected witness, Patsy runs in, this time the pursued. Affecting indignation that a slur should be cast on her reputation, Joey makes the gunner sign a retrac-tion of his imputations, but when Bunny taxes him with steal-ing the affections of Patsy, Joey urges the gunner to go back on his recantation, and shew that it was Patsy who started to woo him. Despite all the protestations, it becomes plain that Patsy is determined to have Joey as a husband, and when he speaks of financial needs, she asks her father to "buy the brute" for her at £1500 a year. Tarleton, who has been re-duced to the verge of hysterics by the ruthless tongue of his daughter, welcomes an opportunity of getting rid of her at the price. Lina Szczepanowska finally declares that she cannot longer remain in a house in which the only concern of the men is love-making; advances have been made to her by Tarleton and his son, and Summerhays and his son; she decides to go off by air, and Bentley, into whom she is instilling the courage of a man, says he will dare to be her passenger.

MRS WARREN'S PROFESSION

"I HAVE shewn that Mrs Warren's Profession is an economic phenomenon produced by our underpayment and illtreatment of women who try to earn an honest living." (Preface to Getting Married.)

Act I, Garden of a cottage at Haslemere, Surrey.—Vivie Warren, an attractive, but resolute-looking girl of twenty-two, who has come down from Newnham, after tying with the third wrangler, is devoting her holiday to preparing for a career in the city. She is joined by her mother, "a fairly presentable old blackguard of a woman", and Sir George Crofts, Bt., "a gentlemanly combination of the most brutal type of city man, sporting man and man about town". Sir George falls in love with Vivie. Frank Gardner, a charming good for nothing young fellow, friend of Vivie, is invited by Mrs Warren to join the party. His father, the Rev. Samuel Gardner, the local rector, is recognized by Mrs Warren as an acquaintance of former days. She was the barmaid to whom he once wrote a series of letters that he offered £50 to recover.

Act II, Inside the cottage that night.—Frank, after engaging in a lively flirtation with Mrs Warren, shows her that he regards himself as her prospective son-in-law, to which Mrs Warren demurs on learning that he is without means or prospects. She also warns Sir George against entertaining any intentions in regard to her daughter. Vivie questions her mother regarding the identity of her father, and learns the secret of Mrs Warren's life and profession. Mrs Warren relates how she was brought up in a fried fish shop; how her half-sister, "one of the respectable ones", worked in a factory for nine shillings a week, and was killed by lead poisoning; how she worked hard as a barmaid, and was induced by her sister Liz to go into partnership with her in the proprietorship of a house in Brussels—a "real high class place where the girls were much better treated than they would have been in a factory or a bar". In justification of her choice of profession, Mrs Warren says that for getting on in the world all she had was her "turn for pleasing men"; if Vivie had been born poor she would have advised her to take the same course; as to being ashamed, that is only good manners; but "what is the use for such hypo crisy? if people arrange the world that way for women there's no good pretending its arranged the other way". Vivie, who had been chilled by her mother's former sentimentality, comes almost to respect her after the straightforward talk.

ACT III, Rectory garden the following morning.—While the Rev. Samuel shews Mrs Warren around the church, Sir George makes love to Vivie, offering to marry her and settle his considerable property on her. Vivie is amazed to learn from him that her mother is still following her avocation; that she is managing proprietor of a business (hotels, he calls it) into which he has put £40,000. She tells Sir George that she is aware of the real nature of the business, and calls him a pretty sort of scoundrel for taking part in it for the 35 per cent he boasts of receiving. Sir George replies that his 35 per cent is no worse earned than the 22 per cent his brother (who founded the Crofts scholarship at Newnham) drew from the factory employing 600 girls, not one of whom was getting enough to live on. Vivie exclaims against the society that tolerates the "unmentionable woman and her capitalist bully". When she seeks to leave him, Sir George, livid with rage, tries to prevent her. Immediately she rings the bell and Frank appears. Crofts is forced to retire at the point of Frank's rifle. He taunts the lovers with being half-brother and half-sister, both children of the Rev. Samuel Gardner. Vivie, disillusioned and sick at heart, runs off to spend the rest of her life in business in the city.

ACT IV, Chambers, in Chancery Lane, of Honoria Fraser, Vivie's friend, with whom she is now in partnership.—Frank tells Vivie that from his father he has obtained a repudiation of the allegation made by Crofts. Vivie replies that this will make no difference to their relations; she is inexorably resolved to have nothing more to do with love's young dream. Learning from her the exact nature of the business her mother and Crofts carry on at Brussels, Berlin and Vienna, Frank realizes that it will be impossible for them to marry and live on her mother's money, and, having no means of his own, he withdraws his suit, leaving the field to the "gilded youth of England". Mrs Warren attempts to effect a reconciliation with her daughter, but in regard to her Vivie is equally determined; in future she will support herself. After cursing her daughter for her hard-heartedness, Mrs Warren vows that henceforth she will do wrong and nothing but wrong. Vivie, after a half-sob, half-laugh of intense relief at the departure of her mother, goes to her work and is soon absorbed in her figures.

Written for the Independent Theatre, but banned by the

censor. (See Play Productions, *infra*.)

Regarding the genesis of Mrs Warren, Mr Shaw wrote in a letter to the *Daily Chronicle* (April 30, 1898): "Miss Janet Achurch mentioned to me a novel by some French writer as having a dramatic story in it. She told me the story, which was ultra-romantic. I said, 'I will work out the truth about the matter some day.' The following autumn a lady suggested to me that I should put on the stage a really modern young lady of the governing class—not the sort of thing that theatrical and critical authorities imagine such a lady to be. I did, and the result was Miss Vivie Warren. I finally persuaded Miss Achurch herself to dramatize the story on the original lines. Her version is Mrs Daintry's Daughter. In the first draft the play was entitled Mrs Jarman's Profession."

Sir Harry Johnston wrote a sequel to the play, called Mrs Warren's Daughter.

Mrs Warren was for many years under the ban of the censor of plays. (See Play Productions, *infra*.)

THE MUSIC CURE

A PIECE OF UTTER NONSENSE

"THIS is not a serious play, it is what is called a variety turn for two musicians."

Hotel drawing room.—Lord Reginald Fitzambey, son of the Duke of Dunmow, is being soothed by his doctor. He is Under-Secretary of State for War, and, having taken advantage of the knowledge that the Army was to be put on vegetarian diet, he bought macaroni trust shares. He has maintained, even before a committee of inquiry, his impenetrable inability to see any reason why he should not have bought the shares. Reginald is in so nervous a condition that he screams at the sound of a piano, and dare not face strangers. After giving his patient a couple of opium pills, the doctor leaves. A lady enters and starts to play the piano, which sets Reginald screaming. It is Strega Thundridge, the female Paderewski, engaged by the Duchess, at a fee of 250 guineas, to play in the room for two hours as a music cure for Reginald. In spite of his protests Strega continues to play; when he starts to make love to her she reduces him to convulsions with a Chopin

67

"study"; then she makes a man of him with the Polonaise in A Flat. As a "clinger", who wishes to be protected from the world, to be a domesticated husband, longing to be mercilessly beaten by a strong, beautiful woman, Reginald implores Strega to become his wife. Strega confesses that throughout her life she has had her dream of having a husband utterly dependent on her, living only to be cherished and worshipped. She accepts him.

O'FLAHERTY, V.C.

"It may surprise some people to learn that in 1915 this little play was a recruiting poster in disguise." (Preface.)

At the door of the Irish country house of General Sir Pearce Madigan.—Having won the V.C. in Flanders, Private O'Flaherty, in the summer of 1915, is having a respite from the trenches as assistant in an Irish recruiting campaign of the General. He asks the General to assist him in maintaining the deception he has practised on his mother, a wild Fenian rebel. Not daring to tell her, when he enlisted, that he was fighting for the English king, he had said that he was going to fight the French and Russians, which she had interpreted as being against the British; it would break her heart, he thinks, to learn the truth. It was she who won the Cross for him—by bringing him up to be more afraid of running away than of fighting. When Sir Pearce suggests that he should explain the rights and wrongs of the war to her, O'Flaherty confesses that, although he has won the V.C., he does not know what the war is about; he killed the enemy, he says, because if he didn't they would kill him. The war has made O'Flaherty see the world in a new light, and he sums it up with the remark, "You'll never have a quiet world till you knock patriotism out of the human race". Mrs O'Flaherty has not been in her son's presence for long before she is roundly abusing him for having deceived her. O'Flaherty is also chilled by the reception he receives from his sweetheart, Teresa, whose chief concern is that she should get a pension, even if he has to be wounded in the getting of it. O'Flaherty vows he will go to France and get a French wife; he'll no longer live in Ireland, where he has been imposed upon and kept in ignorance; he'll no longer stay among a lot of good for nothing divils that'll not do a hand's turn but watch the grass growing. Discovering that her son has presented Teresa with a beautiful gold chain, Mrs O'Flaherty becomes furiously jealous, and an appalling tempest of wordy wrath breaks out between the two women. When they have at last talked themselves out and have been pushed off, O'Flaherty says that he has learnt a lesson from them. "Some likes war alarums and some likes home life; I've tried both and I'm all for war's alarums now; I always was a quiet lad by disposition." As one soldier to another, Sir Pearce agrees with him, remarking, "Do you think that we should have got an army without conscription if domestic life had been as happy as people say it is?"

The production of the play was restrained by the authorities in Ireland, where it was the intention of the Abbey Theatre to produce it, on the ground that it would not be looked on with favour at that time—1915–16.

OVERRULED

"A CLINICAL study (in one act) of how polygamy occurs among quite ordinary people innocent of all unconventional views concerning it." (Preface.)

Gregory Lunn and Mrs Juno are love-making on a chesterfield in the retired corner of the lounge of a sea-side hotel, Gregory being obviously very much infatuated. They had met during a voyage at sea. Each is horrified to find that the other is married, and they feel they ought immediately to separate, but their inclinations are in opposition to their moral promptings. They overhear voices, one of which Mrs Juno recognizes as that of her husband, and the other, Gregory, as that of his wife. They hastily retreat, and Mrs Lunn and Juno occupy the vacated chesterfield. Juno declares his love for Mrs Lunn, who is only mildly interested—she is tired of hearing such declarations. Juno, the conventional, finds this eccentricity hard to bear, preferring either to be repulsed or accepted, so long as it is not out of the ordinary. Gregory and Mrs Juno return, and the party discuss the situation. Gregory finds that, while his intentions were strictly honourable, there was, somehow or other, a disastrous separation between his moral principles and his conduct. Juno holds that there is nothing disastrous about his conduct if his principles are all right; men are not perfect, he says, but it is all right if they keep the ideal before them by admitting when they are in the wrong. Mrs Lunn finds the argument about morality tedious; if Mrs Juno, who seems prepared to endure male sentimentality, will look after Gregory at times, she at times will be pleased to amuse Juno—a proposal which Juno declares to be pure polygamy. Mrs Lunn says she intends to go on receiving Juno, because he amuses her. Mrs Juno refuses to give up seeing Gregory, because she loves being loved. It is finally resolved that the matter must be left at that.

PASSION, POISON AND PETRIFACTION; OR THE FATAL GAZOGENE

A BRIEF TRAGEDY FOR BARNS AND BOOTHS

"THE play has a funny little history, having its origin in a story I once made up for the Archer children, in which a cat lapped up moist plaster of paris and was petrified. It was written at the request of Cyril Maude."

Bed-sitting room in a fashionable quarter in London.—Lady Magnesia Fitztollemache awakens in time to save herself from being murdered by her husband. Adolphus Bastable comes to shew Lady Magnesia his new clothes, which she praises. Fitz (the husband) invites him to drink from the gazogene, and, after Adolphus has pledged Magnesia, he reveals that he had poisoned the drink in a fit of jealousy, because Adolphus' clothes had been praised. Adolphus welcomes his fate as the "first clothes martyr". He declares his love for Magnesia, who says that henceforth he shall have her devotion. Hoping to save Adolphus, they administer lime from the plaster ceiling, but this sets inside him, and he becomes a living statue. The landlord, doctor and policeman who have been summoned are struck dead by lightning.

Originally appeared in Harry Furniss's Christmas Annual for 1905, with illustrations by Harry Furniss.

THE PHILANDERER

A TOPICAL COMEDY

"HERE I have shown the grotesque sexual compacts made between men and women under marriage laws which represent to some of us a political necessity (especially for other people), to some a divine ordinance, to some a romantic ideal, to some a domestic profession for women, and to some that worst of blundering abominations—an institution which society has outgrown but not modified, and which 'advanced' individuals are therefore forced to evade." (Preface.)

ACT I, Drawing room of a flat in Ashley-gardens.—Leonard Charteris, the philanderer, and Grace Tranfield, a widow, two lovers, discuss their previous affairs. Charteris tells Grace that he wishes to marry her in order to demonstrate to Julia Craven, who refuses to give him up, that their old affair is at an end. Julia bursts into the flat and, in jealous fury, attempts to assault Grace, Charteris having forcibly to restrain her. Charteris reasons with Julia, pointing out that she had declined to marry him, as she wished to reserve the right to leave him at any time if she "found the companionship incompatible with her full development as a human being" (as she put the Ibsenist view). As a corollary to that, he claims to leave her now that she has become a jealous termagant. During their argument Grace's father, Joseph Cuthbertson, enters the flat with Colonel Daniel Craven, father of Julia, and an explanation has to be fabricated to explain the absence of Grace. Cuthbertson is pained to learn that the Colonel, a boyhood friend, has been sentenced to death by his doctor, being "celebrated in the medical schools as an example of the newest sort of liver complaint"—Paramore's disease. The Colonel is urged to join the Ibsen Club, for which candidates have to be guaranteed to be not womanly if female, and not manly if male. Colonel Craven is indignant that his daughter Julia should ever have been guaranteed.

ACT II, Library of the Ibsen Club.—Charteris explains his dilemma to the two fathers—that he is between the two fires of Grace Tranfield, the "new" woman, who has written to say that she will not now marry him, and Julia Craven, the old lover, who declines to give him up. Julia enters, and Charteris, wishing to avoid another scene, plays hide and seek with her around the library. When she and the fathers have left for lunch, Sylvia Craven suggests to Charteris that in Dr Paramore, who is deeply in love with Julia, he might find a solution of his problem. Grace gives Charteris confirmation of the letter she wrote him declining to marry him; she is a "new" woman and will not marry a man she loves too much; it would give him a terrible advantage over her.

ACT III, The library.—Dr Paramore finds in the British Medical Journal a complete refutation of the arguments which had led him to believe in the existence of Paramore's disease. Colonel Craven does not share his regrets, and remonstrates with the doctor on having, on the strength of three dogs and a monkey, passed judgment of death upon him and made him an object of public scorn—a vegetarian and teetotaller. Charteris consoles with the doctor, and encourages him to propose to Julia. Grace Tranfield invites the doctor to tell her the latest scientific theories, and Julia, when her attention is directed to them by Charteris, becomes furiously jealous, and causes a disturbance. Mrs Tranfield announces that she is going to lay a complaint before the Club Committee that Julia is a womanly woman. Julia is making protest, when it is mentioned that Dr Paramore has gone home, at which she ascertains his address and hurriedly leaves. The doctor has invited the others of the party to tea, and they start to follow, but Charteris does his utmost to delay them in order that the doctor may have time to propose to Julia.

ACT IV, Paramore's sitting room in Savile-row.—Dr Paramore, while serving tea, makes his proposal to Julia, declaring her to be possessed of sterling qualities that are undeveloped, because she is not understood by those about her. Julia, delighted to find a lover who appreciates something more in her than her beauty, accepts him. When Charteris, who has been successful in delaying the others, learns the news, his congratulations to Julia are so effusive that there is another scene, and Paramore begins to wonder if Julia's heart does not still belong to her old lover. Charteris excuses her by feigning to be the rejected suitor grieving at his rival's happiness. Grace Tranfield delivers the final verdict upon him—"never make a hero of a philanderer".

This play was written in 1893, when "the cult of Ibsen had reached its pinnacle of fatuity". It was intended for the Independent Theatre, but "before I had finished it, it was apparent that its demands on the most expert and delicate sort of acting went beyond the resources then at the disposal of Mr Grein".

PRESS CUTTINGS

TOPICAL sketch compiled from the editorial and correspondence columns of the daily papers during the women's war in 1909.

Room in the War Office of General Mitchener.—In order to escape the attentions of the suffragettes, as he goes from Downing-street to the War Office, Balsquith, the Prime Minister, has pretended to be a suffragette, dressing himself as a woman and padlocking himself to the door scraper. He has come to consult General Mitchener on the situation; Sandstone has resigned from the Cabinet because his plan of dealing with the women by excluding them from within two miles of Westminster has been abandoned. Mitchener supports the plan, and would be prepared to enforce it by shooting down all opposition. Then there is the affair of the curate who was flogged for assaulting a lieutenant; the curate has three aunts in the Peerage, including Lady Richmond, a party hostess. Balsquith declares that Mitchener, to save his country, must don his ceremonial uniform and medals, call on her ladyship and, to propitiate her, promise to promote the curate. Balsquith is also perturbed by the Germans, who have laid down four more dreadnoughts. For dealing with the Germans, Mitchener propounds his short way for dealing with all opponents —"Shoot them down". The General is harangued by his housekeeper, Mrs Banger—who urges that the risks of childbirth are as great as those of the battlefield—and by his orderly —who has reached the Army through compulsory service, to the disgrace of his middle-class family, who have never had a soldier in it before. He is interviewed by members of the Anti-Suffraget League—Mrs Banger and Lady Corinthia Fanshawe—who announce that the League are going to fight the suffragettes, it being no longer possible to trust the men. Mrs Banger declares that the suffragettes are on the wrong track; women want not the vote, but the right to military service; in her view, all the really strong men in history were women in disguise—Bismarck, for instance, and Napoleon. Lady Corinthia, who is the famous singer, the "Richmond Nightin-

gale", believes that it is for the few women of artistic talent to
rule the world through men. Their arguments as anti-suffra-
gettes result in the General's conversion to the idea of en-
franchising women, but when Balsquith announces that the
Labour Party is demanding votes for women, the General says
this makes it impossible to grant women the vote, because it
would be yielding to clamour; the one condition on which the
Government can grant anything is that no one shall presume
to ask for it. Mrs Banger, it is learned, by sitting on his head,
has induced General Sandstone to propose marriage to her—
his ideal of a "really soldierly woman". General Mitchener reflects that the Army is now to all intents and purposes com-
manded by Mrs Banger, and he proposes to the only woman
in the country whose practical ability and force of character
can maintain her husband in competition with the husband of
Mrs Banger—his charwoman, Mrs Farrell, who accepts him.
Lady Corinthia agrees to become an "Egeria" to Balsquith.
The moral of the piece is that Mitchener should give up treating soldiers as schoolboys, and that Balsquith should desist
from treating women as if they were angels.

Shaw was requested to write this piece on the chosen subject
by Forbes Robertson. (Henderson.)

For the censor's action see Play Productions, *infra*.

PYGMALION

"IF the play makes the public aware that there are such people
as phoneticians and that they are among the most important in
England at present, it well serves its turn. . . . I wish to boast
it has been a most successful play. It is so intensely and deliber-
ately didactic that I delight in throwing it at the heads of wise-
acres who repeat the parrot cry that art should never be didactic. It goes to prove my contention that art should never be
anything else." (Preface.)

ACT I, Portico of St Paul's, Covent Garden.—During a
thunderstorm Professor Higgins, teacher of phonetics, is taking dialect specimens among a crowd. Eliza Doolittle, the
cockney flower girl, suspects him of being a policeman's
"nark", and an altercation ensues, during which Higgins impresses the cockney members of the crowd by the facility with

which he identifies their homes from their speech. This facility also attracts the attention of Colonel Pickering, author of Spoken Sanscrit, who has come all the way frcm India to see Higgins.

ACT II, Higgins' laboratory in Wimpole-street.—While the Professor of phonetics is showing Pickering round, Eliza comes in and, to their astonishment, asks to be given a course in correct speaking, as she wishes to become a florist's assistant in a West-end shop; her cockney accent now bars her from getting a place. Higgins wagers Pickering that in six months he will have transformed "this draggletailed guttersnipe" into a Duchess. Having learned that Eliza is being adopted by two rich men, Doolittle, her father, a dustman, "one of the undeserving poor", arrives in the hope of deriving some share in the good fortune which has befallen his daughter. He entertains the Professor with his "undeserving" philosophy, and departs the richer by £5.

ACT III, Drawing room in Chelsea.—Mrs Higgins, the Professor's mother, is about to commence her At Home, when Higgins arrives and asks if she will receive Eliza. His pupil has acquired the speech, but still lacks the manners of society; she had been transformed from a cockney flower girl into a very presentable young woman, and succeeds, in spite of her halting speech, in making a great impression on the party. Freddy Eynsford Hill becomes infatuated. Mrs Eynsford Hill, a very correct lady, and her daughter Clara are puzzled by Eliza's choice of topics for conversation, but Higgins explains to them that this is the "new small talk". The explanation is held to cover the "not bloody likely" which Eliza innocently utters, and which Clara imitates.

ACT IV, Higgins' laboratory.—Eliza has been put on trial as a Duchess, and has passed the test with flying colours. She is discussed by the Professor and Pickering, and resents the impersonal manner in which the Professor refers to her and the patronizing superiority with which he talks of her as his creation, without paying any compliment to her for having contributed to his success by her aptness as a pupil. Eliza is also perturbed about her future, now that her training is over. She is unfitted for resuming her old occupation, and does not see that she is fitted for a new one. She repudiates the Professor's suggestion that she should marry.

ACT V, Mrs Higgins' drawing room.—Eliza has disappeared, and, after informing the police, the Professor has come to his mother for advice. While they are discussing the situation Doolittle enters, resplendent in frock-coat and other marks of affluence. He has, he explains, been left £3000 a year by an American to deliver an annual course of lectures on philosophy; this is the result of a recommendation made by Higgins (who in jest had described him as the "most original moralist in England"), and Doolittle bewails the fact that he has to leave the pleasant ways of "undeserving poverty" for the respectability of the middle classes. One consequence is that he has to marry his wife, and he invites them all to the ceremony. Mrs Higgins, who had concealed Eliza upstairs, sees in the prosperity of Doolittle a solution of the problem of his daughter's future, but the Professor does not approve; Eliza has become a necessity to him to look after his papers, his engagements and his slippers. The play concludes with an angry scene between the Professor and Eliza, in which the student shews the teacher the excellence of his tuition; he has produced a Duchess not only in talk and mannerisms, but also in independence. She will not continue with Higgins and Pickering as "one of three old bachelors"; she will either marry Freddy Hill, or set up as a rival teacher to Higgins, ready to shew others how to develop from flower girls into Duchesses.

The sequel, as sketched in the postscript, is that Eliza marries, not her Pygmalion, but Freddy Hill, and becomes the joint proprietor of a fashionable greengrocer's business.

SAINT JOAN
A CHRONICLE PLAY

"THE combination of inept youth and academic ignorance, with great natural capacity, push, courage, devotion, originality and oddity, fully accounts for all the facts in Joan's career and makes her a credible, historical human phenomenon. . . . Joan was a village girl, without prestige, yet she ordered everybody about from her uncle to the King, the Archbishop and the military general staff. . . . This would have been unbearably irritating even if her orders had been offered as rational solutions of the desperate difficulties in which her social superiors found themselves, but they were not so offered; it was never 'I say so' but 'God says so'." (Preface.)

Scene I, Chamber in the Castle of Vaucouleurs, A.D. 1429.—Joan, after repeated rebuffs, contrives to secure an interview with Captain Robert de Baudricourt, of whom she demands, in the name of God, a horse, armour and soldiers, in order that she may proceed to the Dauphin, raise the siege of Orleans, and expel the English from France. Joan, who has already won the support of many of the soldiers, soon overcomes the opposition of de Baudricourt. When he accedes to her request the steward enters with a basket of eggs; the hens had ceased to lay while Joan had been refused an interview, but now they are "laying like mad"—a circumstance which convinces the simple soldiers and de Baudricourt that the Maid "comes from God".

Scene II, Throne room of Castle at Chinon, in Touraine.—The Dauphin informs the Archbishop of Rheims of the Maid's mission. The Dauphin is advised not to receive Joan, but he decides to do so, and in order to test her powers it is agreed that Gilles de Rais (Bluebeard) shall impersonate the Dauphin. Joan is not deceived, but picks out the real Dauphin from among the crowd of courtiers. Joan persuades the Dauphin to give her the command of the forces at Orleans.

Scene III, On the south bank of the Loire, outside besieged Orleans.—Joan rebukes Dunois, the French commander, for his inaction, and declares that she will raise the siege. Dunois explains to her the English are so securely placed that the only chance of attack is by men on rafts, and these cannot be used until the wind changes. Realizing the truth of this, Joan asks to be conducted to the church, saying that she will tell St Catherine and she will make God give them a West wind. No sooner is she on her way than she is called back; the wind has already changed. Dunois hands his baton to Joan and tells her she commands the King's Army. They rush off to lead the French into battle and victory.

Scene IV, A tent in the English camp.—The Earl of Warwick discusses with his chaplain, de Stogumber, the need for getting rid of the Maid. Because of the successes of the French troops under Joan's leadership it is a political necessity for the

English that the Maid should be disposed of, and the Earl of Warwick receives Peter Cauchon, the Bishop of Beauvais, to discuss this question. The Earl inquires of the Bishop whether, if Joan were captured in his diocese, he would not denounce her to the Inquisition and have her burned as a sorceress. While deprecating the view that the process of the Inquisition can be made subservient to the purposes of the English, the Bishop declares that he regards the Maid as an instrument of the Devil in the mighty purpose of spreading heresy. Warwick explains that, as the representative of the feudal aristocracy, his objection to Joan is that by teaching that Kings should reign as God's bailiffs, she is propagating a cunning device to supersede the aristocracy and make the King absolute autocrat, instead of the first among his peers. The two ideas of Joan's are, says the Earl, the same at the bottom—a protest against the interference of priest or peer between a private man and his God; Protestantism he would call it. To this the Bishop rejoins that the Maid, by thinking of France for the French, is guilty of the heresy of nationalism, which is essentially anti-Catholic and anti-Christian.

Scene V, Ambulatory in the Cathedral of Rheims.—Joan has crowned the Dauphin King of France, but she is sad at heart because the courtiers and soldiers hate her, and Dunois explains to her that she cannot expect them to love her after exposing their inefficiency. When she speaks of returning to her village, the Dauphin does not disguise his relief. She urges a resumption of the war, and Dunois warns her that the English have set a price on her head; should she be captured he will not risk a soldier's life to save her. The Dauphin says that he can afford no money to ransom her, and when Joan declares her trust in the Church, the Archbishop of Rheims warns her that the Church will leave her to whatever fate her presumption may bring upon her.

Scene VI, Rouen, hall in the Castle, arranged for a trial, the time being May 30, 1431.—Warwick greets Cauchon, Bishop of Beauvais, and the Inquisitor, who are about to inquire into the allegations against Joan, and complains of the delay in bringing the Maid to trial, nine months having passed since her capture by the Burgundians, at Compiègne. Cauchon is determined she shall have a fair trial, and if the Church lets her go, woe unto the man who shall dare lay a finger on her. Joan is brought to trial, and the Inquisitor and Cauchon do their utmost to save her from the stake. She is induced to recant, and to sign a confession that her voices were temptations by demons. She is thereupon condemned to lifelong imprisonment, on hearing which she tears up the document, not dreading the fire of the Inquisition as much as the life of a rat in a hole. The Court has then no alternative but to excommunicate her and hand her over to the secular power. The soldiers hurry her out to the market-place, to be burned as a heretic. The penalty inflicted, de Stogumber, an English chaplain, who had been most insistent in clamouring for the execution of the witch, returns in a state of collapse, horrified that he had sought to condemn Joan to such a fate.

EPILOGUE, A windy night in June 1456.—King Charles the Ninth of France, formerly Joan's Dauphin, now Charles the Victorious, is in bed in one of his Royal Chateaux. The monk, Ladvenu, appears before him and announces to the King the result of the inquiry into the case of Joan. The Court has annulled the sentence passed on Joan twenty-five years before, and has declared her judges to have been full of corruption, fraud and malice. To Ladvenu, it is strange that, whereas at the trial which sent Joan to the stake as a sorceress, truth was told and mercy done beyond custom, the result of the inquiry rehabilitating her and setting the great wrong right has been arrived at after shameless perjury and calumny of the dead, who did their duty according to their lights. The King cares not so long as the result is that no one can now challenge his consecration. The Spirit of St Joan appears, followed by the other protagonists in the drama of her life. Another arrival is a ruffianly English soldier from Hell, who is taking his annual day's holiday allowed him for his one good deed—fashioning a rude Cross for a lass that was going to be burned. A clerical-looking gentleman, dressed in the fashion of a twentieth-century parson, announces the decision of the Vatican canonizing the Maid as the Venerable and Blessed St Joan. All kneel and join in paying homage to the new saint—the Archbishop speaking for the princes of the Church, Warwick for cunning counsellors, de Stogumber for foolish old men, and Charles for the unpretending folk. When Joan asks if she shall come back to earth, they all spring up in consternation, and as they make their several exits, indicate that the presence of Joan reincarnate would not be welcomed with enthusiasm. "O God", exclaims Joan in her sadness, "that madest this beautiful earth, when will it be ready to receive thy Saints. How long, O Lord, how long?"

THE SHOWING UP OF BLANCO POSNET

"THIS little play is really a religious tract in dramatic form." (Preface.)

Into a big room, not unlike an English barn, furnished as a court house, where a party of women, their dress and speech those of pioneers of civilization in a territory of the United States, are shucking nuts. Blanco Posnet is marched in. He is a prisoner charged with being the thief of a horse belonging to Sheriff Kemp. The women, whom he reviles, fly at him and are driven out of the building. Blanco declares to Strapper Kemp that as he was taken walking alone, twenty miles from anywhere, they cannot hang him unless they can find a witness to his having been seen with the horse. Elder Daniels, who was left with the prisoner in order to wrestle with his "poor blinded soul", is greeted by Blanco as his boozy brother, who once borrowed money to get drunk and now lends money and sells drink to others. To this the Elder replies that drink and drunkenness save men from worse sins; America is the purest of nations, because when she is not working she is too drunk to hear the voice of the tempter; he fervently thanks God for drink. Blanco warns the Elder against thinking that God has finished with him yet; God is a sly one, a mean one, who plays cat and mouse with a man; he, Blanco, might have been fifty miles away with that horse, but God had a clever trick ready. Strapper Kemp returns with a witness, and is followed by his brother, Sheriff Kemp, and the boys. The trial begins. The witness is Feemy Evans, a woman of ill-fame, who has a grudge against Blanco because he would never have anything to do with her, and she declares she saw him on the horse. Blanco is about to be convicted, when tidings are brought that the horse has been recovered; it was in the possession of a woman, who appears before the court. She states that she took the horse from its rider hoping to save the life of her child, a victim of croup, who is now dead; she denies that the rider was Blanco. The Sheriff divines that she has a delicacy about giving away the man who helped her at the risk of his life, but that is no reason for allowing a horse thief to escape; delicacy is not Feemy's strong point; will she now swear to Blanco? Feemy declares herself ready, but after hearing the woman's pathetic story of how her dying child clutched the horseman by his throat, softening his heart so that he had to surrender the horse though he knew it would cost him his life, Feemy's nerve fails her, and she confesses that she had previously committed perjury out of spite against Blanco. Saved from hanging, Blanco preaches a sermon on the moral of the day—that there are two games being played in the world, the game which is a rotten game and another that is not rotten; formerly he played the rotten game, but the great game was played on him, and now he's for the great game every time.

The censor of plays objected to certain phrases used of God, on the ground that they were blasphemous, and as Shaw refused to mutilate his work to the extent required, the piece could not be performed in England for many years. (See Play Productions, *infra*.)

WIDOWERS' HOUSES

"HERE I have shown middle class respectability and younger son gentility fattening on the poverty of the slum as flies fatten on filth."

ACT I, Garden restaurant of a hotel at Remagen, on the Rhine, in the Eighteen-eighties.—Dr Harry Trench, son of a younger son of a family of title, who is accompanied by William de Burgh Cockane, contrives to get himself formally introduced to Blanche Sartorius, whom he already loves, and her father, a rich but self-made man. The Doctor proposes to Blanche. Her father, from the standpoint of a person socially inferior, is afraid that his daughter may not be well received in the Doctor's aristocratic family, and he will only consent to their engagement when the Doctor produces letters of cordial congratulation from his relations. Sartorius explains that his daughter will inherit his fortune, derived from rentals of real estate in London.

ACT II, Villa, at Surbiton, of Sartorius.—Lickcheese, a rent collector, presents his accounts, shewing that he has spent twenty-four shillings on repairs to a tenement house belonging to Sartorius, who discharges him for such extravagance. Trench brings a batch of congratulations, and the engagement is agreed to by Sartorius. From Lickcheese, Trench learns that it is from slum property that Sartorius derives his wealth, and thereupon the Doctor informs Blanche that it is impossible for him, in the circumstances, to accept any augmentation to his income from her father; but unless his income is thus increased she will not marry him. Sartorius reasons with the Doctor; if the slum property, he argues, were improved, the tenants would only wreck it, and in any case Trench is scarcely the person to raise objections, as his own income is derived from a mortgage on the very property. Trench feels that he cannot maintain his objections, but Blanche, whose pride has been hurt, is no longer prepared to marry him.

ACT III, Drawing room of Sartorius' house in Bedford Square, four months later.—Lickcheese seeks a business interview with his former employer. He is evidently in affluent circumstances, and he explains that, starting with capital acquired by a little judicious blackmail, he has developed a new method of deriving money from slum property—of buying blocks of slums which are likely to become the subject of improvement schemes, and gaining handsome profit by way of compensation. Lickcheese explains to Sartorius how he, with his slum property, can participate. The co-operation of Dr Trench is necessary. Trench at first indignantly refuses to co-operate, but he is out-argued. He is at length induced to join in the scheme, and he is reconciled with Blanche.

With this play Shaw made his debut on the stage. It was commenced in 1885 in (attempted) collaboration with William Archer and was resumed 1892. Archer stated in his account of the collaboration (*World*, December 14, 1892), "I saw that so far from using up my plot he had not even touched it".

YOU NEVER CAN TELL

"WELL, sir, you never can tell—that's a principle in life with me. It is the unexpected that always happens—You never can tell." (William, the waiter.) "This comedy is an attempt to comply with many requests for a play in which the much paragraphed brilliancy of 'Arms and the Man' should be tempered by some consideration for the requirements of managers in search of fashionable comedies for West End Theatres." (Preface.)

ACT I, Dentist's operating room at a fashionable watering place.—Valentine, the young five-shilling dentist, has just performed the first extraction in his six weeks' career. His victim was Miss Dolly Clandon, a visitor from Madeira, and she and her twin brother Phil invite the dentist to lunch. When it is disclosed that they do not know their own father, having been separated from him for eighteen years, Valentine informs them that the conventions make it impossible for him to accept, but the twins have a Dean as grandfather, and the dentist, allowing this relationship to satisfy his scruples, accepts the invitation. The twins are joined by their mother, author of the 20th Century Handbooks, and Gloria, her elder daughter, who has been reared as a twentieth-century girl, to be guided by her reason and to despise her emotions. Gloria immediately inspires Valentine with an infatuation. Valentine is summoned to attend his landlord, Crampton, an elderly and irritable man, to whom the dentist owes six weeks' rent. Crampton wishes to have a tooth removed, but declines gas, remarking that in his day people were "taught to bear necessary pain". Valentine wagers him the owing rent that he will not feel the extraction, and then adroitly administers the gas.

ACT II, Terrace at the Marine Hotel.—Finch McComas, ex-suitor of and friend and solicitor to Mrs Clandon, explains to the children how their mother found it necessary to separate from their father on account of his brutality. To the consternation of the party, the father is disclosed to be Crampton, whom the twins have invited to come with Valentine to lunch. The meal which follows, at which the children and father meet on the footing of absolute strangers, is an extremely embarrassing affair, only saved from disaster by the tactful interventions of the waiter, William (or Walter). Valentine makes ardent love to Gloria. Because she will have none of his sentimentality, he woos her in the "scientific" manner, ridicules her prosaic pose, calling her a feminine prig, and ends by throwing his arms around her and kissing her. To her shame Gloria does not feel the repugnance she considers that she ought to experience.

ACT III, Hotel sitting room.—Mrs Clandon questions Valentine regarding his intentions. Valentine replies that they are marriage with her daughter, but he does not disguise that he is a philanderer, and he expounds his theory of the "duel of sex" —of how modern man, in wooing the girl scientifically educated, has had to improve upon the love-making of the old-fashioned man. Mrs Clandon is disgusted by his levity, and demonstrates to Gloria that his protestations of love have been made many times before. Gloria wrathfully declares that she will never forgive him. McComas espouses the cause of Crampton, who seeks a reconciliation with his family, or the custody of the twins on the ground that the deed of separation has been broken. It is agreed that the matter shall be laid before an eminent Queen's Counsel.

ACT IV, The sitting room.—The eminent Queen's Counsel, Bohun (he turns out to be the son of William, the waiter), quickly provides a solution of the problems submitted to him. Gloria, he says, though she may think otherwise, will marry Valentine; before the legal question of their custody can have been decided the twins will be of age. Gloria is not long in fulfilling the prediction of the Q.C., for, despite the warnings of her reason and of her mother, she finds herself impelled into marriage with Valentine. The ardour of the "duellist of sex" gives way to reluctance on finding that his philanderings are at last to be ended. One by one the others dance away to a ball in progress at the hotel, leaving Valentine, for whom no partner remains, to the sad reflection—"I might as well be a married man already".

Shaw wrote the play for Cyril Maude, and it was put into rehearsal at the Haymarket in the winter of 1897, but was not brought to production at that time.

BIBLIOGRAPHIES

PUBLISHED WORKS OF BERNARD SHAW

1884. Serial publication in *To-day* of "Unsocial Socialist"; English edition, 1887 (Sonnenschein); American edition, 1900 (Brentano); cheap edition, 1914 (Constable); reissue, 1924.

1885–86. Serial publication in *To-day* of "Cashel Byron's Profession"; English edition, 1886 (Modern Press, London); Novocastrian novels, 1889; newly revised, Grant Richards, 1901; Constable, 1914; reissue, 1924. America: 1886 (Harpers); 1899 (Brentano).

1885–87. Serial publication in *Our Corner* of "The Irrational Knot"; English edition, 1905 (Constable); reissue, 1914 and 1924; American edition, 1905 (Brentano).

1887–88. Serial publication in *Our Corner* of "Love Among the Artists"; published Chicago, 1900 (H. S. Stone and Co.); 1909 (Brentano); English edition, 1914 (Constable); reissue, 1924.

1889. ANARCHISM AND STATE SOCIALISM; Revolutionary Reprint No. 1 (Seymour). Unauthorized reprint from *The Anarchist*. The original article was written at the request of the editress and did not (Mr Shaw informs us) represent the author's views.

1889. Edited Fabian Essays in Socialism (Fabian Society) and contributed Economic and Transition sections to the volume. New York edition, 1891 (Humboldt Publishing Co.).

1891. LEGAL EIGHT HOURS' QUESTION; public debate between Mr George Bernard Shaw and Mr G. W. Foote, Hall of Science, London, January 14 and 15, 1891 (Forder). "I have tried to show that a reduction of hours would not raise prices, but would raise wages, and that doing it by law is the only way possible."

1891. QUINTESSENCE OF IBSENISM (Scott). "In the spring of 1890 the Fabian Society finding itself at a loss for a course of lectures was compelled to make shift with a series of papers put forward under the heading of 'Socialism in Contemporary Literature'. I consented to 'take Ibsen'. My paper was duly read at the St James's Restaurant (on July 1,

1890, under the presidency of Mrs Annie Besant), which was the first form of this little book. It is not a critical essay on the poetic beauties of Ibsen, but simply an exposition of Ibsenism." Now completed to the death of Ibsen (Constable, 1913), with new preface and additional chapters. Third edition, 1922. American: 1891 (Tucker); 1904 (Brentano); new edition, 1913 (Brentano).

1892. THE FABIAN SOCIETY: What it has done and how it has done it. Fabian Tract No. 41. Reprint of a paper read at a conference of the London and Provincial Fabian Societies at Essex Hall on February 6, 1892.

1893. IMPOSSIBILITIES OF ANARCHISM; Fabian Tract No. 45 (July 1893). Paper read to Fabian Society, October 16, 1891. "On the whole I do not regard the extreme hostility to existing institutions which inspires Communistic anarchism as being a whit more dangerous to Social democracy than the same spirit as it inspired the Toryism of Ruskin. I leave the matter in the firm conviction that the State, in spite of the Anarchists, will continue to be used against the people by the classes until it is used by the people against the classes with equal ability and equal resolution."—Reprint, 1908, in "Socialism and Individualism", Fabian Socialist Series, No. 3.

1893. WIDOWERS' HOUSES (Independent Theatre Series of Plays, No. 2), with Preface and Appendices (Henry).

1895. INTRODUCTION to the Theatrical World of 1894, by William Archer (Scott). "A few hints to help the reader understand that the real secrets of the theatre are not those of the stage mechanism but of the box office, the acting manager's room and the actor manager's soul." Consideration of economics of the theatre and the gamble of play production; the actor manager; why the theatre lags behind the drama; a protest against the bad conditions under which people are invited to the theatre; women and the stage—highest artistic career is practically closed to the leading ady.

1896. AN ESSAY ON GOING TO CHURCH; The Savoy, January. "No nation working at the strain we face, can live cleanly without public houses in which to seek refreshment and recreation. To supply that vital want, we have the drinking

shop with its narcotic, stimulant poisons, the conventicle
with its brimstone flavoured hot gospel and the Church. In
the Church alone can our need be truly met; nor even there
save when we leave outside the door materializations that
help us to believe the incredible, and the intellectualizations
that help us to think the unthinkable, going in without
thought or belief or prayer or any other vanity so that the
soul, freed from all the crushing lumber, may open all its
avenues of life to the holy air of the true Catholic Church."
Several unauthorized reprints of this Essay have appeared
in America by the Roycroft Shop and others. Luce (Boston)
issued an edition in 1909.

1897. ILLUSIONS OF SOCIALISMS. Reprint of an article (which
originally appeared in *Die Zeit*, Vienna, October 24 and
31, 1896) as one of a number brought together by Edward
Carpenter under the title of "Forecasts of the Coming Century" (Labour Press, Manchester). "Socialism wins its disciples by presenting civilization to them as a popular melodrama, or as a Pilgrim's Progress against the powers of evil
to the bar of poetic justice. . . . By the illusion of the down-
fall of capitalism we shall turn whole nations into joint
stock companies . . . by the illusion of democracy we shall
establish the most powerful bureaucracy ever known."

1898. THE PERFECT WAGNERITE; a commentary on the "Ring
of the Nibelungs" (Grant Richards). "I offer it to those enthusiastic admirers of Wagner who are unable to follow his
ideas, though they are filled with indignation at the irrever-
ence of the Philistines. All I pretend to do is to impart the
ideas which are most likely to be lacking in the conventional Englishman's equipment. I came by them myself
much as Wagner did, having learnt more about music than
about anything else in my youth and sown my political wild
oats subsequently in the revolutionary school. This combination is not common in England; and as I seem so far to
be the only publicly articulate result of it, I venture to add
my commentary to what has already been written by musicians who are no revolutionaries and revolutionists who are
no musicians." Third edition (Constable, 1913), with new
preface; with nine new pages first added to the German
edition of 1907. America: 1899 (Stone); 1909 (Brentano).

1898. PLAYS UNPLEASANT—Widowers' Houses, Mrs Warren, The Philanderer—and PLAYS PLEASANT—Arms and the Man, Candida, Man of Destiny, You Never Can Tell (Grant Richards); third edition, 1913 (Constable). America: 1898 (Stone); 1906 (Brentano).

1900. Edited "Fabianism and Empire", a manifesto on the South African War by the Fabian Society (Grant Richards). The Liberal and Tory politicians are too incompetent to continue the task of Government; the aristocracy is ready to die for the country but not ready to live for it by thinking out a solution of its problems. It is the destiny of conscious Socialism to create a party with a purpose and a faith, and then English statesmen will once more have a craft and master it.—"The proposals as to the South African settlement", writes G. B. S., "are virtually those carried out by Campbell-Bannerman's Government."

1900. DYNAMITARDS OF SCIENCE (London Anti-Vivisection Society); being the report of a speech by Mr Shaw at the Society's annual meeting, May 30, 1900. A reply to the contention that an experiment is justified by merely showing that it is of some use. "If you are prepared to allow a few animals to be tormented by vivisectors on the ground that as a result you are going to relieve the great mass of physical suffering among mankind, you are logically bound to believe that the dynamitard is right to blow up his Cabinet ministers."

1901. THREE PLAYS FOR PURITANS: The Devil's Disciple, Caesar and Cleopatra, and Captain Brassbound's Conversion (Grant Richards); 1906 (Constable). America: 1901 (Stone); 1909 (Brentano).

1901. SOCIALISM FOR MILLIONAIRES, Fabian Tract No. 107 (July); reprinted, with foreword, from *Contemporary Review* (February 1896). There is increasing difficulty for the millionaire to spend his money; it is equally wrong from the point of view of society whether he relieves from the necessity of working his family or a beggar. A safe rule for the millionaire is never to do anything for the public any more than for the individual that the public will do (because it must) for itself without his intervention. The provision of proper hospital accommodation is pre-eminently one of these things. Money is worth nothing to the man who has more than enough, and the wisdom with which it is spent is the sole justification for leaving him in possession of it.

1903. MRS WARREN'S PROFESSION, Stage Society edition; with the author's apology (Grant Richards).

1903. MAN AND SUPERMAN: A Comedy and a Philosophy. With Epistle Dedicatory, "The Revolutionist's Handbook" and "Maxims for Revolutionists" (Constable). Constable's Sixpenny Series, 1908; 1903, Boston (Mass.), printer's copyrighting edition; 1906 (Brentano).

1904. COMMONSENSE OF MUNICIPAL TRADING (Constable). Founded on practical knowledge derived from six years' public work in the committee rooms of a London vestry and borough council. Republished 1908 (Fifield) as No. 5 in the Fabian Socialist Series, with new preface. "Municipal trading is not an evil to be staved off by any possible means, but a highly desirable and beneficial extension of civilization; if it had nothing more to recommend it than its effect in making home investment compulsory, it would be justified by that alone from the patriotic point of view."

1904. FABIANISM AND THE FISCAL QUESTION: an alternative policy by the Fabian Society, drafted by Bernard Shaw. "Though I am the penman of this tract its authorship is genuinely collective. I quite believe that if the counsels given in the following pages be carried into effect by the nation we shall not need trouble about such makeshifts as tariffs." Special edition of Fabian Tract 116.

1905. THE AUTHOR'S APOLOGY FROM MRS WARREN'S PROFESSION, with an introduction by John Corbin, "The Tyranny of Police and Press" (Brentano). A redeclaration of the author's belief that the influence of the theatre in England is growing so great that while private conduct, religion, law, science, politics and morals are becoming more and more theatrical, the theatre itself remains impervious to common sense, religion, science, politics and morals. "That is why I fight the theatre, not with pamphlets and sermons and treatises, but with plays; and so effective do I find the dramatic method that I have no doubt that I shall at last persuade even London to take its conscience and its brains with it when it goes to the theatre, instead of leaving them at home with the Prayer Book."

1905. PASSION, POISON AND PETRIFACTION, or THE FATAL GAZOGENE (Harry Furniss's Annual); Burlesque melodrama to be performed for the benefit of the Actors' Orphanage. America, 1907 (Claflin).

1907. A LETTER published with the translation (by Ernest Crosby) of Tolstoy's critical essay on Shakespear (Funk and Wagnall). Shakespear's literary powers earned him the title of greatness; his philosophy is empty, his morality second-handed, while as a thinker he is weak and incoherent, owing to his snobbery, his vulgar prejudices, his ignorance.

1907. DRAMATIC OPINIONS AND ESSAYS, with an apology; containing as well a word on the Dramatic Opinions and Essays of Bernard Shaw, by James Huneker (Constable). Selections from the dramatic criticisms of Shaw which appeared in the *Saturday Review* from January 5, 1895, to May 21, 1898. Of his attitude as critic, Shaw says, "Weariness of the theatre is the prevailing note of London criticism. Only the ablest critics believe that the theatre is really important; in my time none of them would claim for it as I claimed for it, that it is as important as the Church was in the Middle Ages, and much more important than the Church was in London in the years under review. The apostolic succession from Aeschylus to myself is as serious and continuously inspired as the younger institution, the apostolic succession of the Christian Church." America, 1906 (Brentano).

1907. JOHN BULL'S OTHER ISLAND and MAJOR BARBARA; also How He Lied to Her Husband (Constable). John Bull: Constable's Sixpenny Series (1908); Home Rule edition (1912).

1907. INTERLUDE AT THE PLAYHOUSE. Written for Mr and Mrs Cyril Maude, and delivered by them at the opening of the Playhouse, Mr Maude's new theatre, on January 28, 1907; the text as given in the *Daily Mail* the following day has never been reprinted. Mr and Mrs Maude were playing in "Toddles".

1907. ON SHAKESPEAR, printed with "Tolstoy on Shakespear" (Free Age Press), being a letter written by Shaw before he had seen Tolstoy's essay.

1908. PREFACE to the Autobiography of a Super Tramp, by
W. H. Davies (Fifield). How George Bernard Shaw received in 1900 a volume of poems by "a genuine innocent,
writing odds and ends of things, living quite out of the
world". A letter of encouragement gained Shaw the privi-
lege of reading the autobiography in manuscript.

1908. THE SANITY OF ART; an Exposure of the Current Nonsense about Artists being Degenerate (New Age Press),
with preface; reprinted from *Liberty* (New York), 1895; a
criticism of Max Nordau's "Entartung". Constable (1911).

1909. THE ADMIRABLE BASHVILLE, or Constancy Unrewarded; being the novel "Cashel Byron's Profession" done
into a stage play in blank verse in the Elizabethan manner,
by Bernard Shaw, in 1901 (Constable); with preface giving
account of the genesis of the play, made necessary by the
copyright law, with observations on the copyright laws and
on blank verse dramatists.

1909. THE IDEAL OF CITIZENSHIP, being an address delivered
at the Progressive League Demonstration at the City
Temple Church, October 11, 1909; printed with the new
popular edition of "The New Theology", by the Rev. R. J.
Campbell (Mills and Boon, 1910). A childhood story:
Fabian tactics explained. "What every man has to keep before him is this: In the first place his country's claim on him;
which is to benefit by his life's work, which he must do to
the very best of his ability: in return you must demand
from your country a handsome, dignified and sufficient sub-
sistence."

1909. Evidence given before the Joint Select Committee
(presided over in 1909 by Sir Herbert Samuel) inquiring
into the working of Dramatic Censorship and Regulation
of Amusements. Verbatim report with appendix of statement. (*The Stage*, 1910.) Mr Shaw's own account of the
proceedings is given in preface to Blanco Posnet.

1909. SOCIALISM AND SUPERIOR BRAINS; a reply to Mr Mallock (Fabian Tract 146). Reprint from *Fortnightly Review*,
1894. A reply to the proposition that exceptional personal
ability is the main factor in the production of wealth and
that the Fabian essayists, by failing to grasp this, have
greatly exaggerated the efficiency of mere labour in the

production of wealth. Reprint, Fabian Socialist Series, No. 8 (Fifield, 1910).

1909. PRESS CUTTINGS; A TOPICAL SKETCH COMPILED FROM THE EDITORIAL AND CORRESPONDENCE COLUMNS OF THE DAILY PAPERS, as performed by the Civic and Dramatic Guild at the Royal Court Theatre, London, on July 9, 1909 (Constable).

1911. PREFACE to three Plays by Brieux; English versions by Mrs Shaw, St John Hankin and John Pollock (Fifield). "After the death of Ibsen, Brieux confronted Europe as the most important dramatist west of Russia. In that kind of comedy which is so true to life that we have to call it tragicomedy and which is not only an entertainment but a history and criticism of contemporary morals he is incomparably the greatest writer France has produced since Molière." Consideration of why subjects, usually considered taboo, must be mentioned on the stage.

1911. DOCTOR'S DILEMMA, Getting Married and the Shewing up of Blanco Posnet (Constable), with three extensive prefaces; 1908, Doctor's Dilemma (Constable's Sixpenny Series).

1911. INTRODUCTION to "Hard Times" (Waverley edition of Dickens). Explaining why Ruskin once declared this to be Dickens' best novel; George Bernard Shaw speaks of the Dickens of this novel as "Karl Marx, Carlyle, Ruskin, Morris and Carpenter rising up against civilization itself as against a disease and declaring that it is not our disorder but our order that is horrible". Dickens has awakened to a greater purpose than to be amusing; at the same time his humour has become more abandoned. Dickens' account of Trade Union meeting condemned.

1913. TO THE AUDIENCE OF THE KINGSWAY THEATRE; a personal appeal from the author of "John Bull's Other Island"; a pamphlet; New Year, 1913. The audience are urged to restrain their laughter and applause until the end of each act so that the performance and the performers may not be interrupted. "Will you think me ungrateful and unkind if I tell you that though you cannot possibly applaud my plays too much at the fall of the curtain to please me, yet the more applause there is during the performance the angrier I feel with you for spoiling your enjoyment and my own?"

1914. COMMONSENSE ABOUT THE WAR, a supplement to the *New Statesman*, November 14.

1914. MISALLIANCE, The Dark Lady of the Sonnets and Fanny's First Play; with prefaces on Parents and Children and on Shakespear (Constable).

1914. PREFACE to "Killing for Sport"; essays by various writers, edited by Henry S. Salt, published for the Humanitarian League (Bell, 1914). "Men must be killed and animals must be killed; nay whole species of animals and types of men must be exterminated before the earth can become a tolerable place of habitation for decent folk. But among the men who will have to be wiped out, stand the sportsmen, the men without fellow-feeling—the man so primitive and uncritical in his tastes that the destruction of life is an amusement to him, the man whose outlook is as narrow as that of his dog. He is not even animal; sport is partly a habit to which he has been brought up, and partly stupidity which can always be measured by wastefulness and by lack of sense of the importance and glory of life."

1916. ANDROCLES AND THE LION; Overruled; Pygmalion (Constable), with prefaces "On the Prospects of Christianity" and "On Farcical Comedy". America, 1916 (Brentano).

1916. DER KAISER UND DAS KLEINE MÄDCHEN; eine Marchenerzählung von G. B. Shaw (Freiheitsverlag). This short story, "The Emperor and the Little Girl", was written, Mr Shaw tells us, for a Belgian charity and was sold by it to various periodicals. "Cassells", he adds, "bought the British serial rights for their magazine; but I cannot remember whether they published it or not." We are unable to trace publication.

1917. HOW TO SETTLE THE IRISH QUESTION (Dublin: Talbot Press; London: Constable). Reprint of three articles written at the suggestion of London *Daily Express* and published simultaneously in London, Dublin, Cork and Belfast on November 27, 28 and 29, 1917—a moment chosen in view of the critical stage the deliberations of the Irish Convention were then believed to have reached. "I am only the spokesman of commonsense and of the experience already gained on the integration of distinct nations with distinct creeds into a single power." The settlement advocated is Home Rule on the basis of the British North America Act, 1867, or the South Africa Act, 1909, with Irish representation in a Federal Parliament of the British Isles, and in an Imperial Conference.

1918. PREFACE to Workers' Educational Association Year Book. Fifteen closely printed pages elaborating the views expressed in "Parents and Children".

1918. MY MEMORIES OF OSCAR WILDE; printed with "Oscar Wilde" by Frank Harris (New York). An account of the six interviews Shaw had with Wilde.

1919. INTRODUCTION to "Trade Unionism for Clerks" (Palmer and Hayward). Owing to the trustification of modern business (which results in their working under better conditions and being better paid), clerks have only a remote chance of themselves becoming employers, and individually they are in an utterly hopeless position to obtain or maintain reasonable conditions of employment; therefore they should join their National Union. Autobiographical details of Shaw's own clerking.

1919. PEACE CONFERENCE HINTS (Constable). Recapitulating his arguments, the author says that, as far as the planning of the war and preparations for it are concerned, the parties enter the Conference on equal terms morally; the war was decided by the naval blockade; the United States has declared its intention of building a fleet capable of coping with any existing naval armaments; this may be taken as the first step towards the next war, unless the League of Nations becomes an established fact; the League cannot seriously ensure peace in Europe until Germany is admitted. Disarmament is possible as regards land forces, but delusive; the League cannot make war physically impossible and should not try to.

1919. HEARTBREAK HOUSE, Great Catherine, and Playlets of the War—O'Flaherty, V.C.; The Inca of Perusalem; Augustus Does His Bit; Annajanska, the Bolshevik Empress; with preface, "Heartbreak House and Horseback Hall" (Constable). America, 1919 (Brentano).

1919. PREFACE to "Family Life in Germany under the Blockade", compiled by Lina Richter (National Labour Press). An appeal to the nation at a "climax in National exultation over the most magnificent military triumphs in our long record of victory" to consider whether it can "afford the triumph any further or even to refrain from undoing a good deal of what has been done and so saving as many lives as possible from the wreck".

1920. DYING TONGUE OF THE GREAT ELIZABETH; reprint from an article in the *Saturday Review*, February 1905, with a footnote by William Poel (London Shakespeare League, 1920). A criticism of a production by Mr (Sir Herbert) Tree at His Majesty's of "Much Ado". Tree uses the play as an ancient, dusty, empty house, which it is his business to furnish, decorate and housewarm with an amusing entertainment. He is forced to do this to find a substitute for the charm of Shakespear's language, a dead language to Tree himself and to the majority of theatre goers.

1921. RUSKIN'S POLITICS (Ruskin Centenary Council). A lecture given at the Royal Centenary Exhibition held at the Royal Academy, November 21, 1919. "When we look for a party which could logically claim Ruskin today as one of its prophets we find it in the Bolshevist Party."

1921. BACK TO METHUSELAH: A Metabiological Pentateuch with elaborate preface on creative evolution as the creed of the twentieth century (Constable); America, 1921 (Brentano).

1922. A DISCARDED DEFENCE OF ROGER CASEMENT, suggested by Bernard Shaw, with an appendix of comments by Roger Casement (London, privately printed by Clement Shorter, February 1922; edition limited to 25 copies), with an introduction by Clement Shorter. The line of defence is that the prisoner, an Irishman captured in a fair attempt to achieve the independence of his country, should admit all the facts relied on by the Crown; defend his conduct as an Irish Nationalist and claim to be held as a prisoner of war. Shaw describes Casement's scheme as precisely what might have been expected from an educated professional diplomat, knowing that the only chance of independence for Ireland, a small and military impotent nation among the Great

Powers, was to have its independence guaranteed by a victorious Germany.

1922. PREFACE to "English Prisons under Local Government": by Sidney and Beatrice Webb (Longmans, 1922). Of the three official objects of our prison system—vengeance, deterrence and reformation—only one is achieved, and that is the one which is nakedly abominable. Society claims a right of self-defence, extending to the destruction or restraint of law-breakers, which need have no more to do with punishment or revenge than the caging and shooting of a man-eating tiger. Intolerably mischievous persons can be painlessly killed, or permanently restrained; persons defective in the self-control needed for free life in modern society can, without rancour or insult, be provided with the requisite tutelage and discipline. In all cases where detention and restraint are called for, the criminal's right to contact with all the spiritual influences of the day, all the normal methods of creation and recreation, must be made available, partly because deprivation of these things is severely punitive, partly because it is destructive to the victim and produces what we call the criminal type.

1924. SAINT JOAN: a Chronicle Play in "Six scenes and an epilogue by Bernard Shaw" (Constable), with preface. Saint Joan, with sketches and stage settings by C. Ricketts (Constable, 1924), edition limited to 750 copies; America, 1924 (Brentano).

1925. THE HISTORY OF FABIAN ECONOMICS, published as an appendix to the second edition of The History of the Fabian Society, by Edward R. Pease (Fabian Society). See below.

1925. TABLE TALK OF G. B. S.; Conversation on things in general between Bernard Shaw and his biographer; by Archibald Henderson (Chapman and Hall). On things in general; the drama, the theatre and films; England and America, contrasts; literature and science; the Great War and the Aftermath.

1925. "A critical appreciation of the author" prefaced to "The Mighty Heart, a survey of England as it is and a vision of what it might be", by W. Margrie (Watts); being two letters written by George Bernard Shaw to Mr Margrie, explaining why his play is not acceptable to West End managers.

1926. TRANSLATIONS AND TOMFOOLERIES (Constable); Jitta's Atonement, translation of "Frau Gitta's Sühne", by Siegfried Trebitsch; The Admirable Bashville, or Constancy Unrewarded; Press Cuttings; The Glimpse of Reality; Passion, Poison and Petrifaction, or the Fatal Gazogene; The Fascinating Foundling; The Music Cure.

1926. Cabinet collection of the Plays (The Globe Publishing Company).

1927. Three Plays by William Archer, with a personal note, "How William Archer impressed Bernard Shaw". Contains an account of the attempted collaboration between Shaw and Archer in a play which became "Widowers' Houses".

SELECTED PASSAGES from the works of Bernard Shaw: chosen by Charlotte F. Shaw (Constable, 1912). New popular edition (Fifield, 1915).

THE GEORGE BERNARD SHAW CALENDAR, a quotation from the works of George Bernard Shaw for every day in the year, selected by Marian Nixon; first published in hanging form, December 1908; second edition in book form, December 1909; third edition, 1910 (Frank Palmer).

1927. BERNARD SHAW AND FASCISM; being a reprint in pamphlet form of three letters.—The campaign of abuse against Mussolini's dictatorship is just as stupid as the campaign against the Soviet dictatorship in Russia. The brutalities, retaliations, assassinations and counter-assassinations which accompany the eternal struggle of government against anarchy are not peculiar to Fascism, as the continual harping on them would suggest. The murder of Matteoti is not more an argument against Fascism than that of St Thomas à Becket is against Feudalism.

1928. THE INTELLIGENT WOMAN'S GUIDE TO SOCIALISM (Constable). Dedicated to his sister-in-law, Mary Stewart Cholmondely, the intelligent woman to whose question the book is an answer.—"This book was started by a lady asking me to write her a letter explaining Socialism. I might have referred her to the hundreds of books which have been written on the subject, but the difficulty was they were all written in academic jargon . . . you might read a score of them without even discovering that such a thing as a woman had ever existed. In fairness let me add that you might read a good many of them without discovering that such a thing as a man existed. So I had to do it all over again in my way and yours."—With index by Beatrice White, M.A.

1928. Do we Agree? A debate between G. K. Chesterton and Bernard Shaw, with Hilaire Belloc in the chair (Cecil Palmer).

Mr Shaw informs us that in addition to those listed above several of the earlier tracts of the Fabian Society and election manifestoes were edited and some written by him. There is "A Plan of Campaign for Labour", the literary foundation of the Labour Party, reprinted from the once famous "To Your Tents, O Israel!" as Tract No 49 (in 1894). It was the production of Shaw and Sidney and Beatrice Webb. The authorship of the following anonymous Fabian tracts is attributed to Shaw by E. T. Pease in his "History of the Fabian Society":

1884. A Manifesto (No. 2).

1885. To Provident Landlords and Capitalists a Suggestion and a Warning (No. 3).

1887. The True Radical Programme, Fabian Parliamentary League (No. 6).

1890. What Socialism Is (No. 3).

1892. Fabian Election Manifesto (No. 40).

1892. Vote Vote Vote (No. 43).

1896. Report on Fabian Policy (No. 70).

1900. Women as Councillors (No. 93).

FUGITIVE PIECES

SHAW's first attempt to break into print, so far as has been traced by his biographers, is indicated in the *VaudevilleMagazine* (September 1871), in which Holbrook Jackson found the following among editorial replies:

G. B. SHAW, Torca Cottage, Torca Hill, Dalkey, Co. Dublin, Ireland.—You should have registered your letter; such a combination of wit and satire ought not to have been conveyed at the ordinary rate of postage. As it was, your arguments were so weighty that we had to pay 2d. extra for them.

Shaw's first actual experience in print was in *Public Opinion*, April 3, 1875, in a letter signed "S.", criticizing the methods of Moody and Sankey, then on a visit to Dublin.

During the first ten years of his life in London Shaw contributed occasionally to the periodical press. His first regular contributions were to the *Pall Mall Gazette*, to the reviewing staff of which he was appointed in 1885. The following year he was appointed art critic of the *World*, an appointment he held until 1888. During this period he published many unsigned literary reviews and sallies in the *Pall Mall Gazette*; a number of his criticisms of pictures appear in unsigned paragraphs both in the *World*, 1885–88, and in *Truth*, 1889; a few of his art critiques also appeared in *Our Corner*. The following, in the *Pall Mall Gazette*, are attributed to him by his biographer: 1886, January 26, Failures of Inept Vegetarians, by an expert; 1887, May 7, Marx and Modern Socialism; Hyndman replied on May 11, and Shaw's rejoinder, Socialists at Home, appeared on May 12; May 31, Darwin denounced; 1888, April 16, Songs of a Revolutionary Epoch; 1888, April 28, A Sunday on the Surrey Hills.

He was appointed in 1886 to the *World* as art critic, to the *Star* (1888) as music critic, to the *World* (1890) as music critic, and to the *Saturday Review* (1895) as dramatic critic. The following list includes the more pretentious of his other Fugitive pieces.

1888

Our Corner: November—First publication of "Transition to a Social Democracy", an address delivered to the Economic Section of the British Association at Bath on September 7, 1888.

To-day: August—My Friend Fitzthunder, the Unpractical Socialist, by Redbarn Wash.
  Do. September—Fitzthunder on Himself: a Defence, by Robespierre Marat Fitzthunder. [This is attributed to Mr Shaw by Henderson; but G. B. S. writes, "Surely I did not write this. I think Belfort Bax did."]

1889
Justice: July 20—Letter on Socialism.
To-day: May—Bluffing the Value Theory.

1894
Fortnightly Review: February—Pianoforte Religion of G. B.S.
  Do. May—Socialism and Superior Brains: a reply to Mr Mallock.
New Review: July—A Dramatic Realist to his Critics (Arms and the Man); same in *Eclectic Magazine*—September.

1895
Liberty (New York): July 27—Refutation of Max Nordau's Degeneration.

1896
Contemporary Review: February—Socialism for Millionaires; same in *Eclectic Magazine*, March.
Cosmopolitan: September—Socialism and the International Congress.
Savoy: January—Essay on Going to Church.
To-morrow: February—A Word about Stepniak.

1898
Mainly about People: September 17—In the Days of My Youth.

1899
North American Review: August—Stage Censorship in England.

Saturday Review: May—Works of Neitzsche.
  Do. July—Rent Question in London.

1900

Critic: August—Correspondence with Harper and Brothers.
Current Literature: August—Science and Common Sense.
Humane Review: April—Conflict between Science and Commonsense.
Saturday Review: November 17—Socialism and Republicanism.

1901

Amateur Photographer: October—The Exhibitions.
Anglo-Saxon Review: March—A Word More about Verdi.
Candid Friend: May 18—Who I Am and What I Think.
Humane Review: January—Civilization and the Soldier: on the South African War.

1902

Caxton Magazine: January—The Author's View: a Criticism of Modern Book Printing.
Saturday Review: February—Opposition to Vaccination.

1904

Clarion: September 30, October 21, November 4—The Class War.
Tatler: November—G. B. S.: a Conversation.

1905

Grand Magazine: February—Theatre of the Future; a Satirical Forecast.
Great Thoughts: October 7—Does Modern Education Ennoble.

1906

Clare Market Review: January—Life, Literature and Political Economy.
Metropolitan Magazine: May—Coburn the Camerist.
Star: February 19—In the Days of Our Youth.

1907

Academy: June 29—Solution of Censorship Problem.
Cosmopolitan: September—On American Women (An Interview).

Everybody's Magazine: December—A Nation of Villagers.
Nation (London): November 16—Censorship of Plays.

1908
Clerk: February—Shaw as a Clerk, by himself.
Freethinker: November 1—Open Letter to G. W. Foote.
Review of Reviews: February—Symposium: What to Eat and What to Drink.

1909
Englishwoman: March—The Unmentionable Case for Woman's Suffrage.

1910
Nation (London): March—Elektra of Strauff and Hoffmansthal.
Saturday Review: July—Mr Trench's Dramatic Values.

1914
New Statesman: November 14—Special Supplement: Commonsense about the War.

1915
Review of Reviews: January—Common Sense about the War.

1916
Collier's: June 10—Ireland's Opportunity.
Independent: March—Kings.

1917
English Review: December 1917 to March 1918—What is to be done with the Doctors?
Literary Digest: August—War Thoughts of.
Living Age: June—Professional Association in Literature and the Fine Arts.
   Do. August—Russia's Interest in the War.
New Republic: January—On British Squealing and the Situation after the War.
   Do. February—Artstruck Englishman.

1918
Economic Journal: September—Taxation of Capital.

1919

Fortnightly Review: August—On Cutting Shakespear.

Living Age: July—Shaw and Chesterton: a Challenge and an Answer.

Do. October—Lord Grey, Shakespear, Mr Archer and others.

Do. November—Wanted—Government for Ireland.

Nation (London): December—The Great Fight—Carpentier and Beckett.

1920

Current Opinion: April—Bernard Shaw finds a Churchman after his own heart. (Review of Dean Inge's Essays.)

Hearst's Magazine: September—I am a Classic.

Living Age: October—Logic of Hunger Strike.

Nation (London): September—A Political Contrast.

1921

Living Age: December—Those Washington Futilities.

London Mercury: May—Tolstoy.

Nation (London): November—Limitation Conference.

New Republic: December—Neglected Aspects of Public Libraries.

1922

Collier's: June—Make Them do It Well.—Technical note on stage production.

Fortnightly Review: October—Dialogue with A. Henderson: Literature and Science; same in *Forum*, October.

Library Journal: January—Neglected Aspects of Our Public Libraries; same, December 1921, *New Republic*.

Nation (London): December—Again the Dean Speaks Out.

New Republic: February—Comment on Clive Bell's Article.

Survey: May—Limits to Education.

1923

Living Age: October—On throwing out Dirty Water.

Nation (London): February—Almroth Wright.

Do. February and March—Jenner.

Do. March—Sir Almroth Wright and Scientific Journals.

1924

Fortnightly Review: May and June—On Things in General: Dialogue with Henderson; same in *Harper's*, May.

Do. September—Drama and Films: Dialogue with Henderson; same in *Harper's*, September.

Do. October—Literature and Science; same in *Forum*, October.

Living Age: August—In Days of My Youth.

1925

Bookman: January—England and America Contrast: Dialogue with Henderson.

Century: January—War Record: Dialogue with Henderson; same in *Fortnightly Review*, January and February.

New Leader: July—Fundamentalism, Tennessee and the Theory of Evolution.

Spectator: September 12—Censorship of the Drama.

Annales politiques et littéraires: May 3—Comment écrire une pièce populaire, traduit par M. et H. Hamon.

World To-day: September 25—Shaw *v.* Roosevelt on Birth Control: Unpublished Letters.

Saturday Review: November 7—Theatres and Reviews Then and Now.

1926

Fortnightly Review: April—Conversation with Henderson.

1927

World's Work: April—This Man Lawrence.

REPORTED SPEECHES, LECTURES, LETTERS, Etc.

SHAW's contributions to the daily press have been frequent, and for a bibliographer dispersed to a tantalizing extent. For the most part no record has been kept of their appearance. Shavian references are only to be traced through the innumerable pages of various files, and as they extend over thirty years and more, the compilation of a complete record would be the task of a life-time. Appended is a selection of the principal references in *The Times* of Shaw's letters, reports of his speeches, lectures, etc.:

1898—September 27 (letter), Murder, Juries and Home Secretary.

1901—September 21, Smallpox in St Pancras; October 8, Vaccination Statistics.

1902—February 8, Vaccination; February 22, April 1, August 19, and September 16, ditto.

1903—January 15, On the Imperial Vaccination League; May 10, Borough Councils; May 25, Employment of Children on the Stage.

1904—January 19, Municipal Trading; January 20, Electric Lighting in Marylebone; January 22, Smallpox Hospitals; March 10, Failure of Church's Electioneering for L.C.C.; May 21, Royal Opera; June 14, and September 2 and 14, and October 11, Flogging in Navy; December 1, Minimum Income.

1905—July 3, Sumptuary Regulations at Hospitals; December 7, 8 and 9, Letters on Sir Henry Irving (see also October 25 and 27); November 14, On the Queen's *Coup d'État*.

1906—January 4, Fiscal Policy; February 23, Abolition of Flogging in Navy (letter); March 8, Drama (lecture); May 11, Vivisection; May 23, On Drama; June 29, Poisoning the Proletariat; July 7, Egypt: Denshawi Floggings (letter); July 7, Decision of New York Justices on Mrs Warren's Profession; September 25, Spelling Reform (letter); October 15, Land Nationalization; October 31, Woman's Suffrage; November 30, On Religion.

1907—March 27, Woman's Suffrage; April 26, National Art Collections Fund; May 9, Publishers' Methods; August 30, Biographical article on G. B. S.; September 23, Motherhood; October 5, On Polygamy; October 18, Middle Classes and Politics; October 21, Socialistic Statistics; November 22, Wages of Female Clerks; December 20, Reply to Charge of Anti-Semitism by Dr Nordau.

1908—February 12, Shop-Assistants' Living-in System; March 20, Drink Traffic; March 21, Dramatic Censorship; March 26, Socialism; October 8, Presents Bust of himself by Rodin to Dublin Municipal Gallery; November 16, Literature, Art and the Theatre.

1909—January 25, Emigration; January 26, Anti-vivisection; January 29, Labour M.P.'s; February 1, Socialism; February 5, Wealth Distribution: a reply to W. H. Mallock; February 17, Medical Profession; March 6, Unemployment; May 10, National Shakespear Memorial; May 25, Anglo-German Relations; July 26, Russia: Nicholas II.'s Visit to England; October 13, Poor Law Reform; October 19, Photography; November 25, Woman's Suffrage; November 27, Fiscal Policy and Budget; December 1, National Theatre.

"The Shewing-up of Blanco Posnet"—May 24, Censor's refusal to licence: Mr Shaw's comments; May 29, Lord Aberdeen's Notice to Abbey Theatre Company; August 21, Sinn Fein Party's attitude; August 23, Abbey Theatre Company's statement; August 24, Mr Shaw's letter; Lord Aberdeen interviewed; August 25, Mr. W. B. Yeats interviewed ; August 26, Production; August 27, Statement by Lady Gregory.

Censorship—(Letters) June 4, June 7, June 26, June 30; Evidence before Select Committee, July 31; Committee refuse to accept statement: (Letter) August 2; (Letter) October 11.

1910—January 7, Labour Party Strength; March 17, Publishers' Methods; May 3, Poor Law Reform; May 12 (letter), Mourning for King Edward; June 10, Wives and Income Tax; June 20, Attitude to Critics; June 23 (letter), Reply to special article; October 8 and 10, On Unemployed; November 1 (letter), Dickens Memorial; December 7, On Music.

1911—January 30, Spelling Reform; February 28, On a National Theatre; May 7, Motor Car Accidents to Dogs (letter) quoted; April 1, Dramatic Authors' Rights; May 4 (letter), Copyright Bill; June 10 (letter), Industrial Insurance Bill; *ibid.*, October 24; November 10, Drama; November 15 (letter), Drama; November 17, On Taxation; December 1, Socialism: debate with G. K. Chesterton.

1912—February 16 (letter), On Drama and Censorship; May 8, On Coal Mining Dispute; April 4, Employment of Military in Labour Disputes; June 27, Vivisection; September 27, Women, Taxes and Imprisonment; December 7, Religion in Politics.

1913—May 16, Shakespear Memorial Theatre; June 19, Woman's Suffrage: Imprisonment of Mrs Pankhurst; July 26, On Medical Profession; October 21, Economics of Art: a Trade Union suggested; November 8 and 15 (letters), Censorship and Improper Plays: reply to Bishop of Kensington; December 24, Model added to Madame Tussauds.

1914—January 30, On Picture Palaces; June 20, On Sex Instruction; June 25, Income Tax: Position of Married Persons; December 16 (letter), Suggested British Propaganda in Italy.

1915—April 22, Attitude to Ireland: letter quoted to friend in Vienna.

1916—December 28, Sorrows of the Super-taxed.

1917—January 15, On Taxation of Capital.

1918—May 4, Speech on Absence of Paper for Purposes of Literature; November 15, Speech on Labour Party's Participation in Coalition; December 13, Speech on Coalition.

1919—January 3, Speech on League of Nations or Another War; February 4, Article quoted on British Responsibility for the War; February 6, Letter on Anti-British Propaganda in U.S.; May 5, Speech on Co-operative Societies; May 16, Speech on Proposed Ministry of Fine Arts; November 13, Invitation to Australia by Socialists; December 1, Message on Conscientious Objectors.

1920—March 27, Offer for film rights of plays refused; March 27, Message on Northampton by-Election; May 6, Speech on Municipal Music: at British Music Society's Congress; May 28, Speech on his New Plays.

1921—February 4, Bulgarian Students' Incident: "Arms and the Man"; March 17 and 31 and April 17, Literary Supplement: Letters on Early Texts of Shakespear; April 25 (speech), Failure of Direct Action.

1922—January 19, Speech on Molière, at British Academy; April 29, Signatory to letter on English edition of Tolstoy; August 22, Impression on Irish Situation; December 8, Speech on Shakespear.

1923—October 27, Unveils Memorial at Bath to Sheridan; October 29, Speech on British Drama League.

1924—February 8, Speech on Mr J. R. Macdonald's Interest in Science (at India Office); February 25 and 28, Letters on "Back to Methuselah"; March 28, Speech on Smoke Abatement (at Royal Society of Arts); April 1, Letter quoted on Waterloo Bridge; April 29, Applied for membership of Cremation Society; June 3, Speech on Deterioration of English Language (at Bedford College); October 9, Letter quoted: reply to Bulgarian protest concerning "Arms and the Man".

1925—April 24, Speech on London Audiences (at Stratford-on-Avon); April 25, Letter on Animals' Welfare Week; May 12, Letter on Smallpox and Vaccination; June 11, Speech on Evolution; June 17, Letter on Epstein's Hudson Memorial; October 23 and November 12, Letter on Dr Axham.

1926—July 16, 22, 27, and 28, Seventieth birthday dinner arrangements; July 27, German tributes; Speech on Freedom of Speech; October 7, Letter quoted: opinion of his own popularity; October 23, Litigation; November 12,

Awarded Nobel Prize for 1925; November 19, Proposal for use of money; Letter quoted; November 22, Letter to Baron Palmstierna.

1927—April 9, Granted injunction restraining publication of book containing his letters to Mr William Page; April 27, His portrait by Collier rejected by the Royal Academy; June 17, Speech at Royal Society of Literature, on Dialects; October 11, Attends funeral of Mrs H. G. Wells; October 13, Letter to Herr F. Adler; November 19, Speech at London Pavilion: on Cinematograph; December 31, Speech at Tate Gallery on Art as a Craft.

Among Mr Shaw's other contributions to the daily and weekly press are the following:

Pall Mall Gazette: January 23, 1886, Scotland Yard for Spectres: a Notice of the Proceedings of the Society for Psychical Research; *ibid.*, May 29, 1886, Review of "Stanley Jevons, Life and Letters".

Morning Leader: August 16, 1901, A Plea for Speech Nationalisation; *ibid.*, August 22 and 24, 1901, Phonetic Spelling: a reply to some criticisms.

Evening Standard: September 15, 1924, " Mrs Warren's Profession", thirty years after: a reply to the criticism of Sisley Huddlestone.

Sunday Express: August 7, 1927, an article on Vivisection: "The Science of Imbeciles"; *ibid.*, May 13, 1928, Capital Punishment in the Gutteridge Murder Case: "An Entirely Reasonable Murder".

Daily News: May 8, 1928, On the Gutteridge Murder: Evidence of experts and rewards for apprehension of murderers; *ibid.*, June 6, 1928, Where are the Dead: Am I Immortal?; *ibid.*, June 13, 1928, Reply to Mr Chesterton on the same subject; *ibid.*, June 26, 1928, Woman the Worker.

For the following record of contributions to *The Daily Herald* we are indebted to the Editor of that journal:

1919—April 7 and 8, Article, "Repudiating the National Debt".

1919—November 1, Letter, "Capital Levy".

1922, November 15, Article, "Wreck of the Birkenhead".

1926—August 17, Contribution to the controversy on the effects of deflation, "Blind Leaders of the Blind".

1927—December 5, Article, "Charity and Shoes", with reference of Judge Henry Neill.

HIS TRANSLATORS

French: M. AUGUSTIN HAMON.

German: Herr SIEGFRIED TREBITSCH.

Spanish: Dr JULIUS BROUTA.

Swedish: Herr HUGO VALLENTIN and EBBA BYSTROM (Lady Low).

Danish: Mr J. M. BORUP.

Hungarian: Dr ALEXANDER HEVESI.

Polish: FLORYAN SOBIENIOWSKI.

8

ABOUT BERNARD SHAW

ALREADY a considerable body of literature exists regarding Mr Shaw. The following bibliography is fairly complete as far as the books are concerned. In addition to the articles listed there are also numberless reviews, which appeared at the time of the production of his plays and publication of his books.

The authorized biography is "George Bernard Shaw, his Life and Works, a Critical Biography", by Archibald Henderson, of the University of Carolina. (Hurst and Blackett, 1911.) Other works include:

AAS, L.—Saertryk av Samtiden George Bernard Shaw Socialismens Digter. (1917.)

ARMSTRONG, CECIL FERARD—Shakespeare to Shaw. (Mills and Boon, 1913.) One of six essays; "examination not of the philosophy but of the plays".

BAB, VON JULIUS—Bernard Shaw (Berlin, 1910).

BJORKMANN, E.—Is there Anything New?

BRAYBROOKE, PATRICK—Genius of Shaw. (Dranes, 1925.) Examination of Shaw's work play by play—dramatically and philosophically considered.

BRUGGEN, C. J. A. VAN—(Haarlem, 1908). Mannen en Vroueven van Beteeken is in onze dagen.

BURTON, RICHARD—The Man and the Mask. (New York, 1916.) "Attempt to give a sharply drawn definite idea of the personality, the works and the meaning." Expository and critical; analysis of plays, with dates of production in England, the Continent, and America.

BURTON, RICHARD—Little Essays in Literature: St Augustine and Bernard Shaw.

CARO, JOSEPH—George Bernard Shaw und Shakespeare. (Frankfurt, 1912.)

CASTREN, GUNNAR—G. Bernard Shaw (Helsingfors, 1906).

CESTRE, CHARLES—Bernard Shaw et son œuvre. (Paris, 1912.) An introduction for those of his countrymen who do not know Shaw.

CHASE, LEWIS NATHANIEL—Shaw in France, Bordeaux, 1910. (Reprinted from the Dial, Chicago, April 1910.) A pamphlet recording the earliest critical writings in French.

CHESTERTON, G. K.—George Bernard Shaw. (1910.) "A rough study" under the heads of Irishman, Puritan, Progressive, Critic, Dramatist, Philosopher. "Most people either say that they agree with Bernard Shaw or that they do not understand him: I understand him but do not agree with him."

COLLIS, J. S.—(Cape, 1925). A book examining Shaw's message, by an Irishman who claims to remedy the fact that so far almost all the criticism of Shaw has come from English or foreign pens; and who claim to have "seen straight into the soul of Shaw".

DEACON, RENEE M.—Shaw as Artist Philosopher, an exposition of Shavianism. (Fifield, 1910.)

DUFFIN, HENRY CHARLES—Quintessence of Bernard Shaw. (George Allen, 1920.) "Shaw's art and technique are admirable, his wit is unequalled, his audacity sublime, but these are the sugar to the pill; most people relish the sugar coat hugely but escape swallowing the pill. I present it sugarless." Prologue indicates some of the main tendencies in the thoughts of Samuel Butler, in which he seems to anticipate or resemble Shaw.

ENGEL, FRITZ—Bernard Shaw und seine besten Bühnenwerke: eine Einführung. (Berlin, 1921.)

EULENBERG, H.—Gegen Shaw, Eien Streitschrift mit einer Shaw Parodie des verfassers. (Dresden, 1925.)

FUCHS, J.—The Socialism of Shaw. (Vaughan Press, N.Y., 1926).

GARDINER, A. G.—Certain People of Importance. (Cape, 1926.) "Tolstoy complained that Shaw was treating life as a joke. Shaw replied that it was a joke and he wanted to make it a good joke."

HALE, EDWARD EVERETT—Dramatists of To-day. (Bell, 1906.) One of seven essays, being "an informal discussion of significant work". Appendix gives dates of first productions.

HAMON, AUGUSTIN—Le Molière du XXᵉ Siècle. (Paris, 1913.)

HAMON, AUGUSTIN—The Technique of Shaw's Plays. (Daniel, 1912.) The third of the nine lectures published as "Le Molière", etc.

HENDERSON, ARCHIBALD—Interpreters of Life and the Modern Spirit. (Duckworth, 1911.)

HENDERSON, ARCHIBALD—European Dramatists. (Grant Richards, 1914.) One of six essays, biographical and expository.

HOWE, P. P.—A Critical Study. (Secker, 1915.) With Bibliography. "Shaw's body of work has not been without influence on his generation; the time has come when it is possible to appraise that influence."

HUNEKER, JAMES—Iconoclasts, a book of Dramatists. (Werner Laurie, 1906.) One of twelve essays dedicated to the author's friend, "The Celtic superman to whom the present author (*circa* 1890) played the part of a critical fingerpost for the everlasting benefit (he sincerely hopes) of the great American public".

JACKSON, HOLBROOK—Bernard Shaw. (Grant Richards, 1907.) "This book is designed as an introduction to the work of Bernard Shaw; it is not a piece of criticism; its one and only purpose is an endeavour to induce people to turn from all mere opinions of Shaw and seek him only at the source of those opinions—in his own published works and utterances." Chapter III is a biographical sketch.

KAPTEIJN-MUYSKEN, G.—George Bernard Shaw—Een waardeering en inleiding. (The Hague, 1910.)

MAUDE, AYLMER—Introductory remarks on Tolstoy and Bernard Shaw attached to "Françoise", Tolstoy's adaptation of a story by Guy de Maupassant. (Daniel, 1906.) Whether unpleasant topics and social evils, for which the writings of Tolstoy and Shaw have been denounced as immoral, are to be permitted in works of art.

McCABE, JOSEPH—George Bernard Shaw, a critical study. (Kegan Paul, 1914.) "The message he delivers under the jingle of bells, how he came by it and what it is worth, what he has done and failed to do, and how you may distinguish a momentary paradox from a reasoned conviction, it is the business of this work to relate. It is not a panegyric or a biography, it is a critical interpretation of the man and his message."

MENCKEN, HENRY L.—Shaw and His Plays. (New York, 1905.) "Handbook for the reading tables of America to exhibit the plays as dramas—to describe their plots, characters and general plans, with short account of the novels and short biographical and statistical chapters."

NICOLAYSEN, LORENZ—Eine philosophische Studie. (München, 1923.)

NORWOOD, GILBERT—Euripides and Mr Shaw, an address to the Newport (Mon.) Literary Society, December 1912. (St Catherine Press, 1913.)

OWEN, HAROLD—Common Sense about Shaw, "being a candid criticism of Shaw's 'Common Sense about the War' ". (Unwin, 1915.) Dedicated "To the memory of the Heroic Dead who have fought and died whilst fools at home contend".

PALMER, JOHN—Bernard Shaw, an epitaph. (Grant Richards, 1915.) "The object of this essay is to ask whether we cannot bid farewell" to a man who "is perhaps the most notable of the organically extinct but galvanically active authors to whose existence the Great War has definitely put a term". In time of peace Mr Shaw might be doing salutary work, but when Britain and the Allies had their backs to the wall his writing became "a really injurious heresy".

RICHTER, HELENE—Die Quintessenz des Shawismus. (Leipzig, 1913.)

ROBERTSON, THE RIGHT HON. J. M.—Mr Shaw and the Maid. (Cobden-Sanderson, 1925.) "It has become a matter of some small importance to save history from Mr Shaw in this particular play, and perhaps, incidentally, it may be possible to save something of the Maid as she was imaginable before Mr Shaw adapted her. The critical charge against him, as I see it, is that under the guise (for the young) of champion of a newer enlightenment, he carries on a campaign of new obscurantism. The purpose of this criticism is in the direction of what may be termed the higher commonsense."

SCOTT, D.—Innocence of Bernard Shaw. (Doran, 1914.)

SEGAL, LOUIS—A Study. Thesis presented to the Faculty of Philosophy of the University of Berne, July 1912. (Record Composition Company.)

SHANKS, EDWARD—(In the series "Writers of the Day")—(Nisbet, 1923). With bibliography.

SKIMPOLE, HERBERT—The Man and His Work. (Allen, 1918.) Biographical and critical, with analysis of the plays, plot, and purpose.

SLOSSON, EDWARD E.—Six Major Prophets. (Boston, 1917.)

With Bibliography. This wartime essay commences with consideration of Shaw and the war.

WALKLEY, A. B.—Mr B. Shaw's Plays; in Frames of Mind. (Grant Richards, 1899.)

WHITEHEAD, GEORGE—Bernard Shaw explained: a critical exposition of the Shavian religion. (Watts, 1925.)

Following are among general works on the drama in which special reference is made to Mr Shaw:

CHANDLER, FRANK WADLEIGH—Aspects of Modern Drama. (Macmillan, 1914.) International.

CLARK, BARRETT H.—Study of Modern Drama. (Appleton, 1925.) International.

DUKES, ASHLEY—Modern Dramatists. (Palmer, 1911.) International.

DICKINSON, THOMAS H.—Contemporary Drama of England. (Little, Brown and Co., Boston, 1917.)

HAMILTON, C. M.—Conversations on Contemporary Drama. (Macmillan, 1924.)

MONTAGUE, C. E.—Dramatic Values.

MORGAN, A. E.—Tendencies of Modern English Drama. (Constable, 1924.)

NICOLL, ALLARDYCE—British Drama. (Harrap.)

PHELPS, W. L.—Essays on Modern Dramatists. (Macmillan, 1921.)

SCOTT, JAMES R. A.—Personality in Literature. (Secker, 1913.)

SEE ALSO

ARCHER, WILLIAM—Old Drama and New. (Heinemann, 1923.)

CAMPBELL, MRS PATRICK (Beatrice Stella Cornwallis-West)—My Life and Some Letters. (Hutchinson, 1924.) With letters from Shaw.

CHAPMAN, J. J.—Memories and Milestones—chapter on "Shaw and the Modern Drama".

GRIERSON, F.—The Invincible Alliance includes essay on Shaw. (John Lane, 1913.)

JACKSON, HOLBROOK—The Eighteen-Nineties: a review of art and ideas at the close of the nineteenth century. (Grant Richards, 1913.)

JONES, HENRY ARTHUR—Mr Mayor of Shakespeare's Town.

(1925.) An open letter protesting against the invitation to Mr Shaw to be chief guest of the annual Shakespeare Festival of Stratford-on-Avon. Protest being made on the ground that Shaw had belittled Shakespeare and England.

MACCARTHY, DESMOND (The Court Theatre, 1904–1907)— (Bullen, 1907). With appendix containing reprinted programme of Vedrenne-Barker performances. "Since Shaw's plays are far the most important dramatic contributions the Court Theatre has received, and since its celebrity and success is rooted in them, the critical commentator must give them the largest share of attention. I propose to discuss the characters, the treatment of emotions, and to give a separate account of each play and performance."

MARBURY, ELIZABETH—The Crystal Ball. The author, a dramatic authors' agent, managed the affairs of Shaw when he was "far from being rich in worldly goods".

MAUDE, AYLMER—Life of Tolstoy, Later Years (1910), Chapter XVI, with letters.

MAUDE, AYLMER—Tolstoy on Art and its Critics. (Milford, 1925.) "The most attractive feature of this pamphlet will be found to be the quotation in full of a remarkable review of Tolstoy's 'What is Art?' by Mr Bernard Shaw, which has lain buried in the files of the 'Daily Chronicle' since 1898 and is now reprinted for the first time."

MAUDE, CYRIL (Haymarket Theatre) — (Grant Richards, 1903). Account of the attempted production of "You Never Can Tell" in 1897.

NEVINSON, H. W.—Chances and Changes. (Nisbet, 1923.) A reviewing anecdote.

PEASE, E. R.—History of the Fabian Society. (First edition, 1916, Fabian Society.) Account of the Shaw-Wells controversy following Wells' criticisms in "Faults of the Fabians" —"Was the Society to be controlled by those who had made it or was it to be handed over to Mr Wells? . . ." As Mr Shaw led for the Executive, the controversy was really narrowed down into Wells *versus* Shaw.

STIER, THEDORE—With Pavlova Round the World. (Hurst and Blackett, 1928.) Contains an account of some amusing incidents at the Court during the Vedrenne-Barker partnership.

TERRY, ELLEN—Story of My Life. (1908.) "He drew the character of Lady Cecily Waynflete in 'Captain Brassbound's Conversion' entirely from my letters. He never met me until after the play was written."

UPWARD, ALLEN—Paradise Found, or the Superman Found Out. (Houghton Mifflin, 1915.) A futuristic satire on Shaw in form of a play.

WILSTACH, PAUL—Richard Mansfield. (Chapman Hall, 1908.) Includes account of the production of "Arms and the Man", the first piece by Shaw played in America; and of the first production of the "Devil's Disciple" and the refusal of "Man of Destiny"; with letters from Shaw.

WINTER, WILLIAM—Life of Richard Mansfield. (Moffat, New York, 1910.)

CLARKE, WILLIAM—The Fabian Society and its Work, preface to Fabian Essays. (Bell Publishing Co., Boston, 1908.)

Bernard Shaw et ses traducteurs français, Augustin et Henriette Hamon : a pamphlet. (Paris, 1910.)

ARTICLES ABOUT BERNARD SHAW

1894
Fortnightly Review: April—A Socialist in a Corner.—W. H. MALLOCK.

1898
Academy: April, May, and June—Shaw as Playwright.—G. S. STREET.
Athenæum: May—His Plays.—E. HALE, junr.
Bookbuyer: July—Shaw and his Plays.—T. R. SULLIVAN.
Dial: July—Plays of.—E. E. HALL, junr.

1900
Blackwood's: June—Shaw and Sheridan.—G. S. STREET.
Critic: August—Work as Dramatist.—W. K. TARPEY.
Do. September—Writings of.—J. B. PERRY.
Current Literature: August—Criticism of.—G. S. STREET.

1901
Academy: March—G. B. S.
Bookbuyer: February—Love Among Artists reviewed.—A. S. VAN WESTRUM.
Critic: May—G. B. S. and his Environment.—J. B. PERRY.

1903
Blackwood's: October—Revolutionist Ideas.

1904
Arena (Boston): November—Arnold Daly and G. B. S.: a Bit of Dramatic History.—A. HENDERSON.
Bookman (N.Y.): April—Shaw and the Man of Destiny.—F. M. COLBY.
Harper's: August—Personal Sketch of.—G. KOBBE.
Lamp: January—Apostles of the New Drama.—E. L. CARY.
Overland: January—Point of View of.—AUSTIN LEWIS.
Reader: June—Present Vogue of.—A. HENDERSON.
Sewanee Review: April—Plays of.—E. G. HOFFSTEN.
Tatler: November—G. B. S.: A Conversation.

1905
Bookman: June—Philosophy of.—W. C. FRANCE.

Cosmopolitan: December—His Philosophy.—E. CROSBY.

Critic: November—Popularity of.—L. STRACHEY.

Current Literature: July—His Woman Wooers.

 Do. October—The Socialist Politician.

 Do. November—Is B. S. a Menace to Morals?

 Do. December—Rise and Decline of.

Edinburgh: April—Plays of.

Harper's: May—Impressions of.—A. DALY.

 Do. June—Shaw's Women.—JAMES HUNEKER.

 Do. September—Shaw and Shakespeare.

 Do. November—Influence on Our Embryo Dramatists.
 —J. L. FORD.

Independent: July—As Playwright and Philosopher.—HER-
MAN SIMPSON.

 Do. November—Irish Bull in China Shop.

North American: May—English Dramatists of To-day.—H. A.
BEERS.

Outlook: November—Yellow Dramatist.—R. CORTISSOZ.

Overland: October—Nemesis of.

Spectator: December—Jester to the Nation.

1906

Bibliotheca Sacra: July—Is He among the Prophets.—W. C.
RHODES.

Cosmopolitan: January—Where does He Leave You?—R. LOR-
RAINE.

Current Literature: May—Where Shaw and Barrie Fail.

Fortnightly Review: March—Counterfeit Presentment of
Women.

Independent: January—Note on Gilbert Chesterton.

 Do. March—Contra Mundum.

 Do. July-August—Shakespear, Ibsen and Shaw.—G.
LOWES DICKINSON.

Lippincott's: Some Aspects of.—J. M. ROGERS.

Munsey: March—Shaw and his Plays.—E. GREVILLE (one of
Grein's associates).

Harper's: November—Shaw's Caesar and Comic Relief.

National Review: February—Shaw and Supershaw.—E.
BALFOUR.

1907

Arena: August—Career of.
Atlantic Monthly: April—Shaw as a Critic.—H. W. BOYNTON.
Bookman: November—A Political Allegory.—H. SIMPSON.
Blackwood's: June—Criticisms of.
Contemporary Review: November—Shaw—Lord of Misrule.
    —W. F. ALEXANDER.
Current Literature: January—B. S. as Dramatic Critic.
    Do. February—His Religion.
    Do. August—His Solution of the Problem of Evil.
    Do. July—Case of the Poets *versus* Shaw.
    Do. December—Constructive Side of his Philosophy.
Fortnightly Review: June—As Critic.—ST J. HANKIN.
North American: June—Career of.—A. HENDERSON.
Spectator: April—Dramatic Criticisms of.
Nineteenth Century: November—Prefaces of.—J. A. SPENDER.

1908

Bookman (N.Y.): June—"Collier's Weekly" and G. B. S.
    Do. July—French Estimate of.—GASTON RAGEOT.
    Do. August—Combat with Lord A. Douglas.
    Do. November—Ellen Terry and B. S.
Current Literature: July—Growing Garrulousness of.
    Do. September—His Discovery of a Supertramp.
    Do. October—Gallic Genius of.
Harper's: July—As One of his Own Puppets.
Idler: July—Shaw in Portrait and Caricature.
Independent: January—Clerks, Moralists and G. B. S.
International Journal of Ethics: July—As Social Critic.—W. M.
    SALTER.
Living Age: May—Modern Attacks on Christian Ethics.
Munsey: January—The Real Shaw.—A. HENDERSON.
Putnam's: February—Rodin's Bust of.—B. VAN VORST.
Saturday Review: February—Regicide.
Sewanee Review: April—Shakspear and.—F. GRENDON.
Nineteenth Century: July—Un nouveau Molière.—A. HAMON.

1909

Arena: January—Career of.—A. HENDERSON.
Atlantic Monthly: February—Philosophy of.—A. HENDERSON.

Current Literature: September—In Shakespeare's Shoes.

Dial: October—Chesterton on.—P. F. BUCKNELL.

McClure's Magazine: September—From Lewis Carroll to B. S.—ELLEN TERRY.

Nation (N.Y.): October—Shaw and Chesterton.—S. P. SHURMAN.

Poet-Lore: September—Misconceptions as to.—F. GRENDON.

Saturday Review: August—Shewing-up of Blanco Posnet.—DUNSANY.

1910

Blackwood's: April—Vestryman of Theatre.

Dial (Chicago): April—Shaw in France.—L. N. CHASE.

   Do. October—By and About Shaw.

Hibbert: July—Philosophy of.—A. K. ROGERS.

Review of Current Literature: October—G. B. S. by J. Bab.

1911

Bookman (N.Y.): August—Shaw's Formula.

Current Literature: August—B. S. and his American Boswell.

Educational Review: December—B. S. on Education.

Forum: March—Realiser of Ideals.

   Do. June—New Drama in England.—A. HENDERSON.

   Do. November—Apropos Shaw.—E. BJORKMANN.

Harper's: April—Inspection of G. B. S.

Review of Reviews: April—Serious B. S.—E. BJORKMANN.

Survey: June—Doctor's Dilemma in B. S. and in Fact.—R. C. CABOT.

1912

Bookman: (N.Y.) December—Mistake in Identity.

Catholic World: January—Marriage and G. B. S.—J. GERRARD.

Current Literature: July—Shaw's Drawn Battle with Paris.

Drama: August—Post-mortem; a Note on Bernard Shaw and the Modern English Theatre.—A. DUKES.

Literary Digest: November—How Shaw saw Rodin at Work.

McClure's: April—My Immoral Play; story of first production of Mrs Warren.—MARY SHAW.

Twentieth Century: April—Shavian Socialism.

1913

Bookman: September—Biographical Sketch.—D. SCOTT.

Current Opinion: November—B. S. writes Fable for Christians.

English Review: October—Androcles *v.* (Oh I Say) Potiphar.
Fortnightly Review: July—Dramatic Craftmanship of.—P. P. HOWE.
Forum: August—B. S. and the French Critics.—E. A. BOYD.
Harper's: April—B. S. and Modern Drama.—J. J. CHAPMAN.
Journal of Education: December—B. S. on Art in Schools.—A. L. REYNOLDS.
Literary Digest: February—Shaw for a Mirthless Playhouse.
   Do. September—Christian Martyrs Burlesqued.
Living Age: March—Moral Equivocals.
   Do. December—B. S. and Morals.
Nation (N.Y.): September—Literary Relationships of Shaw.—I. EDELMANN.
   Do. October—Rule that Proves the Exception.
   Do. November—B. S. and the Law.
Spectator: November—B. S. and Morals.

1914

Century: April—Shavian Religion.—P. G. DUFFY.
Current Opinion: January—B. S.'s Boycott of England.
   Do. January—B. S.'s Bout with the Bishop of Kensington.
   Do. February—B. S.'s Disturbing Relation to Modern Religion.
   Do. May—B. S. as a Puritan, Answer to the Paganism of Oscar Wilde.
   Do. May—Makes his Bow in German.
   Do. August—Shaw's Unqualified Approval of Cinematograph.
International (N.Y.): April—Idealism of.—B. DE CASSERES.
   Do. July—As Molière.—L. J. SIMONS.
Literary Digest: December—Shaw Drubbing John Bull Again.
   Do. December—Some of his Errors.
Living Age: Dramatists of To-day.—E. STORER.
Nation: January—Merry Anarchist.
New Republic: December—Shaw's Diverted Genius.—REBECCA WEST.

1915

Catholic World: Martyrs According to G. B. S.—D. A. LORD.
Century: March—G. B. S.—Harlequin or Patriot?—J. PALMER.

Current Opinion: June—Mr Shaw's Utopian Vision of Films of the Future.

Dial: September—Sense and Nonsense about B. S.—A. HENDERSON.

Fortnightly Review: March—B. S.: an Epitaph.—J. PALMER.

Forum: March—German B. S.—H. F. RUBINSTEIN.

Literary Digest: January—Shaw Discovers an Epic.—France's Yellow Book.

Living Age: May—Self-appointed Statesmen.—J. O. P. BLAND (*Nineteenth Century*, March).

New Republic: February—Captain of Revolt.

Opera Magazine (N.Y.): June—As Musical Critic.—D. C. PARKER.

Outlook: June—Shaw Plays in New York.

1916

Bookman (N.Y.): March—B. S. Musician.—F. B. PELO.

Catholic World: March-April—B. S.—D. A. LORD.

Current Opinion: October—Asks us to give Christianity a Trial.

Dial: September—Sense and Nonsense about.—A. HENDERSON.

Harper's: April—Plutarch Lights of History.—F. P. ADAMS.

Independent: April—New Shaw—Recent Phases in Development.—E. E. SLOSSON.

Literary Digest: February—G. B. S. on the Munition-maker.
  Do. May—G. B. S. Writes a Novel.
  Do. July—B. S. Turned Christian.
  Do. September—G. B. S. Adopted.

New Republic: January—Shaw Comedy, Books and Things.—P. LITTELL.
  Do. February—Plato, Dante and B. S.—H. GODDARD.

Pearson's: Personal Reminiscences.—FRANK HARRIS.

Spectator: August—Christianity Upside Down.

1917

Bellman: October—Argumentative G. B. S.—M. J. MOSES.

Bookman (N.Y.): February—Criticism and Creation in the Drama.—C. HAMILTON.

Current Opinion: Barrie *v.* Shaw in the Realm of Wartime Drama.

Literary Digest: March—Shaw at Armageddon.

Do. August—What the Soldier Thinks of Shaw.

New Republic: April—Bondage of Shaw.—P. LITTELL.

New Statesman: March—G. B. S. and Ireland.—J. M. HOWE.

Open Court (Chicago): October 17—B. S.'s Prophecy.—P. CARUS.

Outlook: January—Omniscient Dramatist.

Revue Politique et Littéraire: November—L'Épreuve de B. S. —E. DOLLÉANS.

Seven Arts (N.Y.): July—His Buried Treasure.—ELVA DE PUE.

Do. November—Shaw and Religion.—F. DELL.

Theatre: November—Is He Sincere?

1918

Current Opinion: September—B. S. again Goes to the Opera.

Theatre: May—In Hackneyed Moments.—N. S. SHAPIRO.

1919

Current Opinion: November—Adventures of James Huneker as Literary Steeplejack.

Living Age: May—Mr Shaw and the Peace.

Nation (London): November 19—Wanted a New G. B. S.— W. ARCHER.

New Statesman: June—As Pamphleteer.

Survey: July—Shaw on Jails.

1920

Current Opinion: November—B. S. Admits being a Classic and Assails Illiterate Detractors.

Literary Digest: April—Shaw called a Colossal Joke as a Prizefight Reporter.

New Republic: January—Carpentier Fight—Bennett *versus* Shaw.—F. HACKETT.

North American: May—Some Impressions.—ST J. ERVINE.

Revue des Deux Mondes: February—Six Comédies de B. S.— L. GILLET.

Theatre: March—Humour of Gilbert and Shaw.—F. MOULAN.

Theatre: July and August—Working with Barrie, Pinero and Shaw.—HILDA SPONG.

1921

Independent: July—Conversion of B. S.—P. SLOSSON.

Literary Digest: November—Shaw's Political Pessimism.

Living Age: August—B. S. gets Religion.

Do. November—Interviewing Mr Shaw.

Do. November—Scandal of Mr G. B. S.—HAROLD BEGBIE.

Mentor: April—What Next, as He Sees It?

New Republic: August—Strange Case of Mr Chesterton and Mr Shaw.

Review of Reviews: April—As a Classic.—S. R. LITTLEWOOD.

Revue Politique et Litteraire: June—De Shakespear à B. S.— G. RAGEOT.

Theatre: April—High Priest of Misanthropy: G. H. MELTZER.

1922

Arts and Decoration: December—More Facts about.

Drama: April—Broadway goes back to Shaw.—J. CRAWFORD.

Living Age: September—Re-meeting Shaw; a German's Impression.

Do. B. S. in the Orient.

Literary Digest: April—How Shaw bags the Universe.

Spectator: May—Eternal Need.

1923

Arts and Decoration: March—Shaw Scolds the Writing Craft.

Bookman (N.Y.): February—On not Interviewing Shaw.—V. RICE.

Do. November—Dunsany, Yeats and Shaw—a Trinity of Magic.—S. DESMOND.

Contemporary Review: G. B. S. and Religion.—H. G. WOOD.

English Review: June-August and November—B. S. as a Thinker.—H. A. JONES.

Illustrated London News: October—Works of P. Guedalla.

Living Age: October—G. B. S. v. G. K. C.—H. PEARSON.

Outlook (London): September—Faith and Unfaith.

1924

Bookman: March—Quintessence of Shavianism.—G. SUTTON.

Bookman (N.Y.): August—Mr Shaw and Pure English.

Catholic World: January—G. B. S.—J. M. GILLIS.
Century: September—Fools of God and Doctors of the Church.—C. VAN DOREN.
Do. October—Portraits in Pen and Pencil.—W. TITTLE.
Cornhill Magazine: January—B. S. and a Critic.—H. C. DUFFON.
Current Opinion: June—B. S. Assails American Critics.
English Review: March—B. S. as a Thinker.—H. A. JONES.
Freeman: February—Open Letter to G. B. S.
Living Age: February—Visit to B. S.—S. TREBITSCH.
Do. November—B. S. and the Bulgarian.
Do. November—Interview with, on St Joan.
Nation (N.Y.): October—Catching up with Shaw.
New Republic: August—B. S. since the War.—E. WILSON.
Outlook (London): April—History on the Stage.
Do. June—G. B. S.—C. J. SHERIDAN.
Do. June—Mr Shaw, God and St Joan.—R. B. LAW.
Saturday Review: August—Interpreters of their Age.—R. WEST.
World To-day: June—St Joan and St Bernard.

1925

Century: March—Mark Twain and B. S.—C. VAN DOREN.
Contemporary Review: March—History as Shaw is Wrote.—A. R. ROPES.
International Studio: December—Portrait by Lavery.
Literary Digest: May—Lines on seeing one of Mr Shaw's Comic Tragedies.—ST L. STRACHEY.
Do. November—Shaw, You know nothing about art, said Pennell.
Living Age: January—Psychology of G. B. S.—W. ARCHER.
Do. February—Keeping up with B. S.
Nuova Antologia: September—L' originalità di B. S.—L. TORRETTA.
Outlook: February—Mr Shaw Sits for his Portrait.—W. TITTLE.
Do. March—Mr Shaw Talks of Art, Labour and Neckties.
Do. (London) March—Epitaph on a Writer of Plays.
Saturday Review: July—G. B. S. and Mr Bryan.—G. GOULD.

Spectator: February—B. S. and Immortality.—A. WILLIAMS ELLIS.

1926

Bookman: March—My Favourite Fiction Character—Ann, in "Man and Superman".—T. BOYD.

Do. October—Appreciation of.

Christian Century: February—Disputes Shaw's View of the Inquisition.

Classical Journal: January 26—Mr Shaw and the Apology of Socrates.—W. A. OLDFATHER.

Drama: March—B. S. Proposes the Toast at the Annual Shakespear Celebration at Stratford - on - Avon.—L. STUCKEY.

Fortnightly Review: February—Shaw, Wells and Creative Evolution.—H. E. L. MELLERSH.

Forum: November—G. B. S. Defends Socialism.—C. K. OGDEN.

Humanist: December—Humanity of.—ESMÉ PERCY.

Illustrated London News: August—Notes about Him.—J. T. GREIN.

Journal des Débats: October—La Fausse Gloire de B. S.—M. MURET.

Do. November—B. S.—H. BIDOU.

Literary Digest: October—As a Modern Molière.

Do. December—Mr Shaw and his Bothersome Money.

Living Age: January—Contra Shaw.

Do. May—Fortunes of St Joan.

Do. September—Germany Greets Him.

Do. December—That Man Shaw.—M. MURET and K. A. WITTFOGEL.

Mask: January—The Colossus.

Modern Language Notes: May 26—Note on Peregrine Pickle and Pygmalion.—A. NOYES.

New Republic: July—G.B.S., the Father of the Flapper.

Review of Reviews: September—G. B. S. at Seventy.

Saturday Review: July—Citizen Shaw.—I. BROWN.

Spectator: July 26—His Birthday.

Theatre: September—Superman at 70.

Vanity Fair: April—Explanation of his Celebrity.—A. B. WALKLEY.

ARTICLES ABOUT BERNARD SHAW

World Review: January—G. B. S.

Do. December—Shaw—Master of the Unconventional Play.

1927

Bookman (N.Y.): February—Mr Shaw, Mr Hardy and the Nobel Prize.

Living Age: January—Shaw Impersonated.

Mentor: May—G. B. S., an Exciting Minority of One.

Review of Reviews: January—Introducing G. B. S.

DICTIONARY
TO CHARACTERS, ETC.

THE DICTIONARY

THE references, to acts of the plays and chapters of the novels, are to the first appearances of the characters.

ABENDGASSE, HERR (Cashel, Ch. VI): German socialist and art critic, who, at one of the society gatherings of Mrs Hoskyn, gives a lecture on the "True in Art". Cashel Byron is inspired to reply to the lecture, and uses Lucian Webber as a living object on which to illustrate his arguments, knocking him down with a deft blow, in order to demonstrate that more effort does not necessarily mean more force.

ACHILLAS (Caesar, Act II): General of the troops of the boy-King Ptolemy.

ACIS (Methuselah, Part V): Youth of the race of Ancients (A.D. 30,000) who is three years of age. The Newly Born falls in love with him on the first day of her life, but he explains to her that it is of little use, as in a year's time he will have grown to maturity as an Ancient, and will be past the age of love-making.

ADAM (Methuselah, Part I, Act I): Learns from the Serpent how to set off the dreadful burden of immortality, and resolves to live a thousand years. Reproves Cain for becoming a murderer and a fighter, and is ridiculed by Cain for always digging in the same old furrow. His ghost appears in Part V and muses on the strangeness of the world in A.D. 30,000, saying, "I can make nothing of it; foolishness I call it".

AFRICAN KING (Cashel, Ch. VII): A visitor to London. The Colonial Office arranges for his amusement an assault-at-arms, in which Cashel Byron participates. The King is highly delighted with Cashel's bout with Paradise, and Cashel is presented. Cetewayo (q.v.) in Bashville.

ALEXANDRIA, PALACE IN: Scene of Caesar, Act II; Quay: scene of Act III.

ALTON COLLEGE (Socialist, Ch. I): An Establishment at Lyvern for girls, kept by Miss Maria Wilson, who conducts it on the principle of "moral force".

AMARYLLIS (Methuselah, Part V): Name chosen for the Newly Born (q.v.).

ANA DE ULLOA (Don Juan): Is chagrined to find, after her death, that she has been consigned to Hell. She appears as an ugly crone, having died at the age of seventy-seven, but learns from Don Juan that she can choose to assume the appearance of any age she likes, and elects to be twenty-seven. As a beautiful woman, resembling Ann Whitefield (of Superman, *q.v.*), she is recognized by Don Juan as the girl who screamed for her father (the Statue), whom Juan killed in the duel that followed. She cries to the universe for a father for the superman.

ANARCHIST (Superman, Act III): One of the brigands of the Sierra Nevada.

ANATOLE (Artists, Ch. II): Is ejected with Charlie Sutherland and a young woman from a gambling den in Paris. Charlie offers to fight him, and Anatole fells him with two well-placed kicks.

ANCIENTS (Methuselah, Part V): Race of men developed by the year A.D. 30,000. They are born from eggs at the stage of development reached by short-livers at seventeen, exhaust the pleasures of dancing and sweethearting and tire of the arts and science (in which they shew marvellous proficiency) by the time they are four, when they reach maturity as Ancients. They then lead a life of solitary contemplation for hundreds of years, until their fatal accident kills them. They do not sleep, they do not feed as short-livers, and they are peculiarly susceptible to injury. They have developed the faculty of willing themselves many arms, legs and heads, and have come to regard their body as a tyrant which prevents them from ranging through the stars, their hope being to become pure thought without body—a vortex.

ANDERSON, ANTHONY (Disciple, Act I): Presbyterian minister of Websterbridge, whom the British decide to execute as an example to the American rebels. Richard Dudgeon, the Devil's Disciple, is arrested in mistake for him, and in the hope of saving the minister's life, Richard accepts the identity. On learning of his heroism, Anderson rides off to join the American militia, and to bring help for Richard. In the nick of time he returns, armed with a safe-conduct, to arrange for the surrender of General Burgoyne, commander of the British troops. The minister deeply loves

JUDITH ANDERSON (Act I), his young and pretty wife. When the Devil's Disciple impersonates her husband, prepared to go even to the scaffold in his place, Judith is inspired with love for him, although she had previously scorned him as an evil man.

ANDROCLES: Who gives the name to the play. A Greek tailor, who, as a Christian, is sent to martyrdom, and encounters in the arena the lion from whose paw he once extracted a thorn. A "humanitarian naturalist", he is reckoned a sorcerer.

ANGELS, Choir of Invisible (Passion): Sing Bill Bailey.

ANNAJANSKA: Is the Bolshevik Empress. A member of the family of the Panjandrums of Beotia, who have been superseded by a revolutionary régime, she declares her adherence to the Revolutionaries. Royalty, in her opinion, has become so wicked and so feeble that it has come to will its own destruction.

ANNIE (Widowers'): A maid to Blanche Sartorius, who, in a fit of temper, shamefully illtreats her.

ANTIENT ORPHEUS (Artists, Ch. IX): Musical society, who establish the fame of Owen Jack by producing his Fantasia. "Founded nearly a century ago, it had been regarded as the pioneer of musical art in England. It had begun by producing Beethoven's Symphonies; it had ended by producing a typical collection of old fogeys, who pioneered backwards so fast that they had not finished shaking their heads over the innovations in the overture to William Tell, when the rest of the world were growing tired of the overture to Tannhauser."

APJOHN, HENRY (How He Lied): Boy poet, who falls in love with Mrs Aurora Bompas, and to her addresses poems which come into the possession of her husband. To save her honour, he pretends that they were addressed to the dawn. Bompas is infuriated at this, but is delighted when he learns that the poems really were inspired by his wife.

APOLLODORUS (Caesar, Act III): Handsome Sicilian carpet merchant, and "votary of art". Assists Cleopatra to go to Caesar, rolling her up in a carpet as a means of outwitting the Roman sentinels.

ARCHBISHOP OF YORK (Methuselah, Part III): One of the

first to experience getting "Back to Methuselah". In the
year 2170 he is still recognizably the same as the Rev.
W. Haslam (*q.v.*) when he wooed Savvy Barnabas in the year
1920. During the intervening years he changed his identity
several times, having been forced, through fear of revealing
his age, to arrange "accidental deaths". In this way he was
successively Archbishop Haslam, Archbishop Stickit,
President Dickenson, General Bullyboy, and himself. He
and Mrs Lutestring contemplate matrimony.

ARCHBISHOP (Joan, Scene II): Of Rheims (*q.v.*).

ARCHDEACON DAFFODIL DONKIN (Inca): The widowed
father of Ermyntrude, whom he exhorts not to live beyond
£150 a year.

ARIADNE UTTERWORD (*q.v.*).

ARJILLAX (Methuselah, Part V): Sculptor of the race of Ancients of A.D. 30,000, who is reproached by the art connoisseur, Ecrasia, for having abandoned works of pure beauty
of form for realistic models of the unbeautiful Ancients.

ASSESSORS (Joan, Scene VI): At the trial of the Maid.

AUFSTEIG, GENERAL (Methuselah, Part IV, Act II): Incognito
of the Emperor of Turania of the year A.D. 3000. (See
NAPOLEON.)

AVIATOR (Misalliance): Joey Percival (*q.v.*).

BABSY (Blanco): One of the women shucking nuts, who considers that a man who would steal a horse would do anything,
and wishes to know what right a "brute" like Blanco Posnet has to a trial.

BACCHUS (Socialist, Ch. III): Nickname for the cat Gracchus
(*q.v.*).

BAGHDAD (Methuselah, Part IV, Act I): Capital of the British
Commonwealth in the year A.D. 3000, having superseded
London after the termination of the period of "Exile".

BAINES, MRS (Barbara, Act II): Salvation Army Commissioner, who accepts gifts of £5000 made to the Army by
Bodger, a whisky distiller, and Undershaft, an explosives
manufacturer.

BAKER, MR JULIUS, MASTER JULIUS, MISS LISETTE (aged
eight), MISS TOTTY (aged six and a half) (Irrational, Ch.
I): A concertina quartet who appear at the concert for

working men of Wandsworth.

BAKER, JULIUS (Misalliance): The gunner. He seeks to avenge his dead mother, Lucy Titmus, object of one of the amours of Tarleton. Baker is an overworked city clerk and a ranting Socialist. He attempts to shoot Tarleton, who is rescued by Lina Szczepanowska, a professional acrobat.

BALSQUITH (Press): Balfour-Asquith; Prime Minister during the Suffraget campaign. In order to reach the War Office without being molested he pretends to be a Suffraget, dressing as a woman and locking himself to a doorstep.—To comply with the requirements of the Censor the name was changed to Johnson.

BANGER, MRS ROSE CARMINIA (Press): Organizing secretary of the Anti-Suffraget League, whose view is that the Suffragets are on the wrong track; women want not the right to vote, but the right to military service. She believes that all really strong men of history were women in disguise; for instance, Bismarck and Napoleon. Marries herself to General Sandstone.

BANNAL, FLAWNER (Fanny, Prologue): One of the critics. Although he is only a young man of twenty, his is the voice that counts with the theatrical profession, as he "really represents the British playgoer". "Obviously one of those unemployable of the business class who manage to pick up a living by a sort of courage, which gives him cheerfulness, conviviality and bounce, and is helped out positively by a slight turn for writing, and negatively by a comfortable ignorance and lack of intuition which hides from him all the dangers and disgraces that keep men of finer perception in check."

BARGEE (Socialist, Ch. V): One of the working men whom Sidney Trefusis, the rich Socialist, gets to know when masquerading as a labourer. Trefusis places his wife, Henrietta, on the barge.

BARLOW, JOSEPH POPHAM BOLGE BLUEBIN, O.M. (Methuselah, Part IV, Act I): A visitor from British Baghdad to the land of the long-livers, who inhabit Britain in the year A.D. 3000. He is President of the Historical and Archaeological Society, and is accompanying his son-in-law, the Prime Minister, who has come to consult the Oracle. Claims descent from Joyce Bolge and Hengist Horsa Bluebin, who "wrestled for the Premiership some centuries before". Under the intellectual strain of conversing with the long-livers he suffers from severe attacks of "discouragement" (*q.v.*), and is eventually discouraged to death by the Oracle, from whom he had sought permission to stay in the land.

BARNABAS (Methuselah, Part II): The brothers Conrad, professor of biology, and Franklyn, who was in the Church. They are the propounders of the theory that the term of human life must be extended to at least three centuries, it being certain that the problems of civilization cannot be solved by human mushrooms who decay and die when they are beginning to have a glimmer of the wisdom and knowledge needed for their own government. The force behind evolution, they declare, is determined to solve the problem of civilization, and if it cannot do it through mankind it will produce some more capable agents. Their theory is christened, by Franklyn's daughter Cynthia, "Back to Methuselah".

CYNTHIA BARNABAS (usually called Savvy, "short for savage") is in love with the Rev. W. Haslam. She is a vigorous young lady, with hazel hair cut to the level of her neck. In Part III it is revealed that she married Haslam, who was still surviving her two hundred years later, for he had been one of the first to experience getting "Back to Methuselah".

BARNABAS (Methuselah, Part III): Accountant-General in Britain in the year A.D. 2170. A man "rather like Conrad, but much more commonplace". Discovers that the Archbishop of York had lived many previous lives, and accuses him of cheating the state by drawing working pay for so many years more than the official limit.

BASHVILLE (Cashel, Ch. IV, and Bashville, Act II, Scene II): Footman to Miss Lydia Carew, whom he loves in secret, and whom he attempts to save from the prize-fighter Cashel Byron. When Cashel tries to force his way into Lydia's house, Bashville throws him with a wrestling trick, which Cashel learns from him and uses upon his opponent, Paradise. Bashville leaves Miss Carew's service after declaring his love for her. Robert Louis Stevenson was delighted with the character of Bashville, whom he declared to be "magnifique".

BASTABLE, ADOLPHUS (Passion): Lover of Lady Magnesia Fitztollemache, he is poisoned by her husband, jealous because Lady Magnesia had praised Adolphus' clothes. As an antidote he is given plaster from the ceiling, but this sets inside him and he becomes a "living statue". Adolphus regarded himself as the first clothes martyr.

BASTARD OF ORLEANS (Joan, Scene III): Jack Dunois (q.v.).

BAUDRICOURT, CAPTAIN ROBERT DE (Joan, Scene I): French nobleman. He is persuaded by Joan to grant her facilities to go on her mission to the Dauphin and to the succour of Orleans. Joan finds him (her squire) obdurate at first, but she soon wheedles him into granting her request.

B. B. (Dilemma): Sir R. B. Bonington (q.v.).

BEADLE (Getting Married): Gives away Edith Bridgenorth at her wedding. Touches children to cure them of ringworm for fourpence apiece.

BEAMISH, HORATIO FLOYD (Augustus): Clerk to Lord Augustus Highcastle.

BEATTY, COL. RICHARD (Artists, Ch. III): Is asked by Mary Sutherland to give the bandmastership in his regiment to Owen Jack, the composer. Mrs Beatty, who dislikes Jack, tries to thwart the scheme of Mary, her niece, who, however, carries her point.

BEAUVAIS, BISHOP OF (Joan, Scene IV): Peter Cauchon (q.v.).

BEDFORD (Cashel, Ch. V): Valet to Lord Worthington.

BEEFEATER (Dark Lady): On duty on the terrace of Queen Elizabeth's palace of Whitehall. Shakespear, who seeks to keep tryst with his Dark Lady, bribes him with a season ticket for the Globe Theatre and a piece of gold.

BEL AFFRIS (Caesar, Act I): Young Egyptian nobleman of the court of Cleopatra, who bears tidings of the approach of Caesar and the Romans.

BELZANOR (Caesar, Act I): Captain of the Egyptian Guard.

BENI SIRAS (Brassbound, Act II): Make an attack upon the party of Sir Howard Hallam and Lady Cicely Waynflete, wounding an Italian, Marzo. They are driven off by Captain Brassbound and his men.

BEOTIA: Office in a military station on the Eastern front of—Scene of Annajanska.

BESS (Socialist, Ch. VI): Wife of the shepherd (*q.v.*).

BIJOU THEATRE (Irrational, Ch. I): Where Susannah Conolly appeared.

BILTON (Barbara, Act III, Scene II): Foreman at the explosives factory of Undershaft and Lazarus.

BIRTH of a human being in the year A.D. 30,000 (Methuselah, Part V): By this date human beings of the race of Ancients are born from eggs, from which they emerge at the stage of development reached by normal mankind at the age of seventeen or thereabouts.

BLANCHE SARTORIUS (*q.v.*).

BLENKINSOP (Dilemma, Act I): One of the horns of the dilemma. A general practitioner, of no particular use, but of unimpeachable integrity, so overworked that he has no chance of keeping abreast with science. Sir Colenso Ridgeon undertakes to cure him of consumption in preference to Dubedat, the rascally artist. Blenkinsop's panacea for human ills is "a pound of ripe greengages taken every day half an hour before lunch".

BLOODY: "Not bloody likely", the famous phrase used by Eliza in Pygmalion (Act III). Sir Herbert Tree urged Mrs Patrick Campbell (the original Eliza) to "cut" the word— "but if I must say it to say it 'beautifully'"—("My Life": Mrs Patrick Campbell).

BLUEBEARD (Joan, Scene II): Gilles de Rais (*q.v.*), who "sports the extravagance of a little curled beard, dyed blue".

BLUEBIN, AMBROSE BADGER (Methuselah, Part IV, Act II): Prime Minister of the British Commonwealth A.D. 3000. (See ENVOY.)

BLUEJACKETS, AMERICAN (Brassbound, Act III): From the Santiago; assist at the trial of Brassbound and his men.

BLUNTSCHLI, CAPTAIN (Arms, Act I): Swiss officer from the Servian army, pursued by the Bulgarians, takes refuge in the bedchamber of Raina Petkoff, a Bulgarian girl. He induces her to give him concealment, and she feeds him on chocolate creams and gets him away safely. Ultimately she marries him. He represents the professional as against the amateur soldier, fighting when he has to, and very happy to get out of it when he can. His nerves go to pieces after three days under fire, and he has found it to be far more important to have a few bits of chocolate in his holster than cartridges for his revolver. His proposal for the hand of Raina (as owner of 200 horses, 70 carriages, 9600 pairs of sheets and blankets, etc.) is a paraphrase of the proposal of an Austrian hotel proprietor for the hand of a member of Shaw's family.

BODGER, SIR HORACE SAXMUNDHAM (Major Barbara, mentioned Act II): Whisky distiller who makes a donation of £5000 to the Salvation Army.

BOHUN, WALTER (You Never, Act III): Eminent Q.C. consulted regarding the domestic difficulties of Crampton. His father is Walter the waiter.

BOLSHEVIK EMPRESS: Annajanska.

BOMPAS, AURORA: Reckoned by her husband to be the "smartest woman in the smartest set in South Kensington". The boy poet, Apjohn, falls in love with her and addresses poems to her, which come into the possession of the husband. Bompas is infuriated when Apjohn, to save Aurora's honour, pretends they were addressed to Aurora of the Dawn, and is delighted when the poet owns the truth.

BONINGTON, SIR RALPH BLOOMFIELD (Dilemma, Act I): A bland self-satisfied doctor, of fashionable practice, known to his colleagues as "B. B.". He agrees to treat the rascally artist, Dubedat, but by misapplying the vaccines he hastens instead of retarding death. "A born healer, so cheering and reassuring that disease and anxiety are incompatible with his presence. Imposes veneration and credulity on all but the strongest minds. The professional envy roused by his success, financially, is softened by the conviction that he is, scientifically considered, a colossal humbug."

BOSHINGTON, SIR CARDONIUS (Foundling): Lord Chancellor, approached by two wards of the Court who each desire to be married.

BOWES, GENERAL (Press): Name substituted for General Mitchener to comply with the requirements of the Censor.

BRABAZON, HORACE, is the Fascinating Foundling. A smart and beautiful young man of nineteen, a ward of the Court, he implores the Lord Chancellor (as father of all orphans in Chancery) to provide him with a stage engagement and a wife. He is claimed by Anastasia Vulliamy, another foundling, who is in search of a husband.

BRAILSFORD, SIGISMUND (Artists, Ch. IV): A hot-tempered man who quarrels in a railway carriage with Owen Jack, the composer. Mr Brailsford was bringing home his daughter Magdalen, who had been disgracing the family by running away to go on the stage. Jack gives the girl all the money in his pocket to enable her to fly again. Later Madge takes lessons in elocution from Jack and goes on the stage, gaining fame after a long novitiate. Her family disown her, but her father, in the days of her success, is reconciled with her. She asks Jack to marry her, but he declines.

BRANDON, SIR CHARLES (Socialist, Ch. XI): Seventh baronet, of Brandon Beeches in the Thames valley, husband of Jane Carpenter. He could play a little, sing a little, sketch a little in water colours; had travelled a little, fished a little, shot a little, and had dissipated his energies through all the small channels that his wealth opened and his talents made easy to him. Trefusis, the rich Socialist, induces him to sign a Socialist petition and, to the annoyance of Sir Charles, causes the fact to be announced in the newspapers.

LADY BRANDON, who presented an "immensity of half-womanly half-infantile loveliness", was a disappointment to Sir Charles, falling short of his hopes intellectually and being so languid that she made all his attempts at fondness ridiculous.

BRASSBOUND, CAPTAIN, whose conversion gives the title to the play, is the leader of a smuggling gang in Morocco. Throughout his life he has nursed ideas of vengeance against his uncle, Sir Howard Hallam, a judge, whom he believes to have murdered his mother, a Brazilian woman, and to have stolen his inheritance. Sir Howard visits Morocco with Lady Cicely Waynflete, and Brassbound betrays him to a Christian-hating sheikh. Lady Cicely converts Brassbound from his ideas of vengeance, and also saves him from punishment for the betrayal of Sir Howard.

BRIDGENORTH, ALFRED (Getting Married): Bishop of Chelsea. He is so tolerant of unorthodox views that he scandalizes his conventional brothers, his principle being that in the discussion of all ethical questions "the devil must be given fair play". Presents (though not necessarily subscribes to) the other and anti-clerical side to most of the conventional arguments about marriage, of which institution he is writing a history.

ALICE BRIDGENORTH, his wife, is a pleasant, thoroughly domesticated matron.

EDITH BRIDGENORTH is their youngest and last unmarried daughter. On her wedding morning a pamphlet on the legal position of a wife, married to a criminal lunatic, makes her doubt whether she can go through with the ceremony. She engages in all sorts of social work, and there is a danger that her outspokenness "when her blood boils" will involve her in libel actions, which makes her fiancé, Cecil Sykes, doubt whether he can marry her, in view of the legal liabilities of a husband. They attempt to draw up a contract of marriage, but find it easier to overcome the difficulties of the conventional marriage.

REGINALD BRIDGENORTH, brother of the Bishop, and head of the family, provides evidence in order that his wife, Leo, may obtain a divorce. Belongs to "the large class of English gentlemen of property (solicitor managed) who have never developed intellectually since their schooldays". His wife,

LEO, young and charming, is tired of the conversational and intellectual limitations of her husband, and has decided to replace him by Sinjon Hotchkiss, although with the intention of keeping a motherly eye on Rejjy. She is a young woman who wants to know a lot of men intimately; considers herself clever and superior, but while "always on the high horse about words, is in the perambulator about things". In the end she orders the cancellation of her divorce.

BOXER BRIDGENORTH, GENERAL, another brother, is "faultless and very dull". Unsuccessful suitor of Lesbia Grantham, who refuses him for the "tenth and last time". A man of much natural simplicity and dignity of character, he is "ignorant, stupid and prejudiced, having been carefully trained to be so".

BRIGANDS (Superman, Act III): Gang on the Sierra Nevada who capture John Tanner.

BRITAIN in the year A.D. 3000 (Methuselah, Part IV): Is

inhabited by long-livers, the British, after the period of "Exile" having transferred the capital of their Commonwealth to Baghdad. The British have not succeeded in advancing in the previous thousand years. The pseudo-Christian civilization ended, as a sequel to the war that followed the ten years' war, and the succeeding civilization was brought to a similar pitch of advancement by the year A.D. 3000, except that poison gases had not been rediscovered. The long-liver prophesies that civilization will continue to pass through the same phases of destruction by war and reconstruction.

BRITANNUS (Caesar, Act II): Ancient Briton, secretary to Caesar. "Represents the unadulterated Briton who fought Caesar and impressed Roman observers much as we should expect the ancestors of Mr Podsnap to impress the cultivated Italians of their time." Discussed in a note to the play.

BROADBENT, THOMAS (John Bull, Act I): Civil engineer, English partner of Larry Doyle, a sentimental capitalist and politician. His attitude towards Ireland is dictated by his interest as member of a syndicate for land development, but this is disguised by the declamation of the orthodox views of the Gladstonian Home-ruler, by a man who is inebriated with his own rhetoric. He is adopted as Parliamentary candidate for Rosscullen, and wins the hand of the only "heiress" of the town, Nora Reilly.—A few strokes are taken from A. B. Walkley. (Henderson.)

BURGESS, father of Candida (Act I): A "vulgar, ignorant, guzzling man, offensive to people whose labour is cheap; respectful to wealth and rank; made coarse and sordid by the compulsory selfishness of petty commerce". Because he is a sweating employer, Morell, his son-in-law, secures the rejection of his tenders to the Board of Guardians.

BRUDENELL (Disciple, Act III): Chaplain to the army of General Burgoyne. He tries, without success, to induce the Devil's Disciple to meet death in a becoming spirit, after having lost money to him, when gambling the night before. A brief note to the play describes the Brudenell of history.

BUCKSTONE (Irrational, Ch. XX): Valet to Sholto Douglas.

BULGARIA: Action of Arms and the Man takes place at a house in.

BURGE, JOYCE (Methuselah, Part II): Prime Minister of England under the second Coalition, successor of Lubin, his rival for the leadership of the Liberal Party. Discusses with Lubin the longevity gospel of the brothers Barnabas. Although regretful that there is no specific for achieving longevity, he undertakes to work the "stunt", adapted for fighting an election on the death-rate and Adam and Eve as scientific facts.—Character founded on Mr Lloyd George.

BURGE LUBIN (Methuselah, Part III): A breezily genial man, like Burge, and yet also like Lubin, as if nature had made a composite picture of the two. Is infatuated with the negress Minister of Health, but is no longer prepared to take risks in order to meet her, when he realizes that he may live as long as Methuselah.

BURGLAR (Heartbreak, Act II): Breaks into Heartbreak House and, after his ear has been blown off by Mazzini Dunn, is captured by Hector. When the household shews reluctance to prosecute him, he threatens to give himself up unless it is made worth his while not to. Is killed by a bomb. "The burglar who makes his living by robbing people and then blackmailing them by threatening to give himself up to the police and put them to the expense and discomfort of attending his trial, is a comic representation of a process that is going on every day." (Preface to Prisons Under Local Government.)

BURGOYNE, GENERAL (Disciple, Act III): Takes part in the court-martial of Richard Dudgeon, the Devil's Disciple, whose execution, as an example to impress the American rebels, is, he explains, a political necessity. Burgoyne is delighted at the manner in which his obtuse subordinate, Major Swindon, is ridiculed by Richard, and is humane enough to be pleased when the spirited Richard is saved from death. A note to the play discusses the Burgoyne of history.

BURRIN PIER, GALWAY: Scene of Methuselah, Part IV, Act I.

BYRON, CASHEL, whose profession is that of a prizefighter, marries the wealthy heiress, Lydia Carew, whom he met while he was in training at Wiltstoken, her Dorset estate. Cashel, the son of an actress, ran away from school, and found his way to Melbourne, where he took service with

Skene, a retired pugilist. He soon fights his way to fame and fortune. His last fight, with William Paradise, is interrupted by the police. His marriage is facilitated by the disclosure that he is the heir to Bingley Byron, a miser, from whom he can expect £5000 a year. After the wedding he becomes a member of Parliament. Cashel has little affection for his mother (Adelaide Gisborne of the theatre), whose sentimental ways are tedious to him. In the play (Bashville) he is represented as flying from her and preferring prison to her company. Mrs Byron in the play marries Cashel's backer, Lord Worthington.

CADI OF KINTAFI (Brassbound, Act II): Saves Sir Howard Hallam and Lady Cicely Waynflete from the Christian-hating sheikh, Sidi el Assif.

CAESAR, JULIUS: Is drawn as a man "naturally great", an able civilian taking up arms in middle life, of infinite capacity for work, and of a rare sense of humour, but "He is neither forgiving, frank nor generous: a man who is too great to resent has nothing to forgive; a man who says things that people are afraid to say need be no more frank than Bismarck, and there is no generosity in giving things you do not want to people you intend to make use of". His attitude to Cleopatra is that of an indulgent master to a child—when he has time to spare to notice her at all.

CAIN (Methuselah, Part I, Act I): Reproaches his father, Adam, for always digging in the same old furrow. He declares, with pride, that he is the first murderer, a man of spirit, who, like his brother Abel, took to fighting and killing as a way of life, and found that it reduced the drudgery of living. In Part V his ghost appears and passes judgment on the race of men in the year A.D. 30,000. "There is for me", he says, "no place on earth any longer, yet while it lasted mine was a splendid game."

CAIRNS, MISS LETITIA (Artists, Ch. VIII): Friend of Mary Sutherland, who secures the services of Owen Jack, the composer, to take a singing class at Windsor.

CALATRAVA, COMMANDER OF (Don Juan). (See STATUE.)

CALL BOY (Androcles, Act II): At the Coliseum.

CANDIDA: Mrs Morell (q.v.).

CAPTAIN (Androcles, Act I): Roman patrician in charge of the convoy of Christians being conducted to Rome. He urges them, particularly the handsome Lavinia, whom he admires, to render the homage of incense and save themselves from martyrdom. His is the attitude of the cultivated agnostic, sceptical equally in regard to the old gods of Rome and the new God of the Christians.

CARBURY, JASPER, EARL OF (Irrational, Ch. III): Employs Edward Conolly as electrician. The Earl was a man with no sort of taste for being a nobleman, but had an extraordinary turn for mechanics, and he pottered at every mechanical pursuit as a gentleman amateur in a laboratory and workshop, settling down at last to electrical engineering. He gave up the idea of doing everything with his own half-trained hand, and employed Conolly as a skilled man to help him.

His youngest sister, LADY CONSTANCE CARBURY (Ch. III), had from her youth been regarded among the relatives as the destined bride of Marmaduke Lind. Although it is evident that Marmaduke has no enthusiasm for the match, Constance courts him assiduously, and after the termination of his liaison with Susannah Conolly she marries him.

The DOWAGER COUNTESS of Carbury (Ch. III) was as assiduous as her daughter in engineering the match.

CAREW, LYDIA (Cashel, Ch. I, and Bashville, Act I): Heiress who marries Cashel Byron the prizefighter. She had been brought up by her father to assist him in his philosophical work, and on his death she was left the richest and cleverest woman in Europe. Although she knows Cashel to be something of a ruffian she is attracted to him, and he adores her. After several attempts to break with him she decides to marry him.

CARPENTER, JANE (Socialist, Ch. I): One of the girls at Alton College with whom Trefusis, the rich married Socialist, masquerading as Smilash, the labourer, becomes acquainted. She marries Sir Charles Brandon (q.v.).

CATHERINE THE GREAT, of Russia, is greatly impressed by the English Captain, Edstaston, and appears ready to make him her favourite, but he is engaged to be married, and he disregards her command to attend her. She has him borne before her as a prisoner, and tickles him, which provokes the jealousy of Edstaston's lover, Clàire, who forces her way into the room. Ultimately Catherine sets Edstaston free, and he advises her to set an example to Europe by "marrying some good man".

CAUCHON, PETER (St Joan, Scene IV): Bishop of Beauvais. Approached by the Earl of Warwick regarding the "removal" of Joan. Cauchon regards her as an instrument of the devil in the spreading of heresy. At the trial he does his utmost to save the Maid from a heretic's fate. I the Epilogue he tells how, after his death, when there w a revulsion of popular feeling in favour of Joan, his dead body was dug up and, after excommunication had been pronounced, was flung into a sewer; yet he had been just and merciful according to his light.

CENTURION (Caesar, Act III, Scene I): In command of the Roman sentries on duty on the Mole at Alexandria. He refuses to allow Cleopatra to go to Caesar.

CENTURION (Androcles, Act I): With convoy of Christians proceeding to Rome. A typical army sergeant.

CETEWAYO (Bashville, Act II, Scene II): For his entertainment, during a visit to London, an assault-at-arms is arranged, one of the items being a fight between Cashel Byron and Paradise. Their emotions aroused by the sight of the boxers, Cetewayo and his chiefs run amok among the crowd and are knocked out by Cashel.

CHAPLAIN, ENGLISH (St Joan, Scene IV): Stogumber (q.v.).

CHARLES, DAUPHIN OF FRANCE (Joan, Scene II): Appears a weak and ineffectual figure among his courtiers. The strong-willed Joan has no difficulty in persuading him to appoint her chief of the Army. After his coronation, by her, in Rheims Cathedral, Charles receives without regret her announcement that she is going to return home; she is too resolute a character for him. In the Epilogue he tells Joan that in the twenty-five years since her death he has been inspired by her example to bravery in battle, and is known as Charles the Victorious. He praises the new Saint on behalf of the "unpretending" folk.

CHARLES, PRIVATE (Artists, Ch. III): An Army clarionettist

whom Owen Jack, the composer, engages to assist in a rendering of his Fantasia. His presence, somewhat intoxicated, in the Sutherland drawing room, leads to the dismissal of Jack as tutor.

CHARMIAN (Caesar, Act IV): One of the ladies of Cleopatra's court.

CHARTERIS, LEONARD (Philanderer, Act I): The Philanderer seeks to become engaged to Grace Tranfield, as a refuge from his former lover, Julia Craven, who declines to give him up. When Julia eventually accepts another suitor, Charteris is no longer anxious to marry, and Grace, an advanced woman of the Ibsen Club, feels that she loves him too well to marry him.

CHELSEA, BISHOP OF (Getting Married): Alfred Bridgenorth (*q.v.*).

CHINON: Throne room of Castle (Joan, Scene II).

CHIPS (Socialist, Ch. III): Nickname of one of the girls at Alton College.

CHLOE (Methuselah, Part V): Maiden of the race of Ancients (A.D. 30,000) who is getting tired of dancing and sweethearting with her lover Strephon. She finds fascination in numbers, is abandoning the disgusting practice of sleep; in short, she is approaching the age of four, when maturity commences, and she will be an Ancient.

CHOCOLATE SOLDIER (Arms): Bluntschli (*q.v.*).

CLAIRE (Catherine, Scene III): Accompanies her lover, Captain Edstaston, who seeks audience of Catherine the Great of Russia. When Edstaston is borne off prisoner, Claire follows, even into the presence of the Empress.

CLANDON, MRS LANFREY (You Never, Act I): Authoress of the "Twentieth Century Treatises" on cooking, creeds, clothing, etc., "without which no household is complete". A leader of the sex emancipation movement. Because of his brutality she separated from her husband Crampton, and reared her family in Madeira. She has brought up her elder daughter,

GLORIA (Act I), "scientifically", to be the twentieth-century girl. Gloria, to her shame, succumbs to the love-making of Valentine, the "duellist of sex", who, after many love affairs, is brought by her to matrimony.

151

DOLLY and PHIL CLANDON (Act I), the two younger children, the twins, are a flippant, garrulous, inquisitive and light-hearted pair, who are continually shocking the older and more sedate generation by their lack of respect for age. Dolly is first patient of Valentine, the five-shilling dentist.

CLARA (Artists, Ch. IV): Servant girl to the Sutherlands, complains that Owen Jack, the "chooter", called her names and swore at her.

CLARIONETTIST, DRUNKEN (Artists, Ch. III): Private Charles (*q.v.*).

CLEOPATRA (Caesar, Act I): Is drawn as a very spoilt, petulant and self-willed child, so ignorant that she really believes that the Romans will perform the physical feat of eating her, but she rises to dignity and wisdom through six months' contact with Caesar. She orders her nurse, Ftatateeta, to assassinate Pothinus, who humiliated her before Caesar. She is delighted when Caesar, on leaving for Rome, promises to send Marc Antony to her.

CLEOPATRA SEMIRAMIS (Methuselah, Part V): Consort of Ozymandias. Female figure created by Pygmalion, scientist of the year A.D. 30,000. She bites Pygmalion on the hand, killing him, and is by the Ancients reduced to death by discouragement.

CLERIC (Joan, Epilogue): Of the twentieth century, announces the canonization of the Venerable and Blessed Joan.

COHEN, MRS (Artists, Ch. VIII). (See LAFITTE.)

COKANE, WILLIAM DE BURGH (Widowers', Act I): Friend of Dr Trench. He becomes amanuensis of Lickcheese, the illiterate slum property exploiter, once rent collector.

COLISEUM: Behind the Emperor's Box; scene of Androcles, Act II.

COLLINS, WILLIAM (Getting Married): Greengrocer and alderman, an artist in the arrangement of such social affairs as the weddings of the daughters of Bishop Bridgenorth. He is married to a lady to whom marriage "came natural, being a born wife and mother". His matrimonial philosophy is, "Marriage is tolerable enough in its way if youre easygoing and dont expect too much from it. But it doesnt bear thinking about. The great thing is to get the young people tied up before they know what theyre letting themselves in for."

His sister-in-law, MRS GEORGE COLLINS (christened Zenobia Alexandrina), the Mayoress, is a woman with a varied experience of men. She ran away from her husband many times, but always returned at the end of the affair. In the reckoning of her brother-in-law her experience has made her a wonderfully interesting woman. She is the Incognita Appassionata of Bishop Bridgenorth, having anonymously sent him many love letters. In the presence of the Bishop she goes into a trance. Sinjohn Hotchkiss falls in love with her.

COLONIZERS (Methuselah, Part IV, Act I): One of the political parties of the long-livers. The Conservatives hold that the race should remain in their own islands, wrapped in the majesty of their wisdom; the Colonizers advocate that the race should increase its numbers and colonize other lands, exterminating the short-livers.

COMMANDER OF CALATRAVA (Don Juan). (See STATUE.)

CONFUCIUS (Methuselah, Part III): Chinese Secretary of State to Britain in the year A.D. 2170, at which date the Government is carried on by educated Chinese and negresses. Is revered as a fountain of wisdom by the British.

CONOLLY, EDWARD SEBASTIAN (Irrational, Ch. I): Is an electrical engineer who, after working for the Earl of Carbury, a scientific amateur, makes his fame and fortune with an electro-motor invention. He marries, despite the opposition of her father, Marian Lind, who after a few years elopes with a former lover. Conolly's sister,

SUSANNAH CONOLLY (Ch. I), is an actress (Lalage Virtue) who becomes famous in musical comedy. Marmaduke Lind forms a liaison with her (she declines to marry him) and they establish a ménage at Twickenham, which is maintained largely on Susannah's money. On account of her drinking, Marmaduke leaves Susannah, who makes a hit on the New York stage, but is reduced to poverty by her drinking habits, which ultimately cause her death.

EDWARD CONOLLY is also introduced in "Love Among the Artists" (Ch. XIV). He discusses his own marriage, and advises Mary Sutherland to marry John Hoskyn.

CORNO DI BASSETTO, pseudonym adopted by Shaw when he became music critic to the *Star*. It is the name of a musical instrument which went out in the time of Mozart.

COSSACK (Catherine): Sergeant (*q.v.*).

COURCELLES, CANON DE, of Paris (Joan, Scene VI): Drew up indictment of the Maid on sixty-four counts. To his regret the counts are reduced to twelve, the Inquisitor pointing out that on such an issue as the stealing of a horse he may have to declare Joan innocent, and she may thus escape them on the main issue of heresy. Suggests that Joan should be put to the torture as "it is always done".

CRAMPTON, FERGUS (You Never, Act I): A yacht builder. His wife separated from him on account of his brutality. An irritable and obstinate man, he has little sympathy with the squeamishness of the young generation; he was trained to believe that most things good for him were nasty, and declines to have gas for a tooth extraction, remarking that in his day people were "taught to bear necessary pain". He attempts to effect a reconciliation with his family, of which effort the play is the dramatic record.

CRAVEN, COL. DANIEL (Philanderer, Act I): Victim of Paramore's disease, a new liver affliction, is given a few months to live. Severely dieted, he becomes, after a life of self-indulgence, an enthusiastic member of teetotal societies "making virtue of necessity". The theories of Paramore are exploded, and the Colonel finds he has practised abstinence to no purpose. He is shocked to hear his girls proclaim themselves "unwomanly women" as members of the Ibsen Club. One of the girls,

JULIA CRAVEN (Act I), had declined to marry her lover, Leonard Charteris, the Philanderer, because he might turn out a drunkard or a lunatic, but proves to be a fraud as an unwomanly woman. She reserved the right to leave Leonard as soon as she chose, but when he seeks to exercise the same right, she threatens to assault the other woman—Grace Tranfield. Finally she agrees to marry Dr Paramore.

SYLVIA CRAVEN (Act II), the Colonel's second daughter, is more unwomanly than her sister. She demands that her friends of the Ibsen Club, men and women, shall not call her Sylvia but Craven.

Col. Craven's mannerisms taken from H. M. Hyndman—"now really" in particular. (Henderson.)

CRAWFORD (Irrational, Ch. XVIII): Wife of a General, she befriends Marian Conolly in New York.

CROFTS, SIR GEORGE (Mrs Warren, Act I): Baronet and chief shareholder of the establishments at Brussels, Berlin, and Vienna and Buda-Pesth, of which Mrs Warren is managing director. His investment, he argues, which pays him 35 per cent, is no more open to reproach than that of his brother, who gets 22 per cent out of a factory where none of the girls are paid enough to live on. Woos Vivie Warren, who rejects him with scorn.

CULLEN, SIR PATRICK (Dilemma, Act I): A doctor, representative of the old school, a sceptic regarding the "discoveries" of modern medicine. Most of them, he says, are discovered regularly every fifteen years.

CUSINS, ADOLPHUS (Major Barbara, Act I): Greek professor, lover of Major Barbara, to please whom he plays the big drum at Salvation Army meetings. As the child of a marriage between a man and his deceased wife's sister he is a semi-foundling, and he is chosen to succeed to the Undershaft inheritance in the explosives factory.

CUTHBERTSON, JOSEPH (Philanderer, Act I): A dramatic critic, father of Grace Tranfield, and a member of the Ibsen Club. As critic he passed his life amid "scenes of suffering nobly endured and sacrifice willingly rendered by womanly women and manly men".—A caricature of Clement Scott. (Henderson.)

DADDY (Methuselah, Part IV, Act I): Name given by the long-livers to the Elderly Gentleman whose full title, Joseph Popham Bolge Bluebin Barlow, O.M., is too much for them.

DANBY (Dilemma, Act V): Secretary of one of the smaller Bond-street Picture Galleries, where the works of Dubedat are exhibited.

DANIELS, ELDER (Blanco): Unctuous brother of Blanco Posnet. A reformed reprobate, who turned from borrowing money to get drunk with to lending money and selling drink to others. Had possession of a horse, and Blanco, not knowing it belonged to the Sheriff, rode off with it because

GEORGE BERNARD SHAW

the Elder would not surrender to him their mother's old necklace.

DARK LADY: Mary Fitton (*q.v.*).

DARLING DORA: Delaney (Fanny) (*q.v.*).

DASHKOFF, PRINCESS (Catherine, Scene II): Of the Court of the Empress Catherine of Russia.

DAUPHIN (Joan, Scene II): Charles of France (*q.v.*).

DAWKINS (Music Cure): Doctor who treats Lord Reginald Fitzambey.

DELANEY, MISS (Darling Dora) (Fanny, Act I): Young woman of the streets, whom Bobby Gilbey picks up. She knocks a constable's hat over his eyes, and she and Bobby are sent to prison as "drunk and disorderlies".

DEMPSEY, FATHER (John Bull, Act II): Irish priest of Rosscullen.

DENTIST, FIVE-SHILLING (You Never): Valentine (*q.v.*).

D'ESTIVET (Joan, Scene VI): Canon John, of the Chapter of Bayeux. Promoter (Prosecutor) at the trial of the Maid.

DEVIL (Don Juan): Welcomes the Statue on arrival from Heaven to his kingdom, and attempts to dissuade Don Juan from departing for Heaven. The Devil expresses annoyance of the caricatures of himself drawn by Milton and Dante, and, regarding his departure from Heaven, declares that the notice that he was expelled is ridiculous; the fact was he found life there too tedious, so he left and founded the other place.

DISCOURAGEMENT (Methuselah, Part IV, Act I): Disease, often fatal, which afflicts short-livers who come into contact with long-livers, being the result of intellectual strain. "Daddy" Barlow has several attacks, and ultimately succumbs.

DOCTOR (Passion): Struck dead by lightning.

DOCTOR (Music): Treats Lord Reginald Fitzambey.

DOMESTIC MINISTER (Methuselah, Part III): In Britain in the year A.D. 2170, Mrs Lutestring (*q.v.*).

DON JUAN DE TENORIO decides to leave Hell, where he finds life tedious, for Heaven, where he hopes to be able to assist in helping life on earth in its struggle upwards towards the superman. On this subject he delivers long harangues to the Devil, the Statue, and Ana. In appearance Juan is very like Tanner (of the Superman, *q.v.*). During his earthly career he had an affair with Ana, who screamed for her father, the Statue; Juan killed him in a duel.

DONKIN, DAFFODIL (Inca): Archdeacon (*q.v.*).

DOOLITTLE, ELIZA (Pygmalion, Act I): Cockney flower-girl, who, wishing to be a florist's shop assistant, seeks to become the pupil of Higgins, professor of phonetics. For a wager he undertakes to transform her into the equal of a duchess. When he has succeeded she is piqued to find that he continues to treat her with the indifferent condescension and superiority of a master to a pupil. Makes (in Act III) the famous remark, "not bloody likely". The postscript to the play describes how she marries Freddy Hill and how they establish a fashionable greengrocery establishment.

Her father, ALFRED DOOLITTLE (Act II), a dustman, is one of the "undeserving poor", who, when his daughter is adopted by Higgins, seeks a share in the spoils, and obtains a £5 note. On the recommendation of Higgins that he is "the most original moralist in England", he is left £3000 a year by an American, on condition that he lectures for the Wannafeller Moral Reform World League. The result is that he has to leave undeserving poverty for middle-class morality, and, incidentally, to marry Mrs Doolittle.

DORAN, BARNEY (John Bull, Act II): Miller of Rosscullen, intended to represent the "energy and capacity wasted and demoralized by want of sufficient training and social pressure to force it into beneficial activity and build a character upon it".

DOUGLAS, SHOLTO (Irrational, Ch. I): A haughty, aristocratic person who proposes to Marian Lind. His vanity is sorely mortified when she rejects him. After her marriage to Conolly, Sholto again makes love to Marian and induces her to elope with him. On their flight to New York Marian finds him a jealous and petulant companion, and he informs her that unless she behaves herself he will not marry her after her husband has divorced her, at which she decides she can no longer stay with him. Quite indifferent to her fate, Douglas returns to England.

His mother, MRS DOUGLAS (Ch. VII), is described as "a widow lady with a rather glassy eye and shaky hand, who would have looked weak and shiftless in an almshouse, but who, with plenty of money and unlimited domestic service and unhesitating deference from attendants, made a fair show of being a dignified and interesting old lady".

DOYLE, LAURENCE (John Bull, Act I): Civil engineer, Irish partner of Thomas Broadbent. Son of a small Irish land agent; he makes his fortune in America, and from his larger international experience, develops an attitude of ruthless realism towards his native land. To him small peasant proprietors, though Irish, will be no better than large landlords, though English. Capital and English driving power are to him a necessity for Ireland. His father,

CORNELIUS DOYLE (Act II), is host of Broadbent during his stay in Rosscullen.

MISS JUDY DOYLE (Act II) is housekeeper to Cornelius, her brother.

DRINKWATER, FELIX (Brassbound, Act I): Cockney member of Brassbound's gang, in which he is known as "Brandy-faced Jack". He was once tried before Sir Howard Hallam and "wrongfully acquitted".

DRISCOLL, TERESA: Lover of O'Flaherty. When he returns home on leave, after winning the V.C., she vexes him by her concern that he should get a pension for her, even if he has to be wounded in the getting of it. The gold chain given her by O'Flaherty causes a furious scene between Teresa and Mrs O'Flaherty.

DUBEDAT, LOUIS (Dilemma, Act II): One of the horns of the Doctor's Dilemma. An artist of distinction, but a man without morals—in fact he declares himself to be a disciple of Shaw—he is dying from tuberculosis. Sir Colenso Ridgeon could cure him of his malady, but he would then be unable to save Blenkinsop, a doctor, honest and decent, but of no particular value to the community. The beautiful

MRS JENIFFER DUBEDAT (Act I) persuades Ridgeon to undertake the cure. The doctor discovers what a worthless person the artist is, and eventually resolves his dilemma by leaving the artist to his fate. Sir R. Bloomfield Bonington tries to save Dubedat, but his treatment proves fatal. The real model for Dubedat was Aubrey Beardsley. (Henderson.)

DUCKET, SAM, of Milltown (Cashel, Prologue): Professional

pugilist, against whom Cashel Byron fought his first fight. Cashel by breaking Sam's jaw laid the foundation of his fame.

DUDGEON, RICHARD, is the Devil's Disciple (Act I): During the American War of Independence the British commander, intending to make an example of one of the rebels, orders the arrest of Anderson, a Presbyterian divine. Richard Dudgeon, who is known as the Devil's Disciple because of his evil way of life, is taken in mistake and, in the hope of saving Anderson, he accepts the identity. Only when on the point of being hanged is Richard saved. While Richard boasts of being evil and is a charitable person, his mother,

MRS DUDGEON (Act I), is a woman who prates of her religion but is distinguished by her temper and a fierce pride. She has obtained an unquestioned reputation for piety because she is so exceedingly disagreeable. Her husband, Timothy, in his last hours, was reconciled with his reprobate son, Richard, to whom he left his estate, to the chagrin of Mrs Dudgeon, who dies shortly after the reading of the will. Mrs Dudgeon was left guardian of

ESSIE (Act I), natural daughter of her brother-in-law, Peter Dudgeon, who was hanged as a rebel. Essie feels for Richard a dog's affection for its master, for he alone treats her with kindness.

CHRISTY DUDGEON (Act I), Richard's brother, is a dull young man who is called at the trial as a witness to the identity of Richard. There are two uncles present at the reading of the will.

TITUS DUDGEON (Act I), a horse dealer, a wiry little terrier of a man, with a purse-proud wife; and

WILLIAM DUDGEON (Act I), a bottle-nosed man, obviously no ascetic at the table.

DUNN, MAZZINI (Heartbreak, Act I): Founder of a business which failed. It was ultimately taken over by Mangan, a financier, under whom Mazzini worked successfully as manager. His daughter,

ELLIE DUNN, considers it her duty to marry Mangan, because she believes him to have befriended her father, although she is in love with a man whom she first met at the National Gallery. When she discovers this man, Hector Hushabye, is married, her heart breaks. She finally rejects Mangan and marries herself to Captain Shotover.

Dunois, Jack (Joan, Scene III): Commander of the French forces, known as the Bastard of Orleans. After the apparent miracle of the wind he surrenders his command to Joan and follows her to relieve besieged Orleans. In the Epilogue Dunois tells Joan that it was her "way" of fighting that brought victory to the French.

Duval (Superman, Act III): One of the brigands on the Sierra Nevada.

Duvallet, Lieutenant (Fanny, Act II): A Frenchman, to whom Margaret Knox introduces herself on boat-race night. During a scuffle with the police he fells a constable with a "magnificent moulinet", and is sent to prison, like Margaret.

Ecrasia (Methuselah, Part V): Handsome nymph of the race of Ancients of the year A.D. 30,000, who is reckoned an art connoisseur. She reproaches the sculptor Arjillax for abandoning models of beauty, of nymphs and swains, for realistic studies of the unbeautiful Ancients.

Edith Bridgenorth (Married) (q.v.).

Editor (Androcles, Act II): Of the Gladiators.

Edstaston, Captain Charles (Catherine, Scene I): Of the Light Dragoons. Seeks audience of Catherine the Great of Russia, into whose presence he is carried, unceremoniously, by Patiomkin. Catherine is greatly impressed by the Captain and appears to be ready to adopt him as her favourite, but he is engaged to be married, and ignores the command of Catherine to attend her. He is carried as a prisoner before Catherine, who, after tickling him with her toe, sets him free. Before leaving he gives the Empress a piece of advice —to set Europe an example by "marrying some good man".

Egg (Methuselah, Part V): From which the child of the race of Ancients is born in the year A.D. 30,000. At that date human children exist for two years in the egg, passing in fifteen months through a development that once cost human beings twenty years of awkward stumbling immaturity after birth.

EGYPT: Scenes of Caesar and Cleopatra take place in.

ELDER (BLANCO): Daniels (*q.v.*).

ELDERLY GENTLEMAN (Methuselah, Part IV, Act I): Joseph Barlow (*q.v.*).

ELIZA (Irrational, Ch. XIX): Slipshod Irish girl, servant in the New York house in which Marian Conolly takes lodgings.

ELIZA DOOLITTLE (Pygmalion).

ELIZABETH, QUEEN (Dark Lady): Her features concealed by a cloak, she is mistaken by Shakespear for Mary Fitton, the supposititious Dark Lady of the Sonnets. Mary surprises the Bard as he is in the act of embracing the cloaked lady, and after giving each of them a cuff, she is horrified to find that she has struck her Queen. Shakespear appeals to Elizabeth to support his project for a national theatre, and she predicts that "until every other country in the Christian world has its playhouse at the public charge, England will never adventure".

ELLIE DUNN (Heartbreak).

EMMA (Blanco): One of the women shucking nuts.

EMMY (Dilemma, Act I): Old and trusted serving woman to Ridgeon. "She has only one manner and that is of an old family nurse to a child just after it has learned to walk."

EMPEROR (Androcles, Act II): Who orders the martyrdom of the Christians. "Has no sense of the value of common people's lives and amuses himself with killing as carelessly as with sparing ; is the sort of monster you can make of a silly clever gentleman by idolizing him." He is delighted when the martyr Ferrovius slays six of the gladiators—the record for his reign. If Christians fight like that he will have none but Christians to fight for him.

ENVOY (Methuselah, Part IV, Act II): From British Baghdad, Ambrose Badger Bluebin, Prime Minister of the British Commonwealth in the year A.D. 3000. Comes to Galway to consult the Oracle of the long-livers on behalf of his political party, the Potterbills, regarding the time for a general election, and is given the reply made fifteen years previously to his illustrious predecessor, "Go home, poor fool". "A typical politician, he looks like an imperfectly reformed criminal." Is accompanied by his wife, daughter, Molly, and father-in-law, Joseph Barlow.

ERMYNTRUDE (Inca): Widow of a millionaire, who has been reduced to poverty, and the daughter of an Archdeacon who cannot allow her more than £150 a year. Deciding to take service with Royalty, she succeeds in appointing herself lady's maid to a Princess, and, impersonating her royal mistress, she meets the Inca of Perusalem. The Inca is greatly impressed by her, and offers to turn Mahometan in order to marry her, but she declines the honour because he has bankrupted himself by the war.

ERSKINE, CHICHESTER (Socialist, Ch. XI). Art critic and author of "The Patriot Martyrs", a tragedy in verse, dedicated to the Spirit of Liberty. He is the devoted lover of Gertrude Lindsay, who, on the advice of Trefusis, decides to accept him.

EVANS, FEEMY (Blanco): A woman of ill fame, who is prepared to give evidence that will hang Blanco Posnet, the horse thief, because he had insulted her. Her conscience aroused by the story of how the horse thief, even at peril of his life, responded to the appeal of the mother of the dying child, Feemy finds herself unable to maintain her perjury.

EVE (Methuselah, Part I, Act I): Learns from the Serpent the mystery of death, life and birth. Reproves Cain for his way of life as a killer, and Adam for his as a digger, declaring her belief that it was not for these cheap ways that Lilith set life free. Her ghost in Part V passes judgment on the race of men of A.D. 30,000. The clever ones, always her favourites, have, she finds, inherited the earth.

EXECUTIONER (Joan, Scene VI): Master Executioner of Rouen, present at the trial of Joan, whose burning he carries out. In the Epilogue he complains that, though he was a master at his craft, he could not kill the Maid; she was up and alive everywhere.

FAIRFAX, MRS LEITH (Irrational, Ch. I): Gossipy woman journalist who, twice to his mortification, induces Sholto Douglas to propose to Marian Lind. On the second refusal Sholto accuses Marian of conspiring with Mrs Fairfax to make him ridiculous.

FAIRHOLME (Socialist, Ch. III): Curate at Lyvern: middle-sized, robust, upright and aggressive. Leads a search party for the missing Mrs Trefusis.

FAIRMILE, SERGEANT TODGER (Barbara, mentioned Act II): New "bloke" of Mog Habbijam. Trounces Bill Walker, her old "bloke", while praying for him.

FALSTAFF MONUMENT (Methuselah, Part IV, Act II): "In the war which followed ten years after the war to end war, none of the soldiers were killed, but seven capital cities of Europe were wiped out and statesmen were blown to fragments, while the common people escaped. Later the inhabitants perished, and that was the end of pseudo-Christian civilization. The last civilized thing that happened was that statesmen discovered that cowardice was a great patriotic virtue, and a public monument was erected to its first preacher, an ancient and very fat sage, Sir John Falstaff."

FANNY: O'Dowda (q.v.).

FANSHAWE, LADY CORINTHIA (Press): A famous singer known as the "Richmond Nightingale". She is a member of the Anti-Suffraget League, and she interviews the Prime Minister, Balsquith, and his colleague, General Mitchener, announcing that the League are going to undertake opposition to the Suffragets, it being no longer possible to trust the men. Agrees to become an "Egeria" to Balsquith.

FARRELL, MRS (Press): An Irish charwoman, to whom General Mitchener proposes marriage, considering her to be the only woman of character he knows who can maintain her husband in competition with the husband of Mrs Banger.

FARRELL, PATSY (John Bull, Act II): Young Irish labourer of Rosscullen, who pretends to be dull-witted, "a cunning developed by constant dread of hostile dominance".

FEEMY—EVANS (Blanco) (q.v.).

FERROVIUS (Androcles, Act I): An armourer "with the strength and temper of an elephant", is converted to Christianity and is sentenced to martyrdom. In the arena the Christian spirit of forbearance deserts him and he slays six of the gladiators, to the delight of the Emperor, who appoints him to the Pretorian Guard.

FERRUCCIO, COUNT (Reality): Poses as a friar to the girl Giulia, who confesses to him that her father, Squarcio, a professional assassin, threatens to take his life. From Giulia, who inexorably refuses to save him, Ferruccio obtains, after a life of make-believe, a glimpse of reality. The Count is ultimately spared, the assassins holding him to be a madman, whom it would be unlucky to kill.

FITTON, MARY: The Dark Lady of the Sonnets, an identification adopted (as explained in the Preface, in which the theories are discussed at length) to suit the purposes of the suggested plot. She finds Shakespear, with whom she was to have kept tryst, embracing some other woman, whom she sends sprawling with a cuff, to find to her horror that it is Queen Elizabeth.

FITZAMBEY, LORD REGINALD (Music): Son of the Duke of Dunmow: under Secretary for War. He took advantage of the knowledge that the army was going to be put on vegetarian diet to buy Macaroni Trust shares, and he cannot understand why he is criticized for this action. As a "clinger" he proposes to Strega Thundridge, the "female Paderewski", and is accepted.

FITZTOLLEMACHE (Passion): In a fit of jealousy invites Bastable to drink from the poisoned gazogene. He was jealous because his wife, LADY MAGNESIA, had praised Bastable's new clothes.

FORSTER (Irrational, Ch. XVIII): Name assumed by Sholto Douglas and Marian for the purpose of their elopement.

FRIAR (Reality): Count Ferruccio (q.v.) disguised as.

FTATATEETA (Caesar, Act I): Chief nurse to Cleopatra, a huge grim woman, very tall and very strong, the arrogant power behind Cleopatra's throne, who is humbled by Caesar. At Cleopatra's command she assassinates Pothinus, and is in turn killed by Rufio.

FUSIMA (Methuselah, Part IV, Act I): One of the long-livers, an advanced secondary, being nearly two hundred years of age. Discovers the short-liver "Daddy" Barlow wandering around unattended, and causes him a severe attack of "discouragement".

GALWAY (Methuselah, Part IV, Act II): Site of the temple of the Oracle of the long-livers.

GARDEN OF EDEN: Scene of Methuselah, Part I, Act I.

GARDNER, THE REV. S. (Mrs Warren, Act I): "Pretentious,

booming, noisy parson, hopelessly asserting himself as
father and clergyman without being able to command respect in either capacity." In his younger days he was indiscreet with Mrs Warren, then a barmaid, whom he
re-encounters through the agency of his son,

FRANK GARDNER, a young person of philandering ways
and no occupation, who is in love with Vivie Warren. He is
blessed with "two inches of cheek all over", no means, and
no means of getting any. When he realizes the source from
which Vivie Warren must derive the allowance which will
be the only possible income if they marry, he withdraws his
suit, "leaving the field to the gilded youth of England".

GARNETT, MISS PROSERPINE (Candida, Act I): Typist to the
Rev James Morell. She suffers from what Candida terms
"Prossy's complaint"—of being in love (like many other
women) with Morell.

GENTLEMANLY JOHNNY (Disciple, Act III): General Burgoyne
(q.v.).

GILBEY, BOBBY (Fanny, Act III): Picks up a girl of the streets
and is sent to prison for being drunk and disorderly. Engaged to Margaret Knox, but seeks to free himself of the
engagement, although, to escape the odium of jilting her,
he hopes to make it appear that she is giving him up. His
father,

ROBIN GILBEY (Fanny, Act I), is an eminently respectable man of business, partner of Knox. Discovering from
his son's experience that it is possible to live without being
respectable, he himself kicks over the traces.

MRS MARIA GILBEY (Fanny, Act I), his wife, is equally
respectable, but more human.

GISBORNE, ADELAIDE (Cashel, Ch. IV): Stage name of Mrs
Byron (q.v.).

GIULIA (Reality): A daughter of Squarcio, the innkeeper and
professional assassin. She is the lover of the fisherman Sandro, and in order to gain a marriage dowry she is about to
lure to assassination the young Count Ferruccio. She seeks
absolution for her proposed sin from an aged friar, who reveals himself to be the Count in disguise. Giulia declines to
save Ferruccio, though he offers to make her his countess,
and from her he obtains his first glimpse of reality after a

life of make-believe.

GLORIA—CLANDON (You Never) (*q.v.*).

GOATHERD (Superman, Act III): Look-out of the brigands of the Sierra Nevada.

GOD: Blanco Posnet's opinion of. He's a sly one. He's a mean one. He lies low for you. He plays cat and mouse with you. He lets you run loose until you think you're shot of Him, and then, when you least expect it, He's got you.

GOFF, ALICE (Cashel, Ch. II): A country belle who had been engaged to her cousin, Wallace Parker, a schoolmaster. On being adopted as companion by Miss Carew, she considers herself to have risen socially, and throws him over; ultimately she marries Lucian Webber. Her MOTHER had been left a widow, whereupon she "took refuge in grief". On her father's death Alice formed a dancing class and gave lessons in a language she believed to be current in France, but which was not intelligible to natives of that country travelling through Wiltstoken. Her sister JANET, who had employed herself as a teacher, marries the cousin whom Alice rejects.

GRACCHUS (Socialist, Ch. III): Large pet cat of the old-fashioned schoolmistress, Mrs Miller, whose pupils call it Bacchus.

GRACE—TRANFIELD (Philanderer) (*q.v.*).

GRANDI, GIUSEPPE (Destiny): Innkeeper, host of Napoleon, "a swarthy, vivacious, shrewdly-cheerful, black-curled, bullet-headed, grinning little man of forty, naturally an excellent host". All his life through he has resisted the attempts of those who desired to make a man of him; he taught himself to cook, and "serves a devouring devil who expects to get everything for nothing, sausages, omelettes, grapes, cheese and polenta wine".

GRANTHAM, MISS LESBIA (Getting Married): Sister of Mrs Bridgenorth, who declares that she will ever remain one of the "glorious old maids of old England". A fastidious person, she cannot reconcile herself to marriage with an untidy and pipe-smoking man—visualized in General Bridgenorth. "I should be a good mother to children", she says. "It would pay the country very well to pay me to have children, but the country tells me that I can't have a child in my house without a man too, so I tell the country it will have to do without my children." For the tenth and last time she refuses the General's offer of marriage.

GRASSHOPPER (John Bull, Act II): With which the soliloquizing "Father" Keegan affects to converse, to the amazement of the rustic Patsy Farrell, who credits the "Father" with powers of magic.

GRUFF AND GRUM (Joan, Scene II): Nickname of Joan for Mgr. de la Trémouille (*q.v.*).

GUINNESS, NURSE (Heartbreak, Act I): Ancient retainer of the Shotover family. Discovers the burglar to be her long-lost husband.

GUNN, GILBERT (Fanny, Prologue): One of the critics, an intellectual; considers Fanny's play to have been written by Granville Barker.

GUNNER (Misalliance): Julius Baker (*q.v.*).

HABBIJAM MOG (mentioned Barbara, Act II): Once the girl of Bill Walker.

HAFFIGAN, MATT (John Bull, Act III): A peasant farmer who bought his farm on the Land Purchase System. He and his brother Andy made a farm out of a patch on the hillside, "making a whole field of wheat grow where not even a furze bush had got up its head between the stones". The landlord then put a rent of £5 a year on them, and turned them out because they could not pay.

HAFFIGAN, TIM (John Bull, Act I): "Might be a tenth rate schoolmaster ruined by drink". An indigent, whisky-drinking, Glasgow-born, Irish beggar, who imposes on Broadbent by means of an assumed brogue and Celticisms.

HALLAM, SIR HOWARD (Brassbound, Act I): A judge of the High Court who visits Morocco with his sister-in-law, Lady Cicely Waynflete. Believing him to have murdered his mother and to have stolen his inheritance, his nephew, Captain Brassbound, betrays Sir Howard to a Christian-hating sheikh. Lady Cicely converts Brassbound from his notions of vengeance, and also saves him from punishment for having betrayed Sir Howard.

HANNAH (Blanco): One of the women shucking nuts "elderly and wise".

HASLAM, THE REV. WILLIAM (Methuselah, Part II): Rector of a Hampstead parish in the year 1920, when he wooes Savvy Barnabas. He is one of the first to experience getting back to Methuselah, surviving 250 years later as Archbishop of York (*q.v.*).

HASSAN (Brassbound, Act I): Moor, who acts as porter to Sir Howard Hallam and Lady Cicely.

HAWKINS, LAWYER (Disciple, Act I): Reads the will of Timothy Dudgeon.

HE (How He Lied): Henry Apjohn, the poet, is termed such throughout.

HE-ANCIENT (Methuselah, Part V): Member of the race of mankind developed by the year A.D. 30,000. (See ANCIENTS.)

HEAVEN (Don Juan): The Statue left Heaven because life there was too dull, and Don Juan resolves to go there because he finds existence in Hell, devoted to the vulgar pursuit of happiness, to be too tedious. Juan is informed that "the frontier between Heaven and Hell is only the difference between two ways of looking at things".

HELL: Scene of Don Juan, the play within Man and Superman. It is represented to be a place devoted to gaiety, and Don Juan resolves to leave it, because he cannot endure existence spent in the vulgar pursuit of happiness. To Ana, who is chagrined to find herself there after a most religious life on earth, Juan says that Hell is "the home of honour, duty, justice and the rest of the seven deadly virtues in whose name all the wickedness on earth is done".

HERBERT, ADRIAN (Artists, Ch. I): An artist of no great ability, who is inspired to continue in his career by Mary Sutherland, to whom he engaged himself. He throws her over to marry the Polish musician, Aurelie Szczymplica, with whom he falls wildly in love, and he becomes her devoted slave. His mother,

MRS HERBERT (Ch. III), has no belief in her son's talent for art, and wishes him to adopt a commercial career. Her opposition antagonizes him.

HER HUSBAND (How He Lied): Henry Bompas, is termed such throughout.

HICKLING, MRS (Socialist, Ch. XIII): An old crone from whom Trefusis learns of the medicinal purposes for which hemlock is employed.

HIGGINS, HENRY (Pygmalion, Act I): Professor of phonetics, who, for a wager, undertakes to transform Eliza Doolittle, the Cockney flower girl, into the equal in speech and deportment of a duchess. With Eliza as his Galatea, he repeats the success of Pygmalion. He amazes a crowd of Cockneys by the facility with which, from their speech, he identifies the localities from which they originate. He adores his mother,

MRS HIGGINS (Act III), a cultured woman of "intelligence and grace".

HIGHCASTLE, LORD AUGUSTUS (who does his bit): A distinguished and fatuous member of the governing class who, during the war, persuades himself and others that he is rendering valuable service to his country. Is bamboozled by a lady out of the possession of important state documents, the lady thereby winning a wager.

HILL, MRS EYNSFORD (Pygmalion, Act I): With her family, is first seen taking shelter from the rain in the portico of St Paul's, Covent Garden. In Act III they attend the At Home of Mrs Higgins, at which Eliza is presented. Mrs Hill is "a well-bred woman, with the habitual anxiety of straitened means".

FREDDY, her son, is an amiable but somewhat useless young man, who falls in love with Eliza. The postscript explains that he and she eventually marry and keep a high-class greengrocery establishment.

CLARA HILL, the daughter, is a social "pusher", who has acquired the gay air of being much at home in society, the bravado of genteel poverty. She imitates Eliza's famous "not bloody likely".

HILL, JENNY (Barbara, Act II): Of the Salvation Army, is assaulted by Bill Walker, and prays for him.

HODSON (John Bull, Act I): Valet to Broadbent. In the Irish debates he expresses the view of the lower class English, that it is time the Irish had Home Rule, in order that the grievances of the English may be entertained by the Parliament at Westminster.

HOSKYN, JOHN (Artists, Ch. XIII): A business man in the Conolly electricity firm, who marries Mary Sutherland. He proposes after he has been acquainted with Mary for only twenty-one days, and when she rejects his offer, he writes to her, setting out in businesslike fashion financial inducements in support of his proposal. On the advice of Lady Geraldine Porter, Mary accepts him and, although John does not share his wife's artistic tastes, their marriage is a happy one.

Mrs Hoskyn appears in Cashel Byron. At one of her society gatherings Cashel Byron, the pugilist, upsets one of the guests, Lucian Webber.

Hotchkiss, Sinjon (Getting Married): On the point of becoming the husband of Leo Bridgenorth, who has secured a divorce (collusive) on his account, he falls in love with a married woman, Mrs George (Collins). He is a self-proclaimed snob, described on his card as "the celebrated coward", late Lieutenant in the 165th Fusiliers. He ignored an order to attack at Smutsfontein, because he did not wish his commanding officer, who "was not a gentleman", to gain promotion from a victory.

Hotel Manager (Inca): After treating his customer, the Princess, with "a condescending affability which sails very close to the East wind of insolence", he is rebuked by Ermyntrude, the newly engaged lady's maid.

Hushabye, Hector (Heartbreak, Act I): A very fascinating gentleman, with whom Ellie Dunn falls in love. Her heart is broken when she discovers that "his chief occupation in life" is to be married to

Hesione Hushabye (Act I), daughter of Captain Shotover. Hesione feels no jealousy regarding women who fall in love with her husband. She seeks to rescue Ellie Dunn from her proposed marriage with Mangan, the financier.

Hypatia—Tarleton (Misalliance) (q.v.).

Ibsen Club: Of which most of the characters of the Philanderer are members. The qualification for membership is that men are unmanly and women unwomanly.

Inca of Perusalem, who is seeking to marry his son to a Princess, is received by Ermyntrude, a millionaire's widow, who has engaged herself as lady's maid to the Princess. The Inca is much impressed by Ermyntrude, and offers to turn Mahometan in order that he may marry her, but she rejects him because the war he is waging is bankrupting him.

INQUISITION: Joan before. Scene VI.

INQUISITOR (Joan, Scene VI): Brother John Lemaitre, of the order of St Dominic, acting as deputy for the Chief Inquisitor into the evil of heresy in France; presides with Cauchon at the trial of Joan. Addresses the Court at length on the perils of heresy.

INSPECTOR OF POLICE (Socialist, Ch. IV): Questions Wickens' boy regarding the missing Mrs Trefusis.

IRAS (Caesar, Act IV): One of the ladies of the court of Cleopatra.

ITALY: Edge of a lake in. Scene of Glimpse of Reality.

JACK, OWEN (Artists, Ch. I): Musical composer and unrecognized genius, who makes a precarious living by acting as tutor and music master. Becomes tutor to Charlie Sutherland and is dismissed because of his eccentric ways. His "Fantasia", produced by the Antient Orpheus Society, founds his fame, and after becoming a celebrity he proposes to Mary Sutherland, but divines that she does not love him. Some years later Madge Brailsford, a popular actress, whom he had trained in elocution, suggests that they should marry, but Jack prefers to remain wedded to his art.

JANSENIUS, JOHN (Socialist, Ch. II): A banker, father of Henrietta, first wife of Sidney Trefusis and guardian of Agatha Wylie, Sidney's second wife. A man whose appearance proclaims his Jewish origin, of which he was ashamed. He has a wife, Ruth, and son, Arthur.

JENNIFER—DUBEDAT (Doctor's Dilemma) (q.v.).

JESSIE (Blanco): One of the women shucking nuts. She is tired of lynchings, even of horse thieves, and wants to see a sheriff who "ain't afraid not to shoot and not to hang".

JINGHISKAHN (Misalliance): The Colony of which Lord Summerhays was Governor.

JOAN, the Maid, is shewn in five incidents in her life: persuading de Baudricourt (her squire) to grant her facilities for setting out on her mission; inducing the Dauphin to appoint her head of the army; going to the relief of besieged Orleans; after the Coronation of the Dauphin in Rheims

Cathedral; and tried by the Inquisition and condemned to death. In the Epilogue she learns of her rehabilitation, brought about as the result of the inquiry, twenty-five years after her death, and of her canonization in the year 1920.

JOHNSON (Brassbound, Act II): Member of Brassbound's gang, son of Captain Johnson of Hull.

JOHNSON, Prime Minister (Press): Name substituted for Balsquith in order to comply with the requirements of the Censor.

JOSEPHS (Socialist, Ch. III): A curate at Lyvern—"tall, thin, close shaven, with a book under his arm and his neck craned forward".

JUDGE (Captain Brassbound): Sir Howard Hallam (*q.v.*).

JUGGINS (Fanny, Act I): Footman and butler, younger son of a Duke, entered domestic service as a self-imposed penance for trifling with the affections of a girl of the servant class. Is accepted as suitor of Margaret Knox.

JULIA—CRAVEN (Philanderer) (*q.v.*).

JUNO, SIBTHORPE (Overruled): A solicitor and married man. During a voyage at sea he is inspired with an infatuation for his fellow passenger, Mrs Lunn, who is greatly entertained by him. His wife, MRS JUNO, has similarly become involved in a love affair with Gregory Lunn, and the two couples encounter one another at a hotel, where they discuss their feelings. Juno's verdict is that men are not perfect, but it is all right if they keep the ideal before them by admitting when they are wrong.

KEARNEY, CAPTAIN HAMLIN (Brassbound, Act III): Commander of the American ship Santiago, presides over the court of inquiry on Brassbound and his gang. "A curious ethnological specimen, with all the nations of the Old World at war in his veins. He is developing artificially in the direction of sleekness and culture under the restraints of an overwhelming dread of European criticism. The world, pondering on the great part of its own future which is in his hands, contemplates him with wonder as to what the devil he will evolve into in another century or two."

KEEGAN, PETER (John Bull, Act II): Once a priest. He gave absolution to a black man and ceased to be a priest, but by

training and inclination is incapacitated from being anything else. At Rosscullen he has earned a reputation among
the uneducated of possessing supernatural powers, and
among the educated of being a madman.

KEMP, SHERIFF (Blanco): His horse, lent to Elder Daniels, is
stolen by Blanco Posnet, at whose trial the Sheriff presides.

KEMP, STRAPPER (Blanco): Brother of the Sheriff. He captured Blanco, the horse thief.

KINTAFI (Brassbound): Kadi of (*q.v.*).

KNOX, MARGARET (Fanny, Act II): Daughter of respectable
parents, is sent to prison for assaulting a police constable
on boat-race night. Her prison experiences set her free from
her "silly little hole of a home and its pretences". She breaks
her engagement to Bobby Gilbey and accepts as her lover,
Juggins, the butler, and son of a Duke. Her father,

JOSEPH KNOX (Act II), is an eminently respectable man
of business, partner of Gilbey. The effect of his daughter's
disgrace is to make him kick over the traces. His wife,

MRS AMELIA KNOX (Act II), is a deeply religious woman.
Her life's philosophy is, "If you've happiness within your-
self you don't need to seek it outside; the spirit will set you
free to do what you want and guide you to do right"; for
those who have not, her counsel is, "You'd best be respectable and stick to the ways marked out for you, for you've
nothing else to keep you straight".

LADVENU (Joan, Scene VI): Brother Martin, Dominican
Monk, who at the trial tries to save Joan from the fate of a
heretic. He draws up a recantation and guides her hand as
she signs it. In the Epilogue he informs Charles that the
sentence on Joan was set aside at the inquiry which was
made twenty-five years after her death.

LADY, unidentified (Augustus): For a wager, she bamboozles
Lord Augustus Highcastle into parting with important
documents of State.

LADY, unidentified heroine of the Man of Destiny: Dressed as
a man she tricked a French lieutenant out of the despatches
he was bearing, and she nearly succeeds in playing off the
same confidence trick on Napoleon.

LADY ABBESS (Socialist, Ch. I): Nickname by which the girls

of Alton College know their principal, Miss Wilson.

LADY CICELY—WAYNFLETE (Brassbound) (*q.v.*).

LAFITTE, MISS (Artists, Ch. VIII): Actress (Mrs Cohen in real life) who befriends Madge Brailsford in the early days of her stage career.

LA HIRE (Joan, Scene II): French Captain, a rough war dog who falls under the influence of Joan to such an extent that he abandons his habit of swearing.

LANCASTER, MADGE (Artists, Ch. XIII): Stage name of Madge Brailsford (*q.v.*).

LANDLORD (Passion): To the FitzTollemache's. Struck dead by lightning.

LAVINIA (Androcles, Act I): One of the Christians sent to martyrdom, but reprieved at the last moment. She is a "clever and fearless free thinker", and says that she is not running away from the terrors of life impelled by promised comforts of the life to come; but that religion is so real to her that she cannot, to save her life, render tribute to deities in whom she does not believe. Four Roman officers offered to marry her.

LAZARUS (Barbara, mentioned): Partner of Undershaft in the explosives business. "A gentle, romantic Jew who cares for nothing but string quartettes and stalls at fashionable theatres."

LEMAITRE, BROTHER JOHN (Joan, Scene VI): Inquisitor (*q.v.*), before whom the Maid is tried.

LENTULUS (Androcles, Act I): A patrician, comes to scoff at the Christian martyrs; strikes Ferrovius on the cheek, but ends by apologizing, intimidated by him, the strong man of the Christians.

LESBIA—GRANTHAM (Married) (*q.v.*).

LEXY (Candida, Act I): The Rev Alexander Mill (*q.v.*).

LICKCHEESE (Widowers', Act II): A collector of slum rents, discharged by his employer, Sartorius, for having authorized slight improvements to make some of the dwellings safe to live in. Becomes rich by buying up slum property likely to become involved in improvement schemes, and holding it up to ransom in the form of compensation.

LIEUTENANT, unidentified (Man of Destiny): Tricked out of the despatches he was bearing to Napoleon by a woman in man's attire. "A chuckle-headed man of rank, 24 years of age, with a self-assurance the French Revolution has failed to shake in the smallest degree; without fear, reverence or imagination, stupidly egotistical."

LIGHTHOUSE OF ALEXANDRIA (Caesar, Act III, Scene II).

LILITH (Methuselah, Part V): Mother of mankind, who gives her judgment on the race to which she first gave birth. For many years, she says, her children disappointed her, and she was on the verge of creating a new race to supersede them, when one man learned to live 300 years. After that mankind redeemed themselves of their vileness and took on the burden of eternal life, yet despite all the goals they have passed, they still press on—to redemption of the flesh, to the vortex freed from matter, to the whirlpool in pure intelligence, which, once attained, Lilith will herself be superseded and be only a legend. So because man is still pressing on she will not supersede him.

LIND, MR REGINALD HARRINGTON (Irrational, Ch. II): Grand nephew of the late Earl of Carbury. He attempts to prevent the marriage of Conolly, the electrical inventor (whom he regards as an artisan), and his daughter MARIAN (Ch. I), but withdraws his opposition when he realizes that his daughter is generally regarded as making a good match. Conolly is an ideal husband in many respects, but Marian finds him too coldly rational, and she elopes with Sholto Douglas, a former lover. Sholto abandons her in New York, and Conolly goes to her aid. He offers to take her back, but she sticks to her decision to end the irrational knot.

MARMADUKE LIND (Ch. I) is Marian's cousin. Although it was an understood thing in the family that he was to marry Lady Constance Carbury, he forms a liaison with Susannah Conolly, sister of Edward. They live together for some years at Twickenham, but Marmaduke has to separate from Susannah because of her drinking habits. He finally succumbs to the assiduous courtship of Lady Constance.

Marian's brother, The REV. GEORGE LIND (Ch. I), is sent as family ambassador to induce Conolly to give up Marian, and then to try to get Susannah to leave Marmaduke. A most pious person, he is much scandalized by Susannah.

LINDSAY, GERTRUDE (Socialist, Ch. I): One of the girls at

Alton College, daughter of a retired Admiral. When she leaves school her father considers it to be her duty to marry, but Gertrude, proud of her rank and exclusiveness, is resolved not to have anything to do with anybody who does not share both with her, and throws away her matrimonial opportunities. She is led to believe that Sidney Trefusis is in love with her, and on being undeceived is brokenhearted. Trefusis induces her to accept her devoted admirer, Erskine.

HER MOTHER had learnt by rôle that "the whole duty of a lady is to be graceful, charitable, helpful, modest and disinterested, whilst awaiting passively whatever lot these virtues may induce; she had learnt by experience that a lady's business in society is to get married, and that virtues and accomplishments alike are important only as attractions to eligible bachelorhood".

LION (Androcles, Prologue): The beast of the fable which has the thorn removed from its paw by Androcles. When Androcles, as a Christian martyr, is sent into the arena, the lion recognizes him, and they come dancing out to the amazement (and terror) of the Emperor.

LOIRE, on south bank of, outside Orleans (Joan, Scene III).

LOMAX, CHARLES (Barbara, Act I): Lover of Sarah Undershaft. An ineffective man about town, aged twenty-five, he will be a millionaire at thirty-five. He is allowed £800 a year by the trustees, the allowance to be doubled if he increases his income by his own exertions, but there is no chance of his securing the increase. For Major Barbara he plays the concertina at Salvation Army meetings.

LONG-LIVERS (Methuselah, Part IV, Act I): Inhabitants of the British Isles in the year A.D. 3000. They are divided into primaries, secondaries, and tertiaries, according to the centuries of their age, and short-livers who come into contact with them are subject to attacks of "discouragement" (q.v.). The mere sight of the face of the Oracle, an advanced secondary, reduces Napoleon to prostration and kills "Daddy" Barlow. The long-livers are divided into two parties—the Conservatives and the Colonisers (q.v.)—and are able to communicate with one another through space by means of tuning forks.

LORD CHANCELLOR (Foundling): Sir Cardonius Boshington (*q.v.*).

LOTTIE (Blanco): One of the women shucking nuts, "sentimental, neat and clean".

LOUKA (Arms, Act I): Servant girl to the Petkoffs, engaged to the manservant Nicola, who renounces her on learning that Major Sergius Saranoff desires to marry her.

LUBIN, HENRY HOPKINS (Methuselah, Part II): Leader of the Liberal Party and Prime Minister under the first Coalition Government. Discusses with Joyce Burge, his successor in the Premiership and rival for the party leadership, the Methuselah theory of the Brothers Barnabas. He is interested until he learns that there is no specific for longevity, which nature alone can bring about. He makes himself socially agreeable, particularly to Miss Barnabas, while he approaches politics with the spirit of detachment of a lawyer and literary dilettante, ready to get up the necessary case.—Character founded on Mr Asquith.

LUCIUS, SEPTIMIUS (Caesar, Act II): The tribune who, to Caesar's horror, boasts that he slew Pompey the moment his feet touched the Egyptian shore. He is hostile to Caesar until the reinforcements arrive, when he offers to change sides, and Caesar makes him one of his officers.

LUCY (Irrational, Ch. II): Child of Marmaduke Lind and Susannah Conolly.

LUNN, GREGORY (Overruled): A solicitor and married man, who, during a voyage at sea, falls in love with Mrs Juno, believing that she is a widow. On discovering her to be married, he finds, despite his moral promptings, that his inclinations are against separating from her. His wife,

SERAPHITA LUNN inspires Mr Juno with an infatuation, and the four of them meet at a hotel, where they discuss their feelings.

LUTESTRING, MRS (Methuselah, Part III): Domestic Mini in Britain in the year A.D. 2170, a lady 274 years of age, being one of the first to experience getting back to Methuselah. She was parlourmaid to the Brothers Barnabas 250 years before. She confides to her fellow long-liver, the Archbishop of York, that if the white race is to be saved, their duty is apparent, a matrimonial proposal with which the

Archbishop agrees.

LYDIA—CAREW (Cashel and Bashville) (*q.v.*).

LYVERN (Socialist, Ch. I): Village where Sidney Trefusis takes his retreat, to masquerade as Smilash, the labourer. Near Lyvern is Alton College.

MACLAGAN (Artists, Ch. X): Member of the Antient Orpheus Musical Society, who composed a symphony, laborious and arid, full of unconscious pickings from Mendelssohn. Owen Jack, improvising at the piano, derisively parodies a theme from the symphony in the presence of Maclagan.

MADIGAN, GENERAL SIR PEARCE (O'Flaherty): Assisted during a recruiting campaign in Ireland by O'Flaherty, who has recently won the V.C. in Flanders. Sir Pearce is led to the conclusion that were domestic life as happy as people represented, the authorities would not have got an army without conscription.

MAJOR BARBARA: Undershaft (*q.v.*).

MAJOR DOMO (Caesar, Act IV): Superintends the laying and serving of the banquet.

MALONE, HECTOR (Superman, Act IV): American millionaire, Irish by birth, who hopes his son will marry into the English aristocracy; if he marries a girl of the middle classes, he will be cut off without a penny. He discovers that his son HECTOR (Act I) has fallen in love with and married Violet Robinson, and threatens to cut off supplies; but Violet impresses him as being the equal of ten duchesses, and causes him to withdraw his financial ban. Malone meets his daughter-in-law at Granada, where he was making inquiries regarding the shares he had purchased in Mendoza Limited, which, unknown to him, is a "firm" of brigands.

MANGAN, ALFRED (Heartbreak, Act I): Generally known as "Boss". A financier who advanced money for the conduct of a new business to Mazzini Dunn, and when Dunn went bankrupt Mangan took over the business at a very low figure. Pays suit to Ellie Dunn, who considers it to be her duty to marry the man who helped her father. After her heart is broken by Hector Hushabye she hypnotizes Mangan, and finally rejects him. He is killed by a bomb.

MANLIUS, MR (Artists, Ch. IX): Conductor of the Antient

Orpheus orchestra.

MAN OF DESTINY: Napoleon (*q.v.*).

MARCHBANKS, EUGENE (Candida, Act I): Youthful poet, nephew of an Earl, who falls in love with Candida, and who considers that he understands her soul better than does her husband. For her love he bids his "weakness, desolation and heart's need", but Candida cleaves to her husband, leaving the poet to go out into the night with a secret in his heart.

MARGARET—KNOX (Fanny) (*q.v.*).

MARTELLUS (Methuselah, Part V): Sculptor of the race of Ancients of A.D. 30,000. Moulded, for Pygmalion, protoplasm into shape for the creation of two living human figures. Martellus developed into the world's greatest sculptor, and then became disillusioned with his works of mere beauty, and discarded the fleeting fleshly lure to make images of the mind. Finally the intellectual conscience that tore him away from the fleshly in art tears him away from art altogether, because art is false and life alone is true.

MASTER OF THE REVELS (Bashville, Act II): Announces the fight between Cashel Byron and Paradise.

MARZO (Brassbound, Act I): An Italian member of Brassbound's gang, wounded in an affray with the Beni Siras. He is nursed by Lady Cicely Waynflete, whom he declares to be no "lady but an angel".

MASON (Irrational, Ch. V): Valet to Marmaduke Lind.

MASON (Socialist, Ch. X): Employed by Sidney Trefusis, the rich Socialist, to erect a monument to his first wife. Trefusis finds it extremely difficult to carry out his wish to pay the just value of the work, no more and no less, without regard to the market price. Far from founding the reputation of the mason, the monument, though a good piece of work, gets him into difficulties, as he had contravened trade usages, and is therefore boycotted by his Trades Union and by the employers. Trefusis finds him work to do, and the mason soon saves enough from the liberal payments he receives to start on his own account as employer.

MAX (Socialist, Ch. XIII): St Bernard dog taken out for a walk by Gertrude Lindsay.

McCOMAS, FINCH (You Never, Act II): A solicitor, the rejected suitor of Mrs Clandon, who remains her friend and is summoned by her to tell to her children the story of her unhappy marriage. Acts as intermediary for Crampton, Mrs Clandon's husband, who wishes to be reconciled to his family.

McQUINCH, HARDY (Irrational, Ch. II): Brother-in-law of Mr Harrington Lind and uncle of Marian. A Wiltshire gentleman with a small patrimony, a habit of farming and a love of hunting.

HIS WIFE (Ch. II) had worn many lines into her face by constantly and vainly wishing that she could afford to give a ball every season, and to display other evidences of gentility. They have three daughters,

LYDIA and JANE (Ch. II), and ELINOR (Ch. I), the bad child of the family, whom her cousin, Marian Lind, invites to live with her. Elinor, who is made the bosom friend and confidante of Marian, develops her literary talents, which in her childhood gave much offence to her parents, and becomes a successful novelist. She supports Marian in her resolution to marry Conolly.

MEGAERA (Androcles, Prologue): Wife of Androcles, who is abominably henpecked by her.

MELLISH, BOB (Cashel, Ch. III): Trainer to Cashel Byron. In the play (Bashville) Cashel knocks him out for daring to intrude in his love affair.

MENAGERIE KEEPER (Androcles, Act II): Is furious because Spintho, one of the Christians, has been permitted to become a premature meal for one of his lions, rendering the beast no longer fit to go into the arena.

MENDOZA (Superman, Act III): Chief of the brigands in the Sierra Nevada, who hold up the motor of John Tanner. Once a successful waiter, he became a brigand following a disappointment in love. As a Jew his elaborate sanitary code makes him contemptuous of the Gentile, and no woman can stand a suspicion of indelicacy as to her person. Appears in the "dream" scene as the Devil.

MERCER (Foundling): Faithful clerk of the Lord Chancellor, Sir Cardonius Boshington.

MESOPOTAMIA: Adam (Methuselah, Part I, Act II) is digging in a garden in.

METELLUS (Androcles, Act I): A patrician, comes to scoff at

the Christian martyrs.

MILL, THE REV. ALEXANDER (Lexy) (Candida, Act I): Curate to Morell. "A conceitedly well-intentioned, enthusiastic, immature parson." In love with Miss Garnett.

MILLER, MRS (Socialist, Ch. III): Old-fashioned schoolmistress at Alton College, who "satisfied her affectionate impulses by petting a large cat", named Gracchus.

MINISTER OF HEALTH (Methuselah, Part III): To Britain, A.D. 2170, a negress, the government then being largely carried on by educated negresses and Chinese. The President, Burge-Lubin, becomes madly infatuated with her.

MITCHENER, GENERAL (Press): Head of the War Office during the Suffraget campaign. Proposes marriage to his charwoman, Mrs O'Farrell, as the only woman he knows who can maintain her husband in competition with the husband of Mrs Banger, who marries herself to the Chief of the Army, General Sandstone. The remedy Mitchener invariably proposes for problems of State is to reduce opposition by shooting down his opponents.

"Not the late Lord Kitchener but an earlier and more highly connected commander."

MITCHENS, ROMOLA (Barbara, Act II): One of the poor creatures, known as Rummy, of the East End, who are given bread and treacle at the Salvation Army shelter. She is assaulted by Bill Walker.

MOGADOR: Scene of Brassbound, Acts I and III.

MOLE OF ALEXANDRIA: Scene of Caesar, Act III, Scene I.

MOLESWORTH, GULLY (Cashel, Prologue): One of the fellow pupils of Cashel Byron at Moncrief House. With Cashel he attempts to run away, but unlike Cashel his heart fails him and he surrenders.

MOLLY (Methuselah, Part IV, Act II): Daughter of the Envoy.

MONCRIEF HOUSE (Cashel, Prologue): Scholastic establishment at Panley Common "for the sons of Gentlemen", kept by Dr Moncrief. One of the pupils was Cashel Byron, who ran away.

MOORISH CASTLE: Scene of Brassbound, Act II.

MORELL, THE REV. JAMES MAVOR (Candida, Act I): A Christian Socialist, first rate clergyman of the Church of England,

GEORGE BERNARD SHAW

genial, popular, full of energy, a practised orator. He is
deeply attached to his wife

CANDIDA. The boy poet Morell has befriended Eugene
Marchbanks, falls in love with Candida and claims to
understand her better than her "windbag" of a husband.
Eugene and Morell bid for her affection, and Candida
decides for the weaker of the two—her husband. Candida's
ways "are those of a woman who has found that she can
always manage people by engaging their affection".

MORRISON (Barbara, Act I): A butler.

MUSICIAN (Caesar, Act IV): Engaged by Cleopatra to teach
her to play the harp; after she has had a fortnight's lessons
he is to receive a flogging for every false note she makes.

MYERS, MRS (Irrational, Ch. XIX): Widow with whom
Marian Conolly takes lodgings in New York.

NAPOLEON is the Man of Destiny, and the play is founded on a
supposititious incident in his early days, in which he battles
with a lady for the possession of his despatches, stolen from
their bearer by the lady, disguised in man's attire.

NAPOLEON, CAIN ADAMSON CHARLES (Methuselah, Part IV,
Act II): Emperor of Turania in the year A.D. 3000.
Travelling incognito as General Aufsteig, the greatest military genius of the age, he seeks to have a personal consulta-
tion with the Oracle of the long-livers. He questions the
Oracle as to how he can continue to satisfy his military
genius until he dies, to which the Oracle proposes the
simple solution of trying to kill him, but her pistol shot
misses. He had impressed the Oracle as an exceptionally
strong-willed person for a short-liver.

NARYSHKIN (Catherine, Scene II): Chamberlain to the Empress Catherine of Russia.

NATA (Artists, Ch. II): Ejected with Anatole and Charlie
Sutherland from a gambling den in Paris.

NEGRESS (Methuselah, Part III): Minister of Health (q.v.) in
Britain, A.D. 2170.

NESTOR (Blanco): One of the Boys. He questions the Sheriff's
ruling that there has been no theft of a horse, and is ordered
to pay a dollar for contempt of court.

NEVA: Terrace overlooking (Catherine, Scene III).

NEWLY BORN (Methuselah, Part V): Child of the race of Ancients of A.D. 30,000, born from an egg, from which she emerges at the stage of development attained by persons of short-lived races at the age of seventeen. Falls in love with Acis, a youth of three, who tells her that in a year's time he will have reached maturity and have passed the age of lovemaking.

NEWSBOY (Bashville, Act II): Bears a copy of the "Star" announcing the result of the great fight between Cashel Byron and the Flying Dutchman.

NEWSPAPER MAN (Dilemma, Act IV): Seeking information of the health of the artist Dubedat, he is "in at the death". "A cheerful, affable young man, who is disabled for ordinary business pursuits by a congenital erroneousness, which renders him incapable of describing accurately anything he sees, or understanding or reporting accurately anything he hears."

The reporting incident was founded on an actual occurrence in the life of Mrs Patrick Campbell.

NICOLA (Arms, Act II): Manservant to the Petkoffs, engaged to Louka, the servant girl, whom he renounces when he finds her to be loved by Sergius Saranoff. Nicola has ambitions to become a shopkeeper.

NORA—REILLY (John Bull) (q.v.).

NUBIAN SENTINEL (Caesar, Act I): On duty outside Cleopatra's Palace.

O'DOWDA (Fanny, Prologue): Count of the Holy Roman Empire, is a man who finds modern life to be vulgar, refuses to recognize it, and passes most of his days in Venice. His daughter,

FANNY O'DOWDA (Prologue), is the supposititious author of the "first play", which, as a birthday present from her father, is being given a private performance. A Girton girl, she was sent to prison as a Suffraget, and the play is the result of her experiences. Her father, when he discovers its nature, is "shocked to the very soul".

O'FLAHERTY, PRIVATE DENNIS: After winning the V.C. in Flanders, goes to assist General Sir P. Madigan in a recruiting campaign in Ireland. After having seen life abroad he

GEORGE BERNARD SHAW

is discontented with his native land and vows he'll live in
France. His reception at home increases his discontent. His
lover, Teresa Driscoll, is hoping for a pension, even if he
has to be wounded before she can have it, and his mother
reproaches him with having deceived her when he joined up.
She was a wild Fenian rebel, and he had led her to suppose
he was fighting against the British.

ORACLE (Methuselah, Part IV, Act II): Of the long-livers,
consulted at the Temple of Galway by short-livers. Receives
Napoleon, and propounds a simple solution of his difficulties by attempting to shoot him, but her aim is wide. To
the British Envoy she gives (as she is asked) the reply made
fifteen years previously to his predecessor: "Go home, poor
fool". Joseph Barlow seeks permission to stay in her land,
and she accedes, causing him to die of discouragement.

ORDERLY (Press): Son of a barber; he reaches the army by
conscription, thereby "bringing disgrace" upon a family
which had never had a soldier in it before.

ORLEANS, outside the besieged city (Joan, Scene III).

OSMAN ALI (Brassbound, Act II): Messenger of the Sheikh
Sidi el Assif.

OX-DRIVER (Androcles, Act I): His team of oxen is drawing to
the Coliseum the new lion for the devouring of the Christians.

OZYMANDIAS, King of Kings (Methuselah, Part V): Male
figure created by Pygmalion, scientist of the race of Ancients in A.D. 30,000. Like the female figure, Cleopatra-
Semiramis, Ozymandias is cast in the form of mortals of the
short-living age of the nineteenth century, and he declares
that they are children of cause and effect, free will being an
illusion. He and Cleopatra are by the Ancients reduced to
death by "discouragement".

PAGE BOY (Philanderer, Act II): At the Ibsen Club.

PAGES (St Joan): At the Dauphin's court (Scene II); at the
court of the Inquisition (Scene VI); and with Dunois
(Scene III), before besieged Orleans, who spots the king-
fisher and observes that, following Joan's arrival, the wind
has changed auspiciously for the French.

PARADISE, WILLIAM (Cashel, Ch. X): Prizefighter against

184

whom Cashel Byron fights his last fight. They first meet at a match with the gloves on, but Paradise, who is badly hit, tears off the gloves and goes in real earnest for Cashel, who throws him with a wrestling trick. Later they meet in an illicit encounter, and when Paradise is getting the worst of it the police intervene. On Cashel's retirement from the ring Paradise assumes the championship title, but he drinks himself to beggary and death. Appears in Bashville, Act II.

PARAMORE, DR PERCY (Philanderer, Act I): Is the discoverer of Paramore's disease, a liver affliction of which he pronounces Col. Craven to be a victim. Another doctor proves it, however, to be no disease at all. He is the lover of the Colonel's daughter Julia, who ultimately accepts him.

PARKER, WALLACE (Cashel, Ch. IV): A schoolmaster who was engaged to Alice Goff, until that young lady entered society as companion to Lydia Carew, whereupon she threw him over. Wallace then paid suit to Alice's sister.

PARLOURMAID (Methuselah, Part II): To the Brothers Barnabas, whose service she is about to leave to marry the village woodman. She is one of the first to get "back to Methuselah", surviving 250 years later as Mrs Lutestring (*q.v.*), Domestic Minister of Britain.

PARNASSUS SOCIETY (Irrational, Ch. I): Give a concert for the working men of Wandsworth.

PATIOMKIN (Catherine, Scene I): Favourite of Catherine the Great of Russia, is approached by Captain Edstaston, who wishes to secure audience with the Empress. Patiomkin puts the Captain under his arm, carrying him unceremoniously into the presence of Catherine. When rebuked, Patiomkin feigns drunkenness.

PEARCE, MRS (Pygmalion, Act II): Housekeeper to Higgins.

PERCIVAL, JOEY (Misalliance): An aviator. He wrecks the Tarleton glass house with his machine. Patsy Tarleton jilts her lover, Bentley Summerhays, in his favour. Joey was blessed with three fathers—the regulation one, his mother's confessor, and his father's tame philosopher, who took charge of his conscience; between the three he "got cultivated no end".

PERIVALE ST ANDREWS (Barbara): Explosives factory, in

Middlesex, of Undershaft and Lazarus; scene of Act III, Scene II.

PERSIAN (Caesar, Act I): Young recruit to the Egyptian Guard, who plays dice with his captain, Belzanor. Has a reputation for cunning—"subtlest of serpents".

PERUSALEM. (See INCA.)

PETKOFF, RAINA (Arms, Act I): Romantic Bulgarian girl, in whose bedchamber the Swiss professional soldier, Bluntschli, a fugitive from the Servian army, takes refuge. Raina is forced at the pistol point to conceal him, and she feeds him on chocolate creams and gets him away to safety. After the wars she continues her "higher" love affair with Major Sergius Saranoff, and Captain Bluntschli calls on her. When Sergius renounces her in favour of the servant girl Louka, Raina becomes engaged to Bluntschli. Her parents,

MAJOR PAUL (Act II) and CATHERINE PETKOFF (Act I), are the richest and best-known family in Bulgaria, whose luxury is indicated by the fact that their house is the only private one with two rows of windows; there are also a flight of stairs and a library. Like Bulgarians of good social standing the family wash their hands "nearly every day", although the Major "does not agree with all this washing".

PICKERING, COLONEL (Pygmalion, Act I): Author of a treatise on Sanscrit. He comes from India to meet Higgins, professor of phonetics, and wagers that he cannot transform Eliza, the cockney flower girl, into the equal of a Duchess.

PICTURE GALLERY in Bond Street: Scene of Dilemma, Act V.

PIFFLINGTON, LITTLE: The action of "Augustus Does His Bit" takes place in the Mayor's parlour.

PHOEBE (Cashel, Ch. XII): Servant to Miss Carew.

PHYSICIAN, SIR FRANCIS (Socialist, Ch. IX): Called in to attend the dying Mrs Trefusis. "He believed the general practitioner had treated her unskilfully, but professional etiquette bound him so strongly that, sooner than betray his colleague's inefficiency, he would have allowed him to decimate half London."

PHYLLIS (Passion): Maid to Lady Magnesia FitzTollemache.

PLECHANOFF (Arms and Man, Act I): A Russian officer from the Bulgarian army who searches for the fugitive Bluntschli. His appearance illustrates the fact that the Bulgarians, who at the time of the action of the play had only just been redeemed from centuries of bondage under the Turks, had so little military skill that they had to place themselves under the command of Russian officers. He is described simply as "a Russian officer" in the book, but when the part was played by A. E. W. Mason it was given the name of Plechanoff in the programme as less suggestive of a super. (Shaw.)

POLICEMAN (Bashville, Act III): Enters with Paradise and Mellish in custody. Cashel surrenders to him, preferring prison to the company of his mother.

POLICEMAN (Passion): Struck dead by lightning.

"POLLY" (Joan, Scene I): Poulengey (*q.v.*).

PORTER, LADY GERALDINE (Artists, Ch. XII): Induces Mary Sutherland, against her own judgment, to accept John Hoskyn as a husband. She protests against Mary's romanticism, and advises her not to be deterred from marrying a man because of any supposed incompatibility in tastes or because he is not a genius. In support of her argument she points to her own husband,

SIR JOHN PORTER (Ch. XIV), a genial, double-chinned, white-haired man, with whom she was never romantically in love, but with whom she lives most happily.

PORTER'S WIFE (Artists, Ch. II): Adrian Herbert learns from her that Charlie Sutherland spent a night in his wife's rooms.

POSNET, BLANCO, is "shewn up" by his conscience. He was riding off on a stolen horse, when a woman asks him to lend her the animal to take her dying child to the doctor. Although he knows that it is imperilling his life, in a state where hanging is the fate of the horse thief, Blanco surrenders the animal. He is caught and tried by the Sheriff, and is about to be hanged on the perjured evidence of Feemy Evans, when the woman is brought into the court and gives evidence that saves him. Blanco's opinion of God is that He is sly and mean, ready to trick a man.

POTHINUS (Caesar, Act II): Guardian of the boy king, Ptolemy. Offers to plot with Cleopatra, but is rebuffed, and after he has humiliated the Queen in the presence of Caesar, he is, by her order, assassinated by Ftatateeta.

POTTERBILLS (Methuselah, Part IV, Act III): One of the political parties in the British Commonwealth in the year A.D. 3000, then led by Badger Bluebin, the Prime Minister, and opposed by the Rotterjacks.

POULENGEY, BERTRAND DE (Joan, Scene I): French gentleman-at-arms, one of the first converts of Joan, who calls him "Polly". Such is his belief in her that he is ready to pay for a horse to take her on her mission to the Dauphin.

PRAED (Mrs Warren, Act I): An architect whose introduction in the play is only necessary to make the stage wheels go round. Friend of Mrs Warren.

PRICE, BRONTERRE O'BRIEN (Barbara, Act II): Unctuous rogue who, for the sake of what he can get out of it, pretends to be a convert to the Salvation Army. To please his converters he invents confessions. He is known as "Snobby".

PRIMARY (Methuselah, Part IV, Act I): Long-liver in his first century.

PRINCESS (Inca): To whom Ermyntrude engages herself as lady's maid. She is sought in marriage by a son of the Inca of Perusalem, and permits Ermyntrude to interview the Inca in her stead.

PROSSY: Miss Proserpine Garnett, typist to Morell, who is afflicted, like many women, with Prossy's disease—of being in love with Morell.

PTOLEMY, DIONYSIUS (Caesar, Act II): The boy king of Egypt. He tries to recite to his court a proclamation (which he has imperfectly memorized) regarding his rival on the throne, Cleopatra. When Cleopatra drags him from the chair of state his distress appeals to Caesar, whose kindness to her brother makes Cleopatra jealous. "Looks much older than an English boy of ten, but he has the childish air, the habit of being in leading strings, the mixture of impotence and petulance, of being excessively washed, combed and dressed by other hands, which is exhibited by Court bred princes of all ages."

PYGMALION (Methuselah, Part V): Scientist of the race of Ancients (A.D. 30,000), who discovers how to create human beings, manufacturing the protoplasm, which the sculptor, Martellus, moulds for h m into human shape. Pygmalion produces two human figures, Ozymandias and Cleopatra-Semiramis. The latter bites him on the finger, causing him to die.

PYTHONESS (Methuselah, Part IV, Act III): Oracle (*q.v.*).

Q.C. (Cashel, Ch. XV): Briefed to defend Cashel Byron on the prizefighting charge. Cashel is astounded at the manner in which the lawyer "rearranges the facts" of the meeting and secures an acquittal.

Q.C. (You Never, Act III): Bohun (*q.v.*).

RAINA—PETKOFF (Arms) (*q.v.*).

RAIS, GILLES DE (Joan, Scene II): Bluebeard. To test Joan it is arranged that he shall impersonate the Dauphin, but the Maid is not deceived by the impostor.

RAMSDEN, ROEBUCK (Superman, Act I): Left Guardian of Ann Whitefield, to act to his disgust with Tanner the revolutionary. A man proud of his liberal views, but of eminent respectability—"a president of highly respectable men". His sister,

MISS RAMSDEN (Superman, Act I), is a "hard-headed old maiden lady". Ramsden appears in the dream scene as the Statue.

RANKIN, LESLIE (Brassbound, Act I): Presbyterian missionary in Morocco who, as the result of many years of missionary endeavour, secures one convert, a cockney hypocrite from Brassbound's smuggling gang. Learns of the plot against Sir Howard Hallam and Lady Cicely Waynflete, and takes steps to save them.

RECORDING ANGEL (Socialist, Ch. I): Name given by the girl students of Alton College to the fault book, in which they are required to make admission of their transgressions.

REDBROOK, "KIDDY" (Brassbound, Act II): Son of a Dean who reached Brassbound's gang of smugglers by way of drink and cards.

REDPENNY (Dilemma, Act I): Medical student under Ridgeon.

REILLY, NORA (John Bull, Act II): "The only heiress of Rosscullen". She and Larry Doyle were boy and girl lovers, but he leaves her to make his fortune, and does not come back for eighteen years. When she finds that Larry is not ready to marry her, she accepts Broadbent, his partner.

REMAGEN, on the Rhine: Garden restaurant of hotel at. Scene of Widowers' Houses, Act I.

RETIARIUS (Androcles, Act II): The net thrower. Instead of making the conventional throw, he caused his net to throw dust in the eyes of Secutor, and thus vanquished him.

REVOLUTIONISTS' HANDBOOK: Supposititious work of the Socialist, John Tanner; it forms an appendix to Man and Superman.

RHEIMS: Ambulatory in the Cathedral of (Joan, Scene V).

RHEIMS, ARCHBISHOP OF (Joan, Scene II): Commands the Dauphin to refuse to see Joan. After the Coronation he admonishes Joan for her presumptuous attitude to the Church, and warns her that she is in danger of a heretic's fate. In the Epilogue he praises St Joan on behalf of the Princes of the Church.

RIDGEON, SIR COLENSO (Dilemma, Act I): Doctor who is knighted for his consumption cure; advocate of vaccines and innoculation; inventor of the use of opsonin to stimulate the phagocytes to destroy disease germs. He refuses to cure Dubedat, the artist, partly because of Dubedat's lack of morality, and partly because he would prefer Mrs Dubedat to be a widow. On learning after Dubedat's death that the widow has already remarried, he confesses that he has "committed a purely disinterested murder" in allowing the artist to die.—A character founded on Sir Almroth Wright. (See PREFACE.)

ROBINSON, OCTAVIUS (Superman, Act I): Poet, falls in love with Ann Whitefield, who rejects him for Tanner. His sister,

VIOLET ROBINSON (Act I), is married to Hector Malone. Her father-in-law, an American millionaire, had wished Hector to marry a girl of the English aristocracy, and threatens to beggar him because he has married into the middle classes. Violet impresses the father as being the equal of ten duchesses, and secures the withdrawal of the financial ban.

ROME: Roads converging on. Scene of Androcles, Act I.

ROOSENHONKERS-PIPSTEIN (Inca): American millionaire who

died leaving his widow, Ermyntrude (*q.v.*), in poverty.

ROSSCULLEN (John Bull, Act II): The scene of the principal events (and debates) of the play.

ROTTERJACKS (Methuselah, Part IV, Act III): One of the political parties in the British Commonwealth in the year A.D. 3000, opposed to the Potterbills.

ROUEN: Hall in castle. Trial of Joan (Scene VI) takes place there.

RUFIO (Caesar, Act II): "Caesar's shield", his chief military executive officer. A burly middle-aged man, very blunt, prompt and rough, intensely loyal to Caesar, whose ideals he often cannot understand. He murders Ftatateeta, Cleopatra's nurse, because he thought that one day she might be ordered to kill his master.

RUMMY (Barbara): Nickname of Romola Mitchens (*q.v.*).

RUM TUM TRUMPLEDUM (Joan, Epilogue): Song of the soldier from Hell.

ST PAUL'S, Covent Garden: Pygmalion, Act I, takes place before the portico of.

ST PETERSBURG, Palace of: Scene of Catherine.

SALLUST'S HOUSE (Socialist, Ch. XV): Home of Sidney Trefusis.

SALVATION ARMY: Barbara Undershaft is a major of the Army, which she deserts because it will accept for its funds the profits of war and drink. Act II of the play takes place in an Army shelter.

SANDRO (Reality): A fisherman who wishes to marry Giulia, the innkeeper's daughter. Sandro is prepared to arrange assassinations by drowning, and assists in the capture of the young Count Ferruccio.

SANTIAGO: American battleship, scene of Brassbound, Act III, the court-martial of Brassbound and his gang taking place in the ship.

SARANOFF, MAJOR SERGIUS (Arms, Act II): "Amateur" Bulgarian soldier, engaged to Raina Petkoff. In the war with the Servians he wins the battle of Slinitza "in the wrong way", by leading a cavalry charge. Returning from the wars he tries to continue his higher love affair with the romantic Raina, but he jilts her for the servant girl Louka.

Sergius is described as a product of Balkan Byronism, who can neither live up to his ideals nor realize them to be false posturings.

SARTORIUS (Widowers', Act I): The widower, whose fortune is derived from slum property—the personification of "middle-class respectability fattening on the poverty of the slum as flies fatten on filth". His daughter,

BLANCHE (Act I), is a spoilt child of tempestuous temper. Dr Trench seeks to marry her, but when he discovers that her father's wealth is derived from slum property he declines to receive that augmentation of his income without which Blanche will not marry him. Ultimately the lovers are reconciled.

SAUNDERS, MRS (Artists, Ch. XII): Informs Owen Jack that his patroness, Mary Sutherland, has been jilted by Adrian Herbert. Mrs Saunders was a born Irish protestant, a Roman Catholic by conversion, and a sort of free thinker by habit, by conviction nothing at all, and very superstitious by nature.

SAVOYARD, CECIL (Fanny, Prologue): Impressario who arranges for the production of Fanny's play. Is strictly limited to the professional view of life, and outside theatrical matters is shockingly ignorant.

SAVVY—BARNABAS (Methuselah, Part II) (q.v.).

SCHNEIDEKIND, LIEUTENANT (Annajanska): Subordinate of General Strammfest.

SCHUTZMACHER, LOONY (Dilemma, Act I): Doctor who made a small fortune in a Midland town from his simple secret of announcing "cure guaranteed". As a Jew he is unable to understand the average Englishman's lack of honour in financial borrowings which turn out badly for him.

SECONDARY (Methuselah, Part IV, Act I): Long-liver in his second century.

SECUTOR (Androcles, Act II): The gladiator, vanquished by Retiarius, the net thrower, by a trick.

SENTINELS (Caesar, Act III, Scene I): On duty on the Mole at Alexandria, refuse to allow Cleopatra to go to Caesar.

SENTRY (Joan, Scene III): At Orleans, accosts Joan.

SERGEANT (Disciple, Act II): Carries out the arrest of the Devil's Disciple, mistaking him for the minister, Anderson.

SERGEANT (Catherine, Scene I): An old Cossack on duty at the Court of Catherine the Great, is kicked downstairs by Patiomkin. He is severely handled by the English captain, Edstaston, whom he makes prisoner under the orders of the Empress.

SERPENT (Methuselah, Part I, Act I): Talks with Adam and Eve in the Garden of Eden, telling them of the mysteries of life and death; shews Adam how to create marriage, and instructs Eve in the mystery of birth. In Part V the ghost of the Serpent passes judgment on the race of men in the year A.D. 30,000, finding itself justified in having chosen wisdom, the knowledge of good and evil.

SEX, duellist of (You Never): Valentine (*q.v.*).

SHAKESPEAR, WILLIAM (Dark Lady): Mistakes Queen Elizabeth, who is cloaked, for Mary Fitton, supposititious Dark Lady of the Sonnets, with whom he was keeping tryst on the terrace of Whitehall Palace. On discovering the Queen's identity he invokes her patronage for the institution of a public playhouse.

SHE (How He Lied): Mrs Bompas is termed such throughout.

SHE ANCIENT (Methuselah, Part V): Assists in the birth from an egg of the child of her race. She is a being of seven hundred years of age. (See ANCIENTS.)

SHEIKH SIDI EL ASSIF (Brassbound, Act II): Anti-Christian fanatic to whom Brassbound, for the sake of vengeance, betrays his uncle, Sir Howard Hallam. The Sheikh agrees to surrender Sir Howard to Brassbound, in exchange for his daughter-in-law, Lady Cicely Waynflete.

SHEPHERD (Socialist, Ch. VI): Tom by name, whose hut was blown down in a storm, and who, with his wife Bess and two children, is brought by Trefusis, the rich Socialist, to seek shelter at Alton College. Because he was allowed to live in the hut, Tom had been paid less than the other shepherds on the estate of their employer, Sir John. Trefusis advances money to send Tom to Australia.

SHERIFF (Blanco). See KEMP.

SHIRLEY, PETER (Barbara, Act II): One of the honest poor, discharged from his job as too old at forty-six. He is a Secularist.

SHOTOVER, CAPTAIN (Heartbreak, Act I): An eccentric old

man who has retired from the sea and is trying to invent a psychic ray which will explode dynamite. He lives with his daughter, Hesione Hushabye, and her husband Hector, in a villa in which the principal room resembles the poop of a ship. At sea he was credited with having sold himself to the devil, and he married a black woman. After her heart has been broken by Hector Hushabye, Ellie Dunn decides to become the Captain's white wife.

SIDI EL ASSIF (Brassbound): Sheikh (*q.v.*).

SIERRA NEVADA (Superman, Act III): Scene of the capture of John Tanner by the brigands.

SIMPSON, MRS (Artists, Ch. V): Goodnatured landlady to Owen Jack, who tries her sorely with his eccentric ways.

SKENE, NED (Cashel, Prologue): Prizefighter, ex-champion of England. Cashel Byron takes service as male attendant at his establishment in Melbourne, and Skene backs him in his first fight. Cashel comes to regard Mrs Skene as more of a mother than his proper parent, and when Lydia Carew dismisses Cashel, Mrs Skene goes to her to plead his cause.

SLINITZA, Battle of (mentioned, Arms, Act I): Engagement in which Major Saranoff leads a Bulgarian cavalry charge against the Servians in most unprofessional manner. The charge ends in victory because the Servians have been served with the wrong cartridges for their rifles.

The description of the charge was taken almost verbatim from an account given privately to a friend of Shaw's by an officer who served in the Franco-Prussian war.

SMALL BOY (Cashel, Ch. VII): Involves Lydia Carew in a street altercation in which Cashel Byron comes to her aid.

SMILASH, JEFF (Socialist, Ch. III): Name assumed by Trefusis, the rich Socialist, when masquerading in Lyvern as a labourer. He took great pains in constructing the pseudonym, a compound of smile (suggesting good humour) and eyelash (they soften the expression)—"hence it is a sound that should cheer and propitiate".

SNOBBY (Barbara): Nickname of the unctuous Price (*q.v.*).

SOAMES, FATHER ANTHONY (christened Oliver Cromwell) (Getting Married): An ex-solicitor, chaplain to Bishop Bridgenorth. A very devout person, who thinks it is the duty of all Christians to take vows of poverty and celibacy, marriage being "an abomination which the church was founded to cast out and replace by the communion of saints".

SOCIAL DEMOCRATS (Superman, Act III): Members of the gang of brigands of the Sierra Nevada who capture John Tanner.

SOLDIER (Joan, Epilogue): An Englishman from Hell, who appears before Joan and the Dauphin. He is enjoying his one day's annual leave, granted him for the one good action of his life—fashioning a rude Cross for a lass that was going to be burned at the stake.

SPHINX: Caesar addresses it and finds Cleopatra sleeping between its paws.

SPINTHO (Androcles, Act I): A cowardly debauchee, embraces Christianity, believing that martyrdom will expunge the record of his past excesses—"every martyr goes to Heaven no matter what he has done". At the last his spirit fails; he will have one more debauch before martyrdom; but hurrying off to perform the heathen sacrifice, he takes the wrong turning, rushes into a cage, and is devoured by the lion.

SQUARCIO (Reality): Innkeeper and professional assassin, who threatens to take the life of Count Ferruccio. He is the father of Giulia, who, in order to earn the dowry which would enable her to marry, had contemplated the sin of luring the Count to his death.

SQUINTY (Blanco): One of the Boys who assists in guarding Blanco Posnet.

STAR AND GARTER, Richmond: Terrace of. Is the scene of Dilemma, Act II.

STATUE (Don Juan): Late illustrious Commander of Calatrava, leaves Heaven, where he finds life tedious, to go to Hell. In appearance he resembles Roebuck Ramsden of Superman (q.v.). He was slain in a duel by Don Juan, who had an affair with his daughter, Ana de Ulloa. He explains that in his after life he assumed the form of the Statue which his daughter erected to him because he was "so much more admired in marble than ever he was in his own person".

STEWARD (Joan, Scene I): Of the Castle of Vaucouleurs. He is convinced that the Maid is a witch because his hens gave no eggs when she was refused an interview with his master. After the Maid has had her desire granted he announces that the hens "are laying like mad".

STOGUMBER, JOHN BOWYER SPENSER NEVILLE DE (Joan, Scene IV): English chaplain, Keeper of the Seal to the Cardinal of Winchester. Clamours for the burning of Joan, whose witchery alone, he believes, is the cause of the French victories, for "no Englishman is ever beaten fairly". After witnessing the burning he is overcome with remorse at having contributed to the condemnation of the Maid to such a fate. "If you only saw what you think you would think differently about it", he declares in the Epilogue.

STRAKER, HENRY (Superman, Act II): Chauffeur to Tanner, to whom he is an interesting phenomenon. "The new man", the educated artisan product of a board school, where boys actually learn something, and of a polytechnic, his equivalent of Oxford and Cambridge.

STRAMMFEST, GENERAL (Annajanska): After his family has served the Panjandrums of Beotia for seven centuries, he, to his sorrow, has to serve the revolutionary party. He is further pained by discovering that the Grand Duchess, Annajanska, is a supporter of the revolution, being, in fact, the Bolshevik Empress.

STREPHON (Methuselah, Part V): Youth of the race of Ancients (A.D. 30,000), whose heart is broken when his beloved Chloe, on reaching maturity at the age of four, grows tired of sweethearting. They had sworn in the temple of love never to let their hearts grow cold.

SUMMERHAYS, LORD (Misalliance): Retired governor of Jinghiskahn, a widower of charming manner. He falls in love with Hypatia Tarleton, not knowing that she is engaged to

    BENTLEY SUMMERHAYS, the son of his middle age. Bentley is a young man whose brains have developed at the expense of his body. He is termed a "squit of a thing" by Hypatia, who jilts him.

SUSAN (Socialist, Ch. III): Domestic servant at Alton College.

SUTHERLAND, MR (Artists, Ch. I): Discusses, in Kensington Gardens, the appointment of a tutor for his son Charles. Overhearing the conversation, Owen Jack, an indigent composer, proposes himself for the position, and is appointed, largely through the influence of the daughter,

MARY SUTHERLAND (Ch. I). Mary is an amateur artist, and she encourages Adrian Herbert, to whom she becomes engaged, to persevere in his career as artist. After Adrian has thrown her over for Aurèlie Szczymplica, Owen Jack proposes to Mary, but she feels no love for him. She eventually marries the commonplace man of business, John Hoskyn, who is devoted to her, and although she is not romantically in love with him their marriage is a happy one. Her brother,

CHARLIE SUTHERLAND (Ch. II), is injured in a drunken brawl in Paris, and is succoured by Aurèlie, with whom he falls in love. He tries to kiss her, and she reproves him for acting dishonourably. He decides to go into the Conolly electric business.

SWINDON, MAJOR (Disciple, Act III): Presides at the court-martial on the Devil's Disciple. An officer whose loyalty without brains evokes the sarcasm of General Burgoyne.

SYKES, CECIL (Getting Married): Fiancé of Edith Bridgenorth. On his wedding morning a pamphlet on the legal position that makes a husband responsible for his wife's torts makes him doubt whether he can go through with the ceremony, particularly as he has a widowed mother dependent on his limited income. Solves the difficulty by having recourse to an insurance company.

SYLVIA—CRAVEN (Philanderer) (*q.v.*).

SZCZEPANOWSKA, LINA (Misalliance): A professional acrobat, Pole by birth. It is a tradition in her family that never a day shall pass without life being risked by one member of it. For this reason she goes for a trip in an aeroplane, which crashes in the glass house of John Tarleton. She is asked to stay as a guest, but finds the atmosphere impossible, because all the men make advances to her.

SZCZYMPLICA, AURÈLIE (Artists, Ch. IX): Polish pianist, who takes part in the production of Owen Jack's Fantasia. Adrian Herbert falls madly in love with her, and forsakes Mary Sutherland to marry her. Aurèlie is too devoted to her art to be a compliant wife, and Adrian has to be content with seeing his wife in between her tours abroad. She will not permit him to accompany her, but is chaperoned by her mother.

TANNER, JOHN (Superman, Act I): Supposititious author of the "Revolutionists' Handbook". A man whose advanced ideas make him appear a most immoral person to the respectable Ramsden, with whom he is appointed to act as guardian of Ann Whitefield. When Tanner realizes that Ann intends to marry him, he flies across Europe in his motor, and is captured in Spain by a gang of brigands. He is not able to escape his destiny as the bridegroom victim of Ann. In the "dream" scene he appears as Don Juan (*q.v.*).—In Tanner, with all his loquacity, Shaw satirized Hyndman. (Henderson.)

TARLETON, JOHN (Misalliance): Has made a fortune by making underwear. He is a man of superabundant vitality, intellectual curiosity, and unconventional views, with a quotation ready for all the chances of life. His wife,

MRS "CHICKABIDDY" TARLETON, is a shrewd motherly old lady, once his shop girl, still very pleasant and unaffected in spite of the advance in her social position. Their son,

JOHNNY TARLETON, is an ordinary dull and conventional young man of business. He infuriates Lina Szczepanowska, the Polish acrobat, by offering to marry her.

HYPATIA TARLETON, their daughter, "a glorious brute" her father calls her, bewails the fact that she is the child of a house where they are all old, and do nothing except argue whether what others do is right. She is engaged to the squit of a thing, Bentley Summerhays (unbeknown to Lord Summerhays, who proposes to her), but jilts him for the more masculine Joey Percival.

TAVAZZANO: An inn at. Scene of Man of Destiny.

TEDDY (Cashel, Ch. VII): London tough who accosts Lydia Carew in the street. Cashel Byron comes to Lydia's rescue, and the tough is ready to fight him until he learns that it is the famous prizefighter.

TELEPHONE OPERATOR (Methuselah, Part III): Controls the mechanism by which, in the year A.D. 2170, man is able to see as well as hear by telephone.

TEMPLE IN GALWAY: Scene of Methuselah, Part IV, Act II, and Act III.

TENORIO: Don Juan de (*q.v.*).

TERTIARY (Methuselah, Part IV, Act I): Longer-liver in his third century. "A short-liver would drop dead if a tertiary as much as looked at him."

THEODOTUS (Caesar, Act II): Tutor of the boy king, Ptolemy.

THUNDRIDGE, STREGA (Music): "The female Paderewski". Her life's dream has been to marry a man absolutely dependent on her, and she accepts the "clinging" Lord Reginald Fitzambey.

TINWELL, MINNIE (Dilemma, Act II): Waitress at Star and Garter, bigamously married by Dubedat, who left her after they had spent on their three weeks' honeymoon her life's savings of £30.

TRAGEDIAN (Artists, Ch. VIII): Eminent and exacting, who terrorizes the stock company with whom Madge Brailsford appears. Offers to take Madge on tour with him, but she declines.

TRANFIELD, GRACE (Philanderer, Act I): A widow, daughter of Cuthbertson. She loves Leonard Charteris, the philanderer, but being a "new" woman member of the Ibsen Club, she will not marry him. "I will never", she says, "marry the man I love too much; it would give him a terrible advantage over me; I should be utterly in his power."

TREFUSIS, SIDNEY (Socialist, Ch. II): A young Socialist who inherits much wealth from his father, a cotton merchant. Within six weeks of his marriage he flies from his wife, Henrietta, finding that in her presence he is not able to pursue his life's purpose of serving the cause of the working men. He runs away and finds a retreat at Lyvern, masquerading as a labourer under the name of Smilash (*q.v.*). He becomes acquainted with some of the girls of Alton College, and one of them, Agatha Wylie, informs Henrietta that he is in love with her, not knowing that "Smilash" is Henrietta's runaway husband. Henrietta makes a hurried journey to Lyvern to see Trefusis, and dies from the chill she catches. Trefusis ultimately marries Agatha.

TRÉMOUILLE, MGR. DE LA (Joan, Scene II): Lord Chamberlain to the Dauphin, who borrows money from him but does not repay. He is in command of the army at Orleans, and when Joan is appointed to supersede him he curses fluently. Joan calls him "old Gruff and Grum". His wife

(Scene II), in the imposture arranged to test Joan, impersonates the Queen.

TRENCH, DR HARRY (Widowers', Act I): Son of a younger son of a family of title, is a personification of "gentility fattening on the slum as flies fatten on filth". He wishes to marry Blanche Sartorius, but indignantly refuses to share the fortune of his prospective father-in-law, drawn from slum property. He is shewn, however, that his own income is derived from a mortgage on the very property, in the face of which he feels unable to maintain his objections.

TROTTER (Fanny, Prologue). One of the critics invited to see the private presentation of Fanny's first play. He alone solves the secret of the authorship.

TUNIC BEARER (Methuselah, Part V): Assists at the birth of the Newly-born.

TURANIA (Methuselah, Part IV, Act II): Cain Adamson Charles Napoleon (*q.v.*), Emperor of, in the year A.D. 3000.

TWINS (You Never, Act I): Dolly and Phil Clandon (*q.v.*).

ULLOA (Don Juan): Ana de (*q.v.*).

UNDERSHAFT AND LAZARUS (Major Barbara): Firm of explosives manufacturers, founded by a man who established a tradition of inheritance that the business shall pass not from father to son but from foundling to foundling. It descends to the seventh holder, ANDREW UNDERSHAFT (Act I), who was born an East Ender, and swore that he would be a full-fed, free man at any cost, neither reason, morals or lives of other men to stop him. He scoffs at the sentimental morality that condemns his trade as brutal, and develops his own religion, that poverty is the greatest crime, and that riches alone can afford the opportunity for honour, justice, truth, love and mercy, "graces and luxuries of a strong safe life". On account of the inheritance custom he is separated from

LADY BRITOMART UNDERSHAFT (Act I), his wife, daughter of the Earl of Stevenage, a charming representative of the aristocracy, in principle a Whig, in practice the genial autocrat of whatever circle in which she happens to move.

BARBARA UNDERSHAFT (Act I), their younger daughter, is a Major in the Salvation Army, an expert in wooing the souls and touching the pockets of the poor in the cause of the Army. Because the Army is ready to accept for its funds donations from her father and a whisky distiller, profits from war and drink, she loses her faith, but a visit to her father's factory discloses to her a new field for saving souls. Her brother,

STEPHEN UNDERSHAFT (Act I), is a priggish young man whom Eton and Cambridge have left without any qualifications for entering the professions, and he elects to become a politician. He has no resentment against his father for disinheriting him, as he has no intention to "go in for trade", as he describes the cannon business.

SARAH UNDERSHAFT (Act I), the elder daughter, "slender, bored and mundane", is engaged to Charles Lomax.

UTTERWORD, LADY ARIADNE (Heartbreak, Act I): Daughter of Captain Shotover. Brought up in the Bohemian atmosphere of Heartbreak House, which she loathed, she married, in order to escape it, Sir Hastings Utterword, a colonial governor. She carries on a flirtation with her brother-in-law,

RANDALL UTTERWORD (Act I), who becomes jealous of Hector Hushabye, with whom Ariadne commences another affair. Randall is an amateur flute player.

VALENTINE (You Never, Act I): Five-shilling dentist and "duellist of sex". After many love affairs he is finally brought to matrimony by Gloria Clandon.

VARINKA (Catherine, Scene I): A pretty young lady of the Russian Court, favourite niece of Patiomkin, whom she assists in carrying the English officer, Edstaston, into the presence of Catherine the Great.

VAUCOULEURS: Chamber in Castle of (Joan, Scene I).

VAUGHAN (Fanny, Prologue): One of the critics; considers Fanny's play to have been written by Pinero.

VICTORIA PARK (Candida): Morell is the hardworking vicar of St Dominic's.

VIRTUE, LALAGE (Irrational): Stage name of Susannah Conolly (*q.v.*).

VIVIE: Warren (*q.v.*).

VORTEX (Methuselah, Part V): The final goal set before them-

selves by the race of Ancients in the year A.D. 30,000—
mind without matter, freed from the tyranny of the body,
able to range the stars.

VULLIAMY, ANASTASIA (Foundling): Found as a baby on a
doorstep in Park Lane. She approaches the Lord Chancellor
to find her a husband, and claims Brabazon, another foundling, as "the very thing".

WAGGONER Jo (Blanco): Discovered the woman with the
horse Blanco Posnet is accused of stealing.

WAITER (Inca): Formerly an eminent medical man, who found
that the war, which robbed him of all his patients, closed
every career to him except that of waiter.

WAITER (You Never, Act II): At the hotel where the Clandons
are staying. His tact averts disaster at the luncheon at which
Fergus Crampton meets his family for the first time for
many years. A remarkable person in his way, the waiter "has
a certain expression peculiar to men who are pre-eminent in
their callings". His life's philosophy provides the title to
the play, that it is the unexpected that always happens, and
that in regard to most of the chances of life "you never can
tell".

WALKER, BILL (Barbara, Act II): A rough customer, who as-
saults two women at a Salvation Army shelter because the
Army has taken his girl from him. After the assault he tries
to buy forgiveness; but while the millionaires' thousands
(profits from war and drink) are accepted, Bill's pound is
rejected.

WALPOLE, CUTLER (Dilemma, Act I): Surgeon, whose dis-
covery is that "95 per cent of the human race suffer from
chronic blood poisoning" caused by the nuciform sac. His
panacea for all ills is to operate for the removal of the sac.

WALTER (You Never, Act II): The Waiter (q.v.).

WARD, MISS (Socialist, Ch. III): One of the teachers at Alton
College. She goes skating on Wickens's pond.

WARDER (Dark Lady): At Queen Elizabeth's Palace of Whitehall, whom Shakespear bribes, when keeping tryst with his
Dark Lady. From the warder the Bard obtains for his
tablets several jewels of speech such as "frailty thy name is
woman".

WAR OFFICE: Room in. Scene of Press Cuttings.

WARREN, MRS, is the managing director of a business, with establishments in Brussels, Paris and Vienna, in which Sir George Crofts has invested £40,000. Her daughter, VIVIE, brought up alone in England, who has just finished her career at Cambridge, learns the secret of her mother's profession. Mrs Warren tells her that she had to choose between immorality and poverty, and she would, were Vivie in a similar position, advise her to make a decision similar to her own. After hearing the explanation Vivie comes almost to respect her mother, but, on learning that she is still following her profession, decides that she cannot live with her, and is cursed by Mrs Warren for her hardness of heart. Sir George Crofts makes love to Vivie, who scornfully rejects him. Frank Gardner, her lover, withdraws his suit because he cannot afford to marry Vivie except on her mother's money.

WARREN LODGE (Cashel, Ch. II): In Wiltstoken Park, leased for Cashel Byron, the pugilist, as his training quarters, it being represented to Miss Carew, the owner, that it is required by a young man who wishes to recruit his health in solitude. Scene of Bashville, Act III.

WARWICK, EARL OF (Joan, Scene IV): Discusses with the Bishop of Beauvais the possibility of having Joan burned as a sorceress, her removal being to him a political necessity. In addition to attributing the French victories to her leadership, the Earl regards her as the exponent of political ideas which would make Kings the superior instead of the equal of their peers. Confesses to Joan, in the Epilogue, that the political necessity had proved to be a political mistake, and he praises the new Saint on behalf of "cunning Counsellors".

WATERS OF MARAH (Irrational, Ch. XIV): One of the novels of Elinor McQuinch.

WAYNFLETE, LADY CICELY (Brassbound, Act I): A famous and fearless traveller, visits Morocco with her brother-in-law, Sir Howard Hallam, a judge. Sir Howard is betrayed to a Christian-hating sheikh by his nephew, Captain Brassbound, and Lady Cicely successfully undertakes the conversion of Brassbound from his lifelong designs of vengeance. She also saves Brassbound from the hands of justice

GEORGE BERNARD SHAW

for having betrayed his uncle. Lady Cicely is a charming and dominating woman, and, according to her brother-in-law, half a dozen such would "make an end of the law of England in six months".

Character drawn from letters to Shaw from Ellen Terry, for whom the play was written.

WEBBER, LUCIAN (Cashel, Ch. II): Secretary to a Cabinet Minister, cousin of Lydia Carew, who rejects his proposal of marriage. Lucian eventually marries Alice Goff. At a society gathering Cashel Byron, the pugilist, uses Lucian to illustrate his argument that more effort does not necessarily mean more force, knocking him down with a deft blow. Appears in Bashville, Act II.

WEBSTERBRIDGE: Scene of the action of the Devil's Disciple.

WHITEFIELD, MRS (Superman, Act I): A pleasant widow, left with two daughters, the elder of whom,

ANN WHITEFIELD (Act I), is courted by Octavius Robinson, the poet, but she marks down John Tanner as her "intended victim". She pursues him when he flies across Europe, and overcomes his objections to marrying a woman whom he calls a liar, bully, coquette and, worst of all, hypocrite. Ann appears in the dream scene as Ana de Ulloa.

WHITEHALL: Terrace of the Palace (Dark Lady). Shakespear, keeping tryst there with his Dark Lady, meets Queen Elizabeth.

WICKENS, FARMER (Socialist, Ch. IX): One of the country people with whom Trefusis, the rich Socialist, masquerading as the labourer "Smilash", becomes acquainted. Trefusis instructs him in Socialistic principles in regard to landlords. On the farm is Wickens's pond, on which "Smilash" and the girls of Alton College skate. Wickens's boy (Ch. IV) gives information regarding the missing Mrs Trefusis, whom he saw kissing "Smilash".

WILLIAM (You Never, Act II): The waiter (q.v.), so called by Dolly Clandon because of his "likeness to Shakespear".

WILSON, MISS (Socialist, Ch. I): Principal of Alton College for girls, an establishment she attempts to conduct on the principle of moral force, without recourse to physical force.

WILSON, MR (Cashel, Prologue): Professor of mathematics at Moncrief House, the school from which Cashel Byron runs

204

away. He attempts to stop Cashel, who knocks him down.

WILTSTOKEN CASTLE (Cashel, Ch. I): Standing in the park of thirty acres, the property in Dorset of Lydia Carew. Wiltstoken Park is the scene of Bashville, Act I.

WORTHINGTON, LORD (Cashel, Ch. II): A patron of the boxing ring, backer of Cashel Byron, whom he introduces to Miss Carew. In the Play (Bashville) he proposes to Cashel's mother, Adelaide Gisborne, the actress, who accepts him.

WYLIE, AGATHA (Socialist, Ch. I): One of the girls at Alton College with whom Sidney Trefusis, the rich Socialist, masquerading as the labourer "Smilash", becomes acquainted. She falls in love with him and writes about him to her friend Henrietta, not knowing that "Smilash" is Henrietta's runaway husband. Some years later, after leaving school, Agatha again meets Trefusis, who induces her to marry him.

YORK (Methuselah, Part III): Archbishop of (*q.v.*).

Zoo (Methuselah, Part IV, Act I): One of the long-livers, a young thing of fifty, who takes charge of "Daddy" Barlow and threatens to kill him when he says things to hurt her, causing her a sensation, utterly evil, she had never experienced before. She "specializes in babies", her first having been such a success.

ZOZIM (Methuselah, Part IV, Act I): A long-liver appointed to take charge of the short-liver "Daddy" Barlow. He is an advanced primary (ninety-five years of age), and the intellectual strain of conversing with him causes Barlow "discouragement".

PLAY PRODUCTIONS

PLAY PRODUCTIONS

Mr J. T. Grein's Independent Theatre, founded in 1891, secured in 1892 (on December 8 at the Royalty) Mr Shaw's first hearing on the stage by producing "Widowers' Houses". Two years later "Arms and the Man" was produced at the Avenue Theatre. The enterprise was backed up at a considerable loss by Miss Horniman. "Arms and the Man" was first given on April 21, 1894, at the Avenue Theatre, where it ran until July 7, the receipts amounting to £1777. The next Shavian premières were at South Shields, where "Candida" was produced in 1895, and at the Bayswater Bijou, where "The Devil's Disciple" was played in 1897.

The first long run of Shaw plays in London took place under the Vedrenne-Barker management, at the Court. In the course of three seasons (1904–6) eleven of the plays were presented, 701 performances being given of them against 287 of plays by other authors.

The most recent Shaw premières in London were those of "Back to Methuselah", February 18-22, 1923, and "A Glimpse of Reality", November 20, 1927.

The Longest Runs.—The longest run of any Shaw piece was that of "Fanny's First Play", commenced at the Little Theatre on April 19, 1911, and shewn for 624 performances. The other runs of more than 100 performances were: "St Joan", New, commenced March 26, 1924—244; "Pygmalion", His Majesty's, April 11, 1914—118; and "Man and Superman", Lyric, April 16, 1914—105.

On the Halls.—In the variety theatre Mr Shaw made his début with "How He Lied to Her Husband", produced at the Palace, December 4, 1911.

Wireless.—The first Shaw play broadcast in England—"Passion, Poison and Petrifaction"—was sent over the wireless on January 15, 1926. On March 28, 1928, "The Man of Destiny" was broadcast from the London Studio, the cast being composed of the Macdona players, with Esmé Percy as Napoleon.

In America.—The first production of a Shaw piece abroad took place in the United States, "Arms and the Man" being

14

played by Richard Mansfield in the Herold Square Theatre, New York, on September 17, 1894. "The Devil's Disciple" was first seen in America, and "How He Lied to Her Husband" was first produced in New York. So also were "Heartbreak House", "Back to Methuselah" and "St Joan".

ON THE CONTINENT.—The first performance in the German language was on April 20, 1903, when "The Man of Destiny" was given at Schauspielhaus, Frankfurt. "Candida" was the first Shaw piece played in French—at Brussels, on February 7, 1907, at the Théâtre Royal du Parc; and also in France— Théâtre des Arts, Paris, May 7, 1908. "Androcles and the Lion" and "Pygmalion" were seen in Berlin before London.

THE SATIRIST SATIRIZED.—In "His Wild Oat", a farce by Mr Sydney Blow, produced at Portsmouth, November 29, 1926, Ronald Simpson impersonated Shaw.

BANNED BY THE CENSOR.—Three of the plays were banned by the Censor. The first was "Mrs Warren's Profession", written for the Independent Theatre. When it was produced in America the authorities, no doubt influenced by the Censor's decision, caused the company to be prosecuted; the magistrate acquitted them, holding that there was nothing indecent, and venturing the opinion that "the playwright's attack on social evils is one that may result in effecting some reform". That was in 1905, but the English interdict was not withdrawn until September 1924. Regarding the American production Shaw has written: "The prosecution was so far successful that it ruined the management. I myself, in addition to the loss of author's fees, had to forgo fees on other plays to the amount of £1000 to alleviate the situation. On the Continent the play was very successful in Berlin. I am told that it is also played a good deal in Holland. It has been produced in the Imperial Theatre in St Petersburg; some of the Russian critics ridiculed it as a goody-goody sample of English puritanism."

The Censor objected, in 1909, to "The Showing Up of Blanco Posnet", condemning a number of phrases as blasphemous, and was only prepared to license it on condition that certain phrases regarding God (for instance, "He's a sly one, He's a mean one, He plays cat and mouse with you") were expunged. Mr Shaw was not prepared to mutilate the work to the extent required. The play was produced in Dublin, where "an attempt was made to prevent its performance by some indiscreet officials in the absence of the Lord Lieutenant. The Directors of the Irish National Theatre, Lady Gregory and Mr W. B. Yeats, rose to the occasion with inspiriting courage. Their triumph was as complete as they could have desired. The performance exhausted the possibilities of success and provoked no murmur, though it inspired several approving sermons."

The third play was "Press Cuttings". The Censor took objection to the characters, and it was banned on the ground that Shaw was guilty of employing personalities expressed or implied. The Civic and Dramatic Guild was immediately created to evade the interdict, and the play was produced for the first time on July 9, 1909. The reader of plays allowed the production after the change of the names Balsquith (Balfour-Asquith) and Mitchener to Johnson and Bones. In a speech to the Society of Authors, Playwrights, and Composers in 1926 Mr Shaw said: "The most extraordinary adventure I have ever had with the Censor was with a play in which I wanted to call a General 'Mitchener'. This was objected to because the Censor thought I was alluding to Kitchener. As a matter of fact anybody who read the play could see that my character was not in the least like Kitchener's, and the reason I chose the name was because I wanted to throw the Censor right off the scent. I was really alluding to the late Duke of Cambridge."

Mr Shaw discusses the censorship at length in the Preface to "Plays Unpleasant" and to "How He Lied to Her Husband". See also "Censorship in England", Frank Fowell and Frank Palmer (Palmer, 1913). In *McClure's* (April 1912), under the title of "My Immoral Play", Mary Shaw, who took the part of Mrs Warren, gives an account of the production by Arnold Daly of "Mrs Warren's Profession" at the Garrick, New York, October 1905, and the prosecution that followed.

The following selection of principal productions takes no account of performances by repertory companies or of later revivals of the earlier plays.

ADMIRABLE BASHVILLE

First performed June 3, 1903, by the Imperial Stage Society, and repeated the following day at the Imperial Theatre. Cast:

LYDIA	.	.	.	Henrietta Watson.
CASHEL BYRON	.	.	.	Ben Webster.
MELLISH	.	.	.	William Wyes.
LUCIAN	.	.	.	Charles Quartermaine.
BASHVILLE	.	.	.	J. Farren Soutar.
CETEWAYO	.	.	.	James Hearne.
PARADISE	.	.	.	William Pilling.
LORD WORTHINGTON	.	.	Douglas Gordon.
MASTER OF THE REVELS	.	.	A. Lingham Power.
POLICEMAN	.	.	.	C. Aubrey Smith.
ADELAIDE GISBORNE	.	.	Fanny Brough.

Revivals: January 26, 1909, His Majesty's, Matinee. Cast included Marie Löhr (Lydia), Ben Webster (Cashel), Henry Ainley (Bashville).

ANDROCLES AND THE LION

First production in England: September 1, 1913, St James'. Cast:

EMPEROR	.	.	.	Leon Quartermaine.
CAPTAIN	.	.	.	Ben Webster.
ANDROCLES	.	.	.	O. P. Heggie.
LION	.	.	.	Edward Sillward.
LENTULUS	.	.	.	Donald Calthrop.
METELLUS	.	.	.	Hesketh Pearson.
FERROVIUS	.	.	.	Alfred Brydone.
SPINTHO	.	.	.	J. F. Outram.
CENTURION	.	.	.	H. O. Nicholson.
EDITOR	.	.	.	Herbert Hewetson.
CALL BOY	.	.	.	Neville Gartside.
SECUTOR	.	.	.	Allan Jeayes.
RETIARIUS	.	.	.	J. B. Turnbull.
MENAGERIE KEEPER	.	.	Baliol Holloway.
SLAVE DRIVER	.	.	.	Ralph Hutton.
MEGAERA	.	.	.	Clare Greet.
LAVINIA	.	.	.	Lillah McCarthy.

New York: 1915, January 22, Wallacks. Granville Barker production.

Berlin: 1912, November 25, Kleines.

ANNAJANSKA

First performed January 21, 1918, Coliseum: "Anna-janska, the Wild Duchess, play in one act from the Russian of Gregory Biessipoff". Cast:

ANNAJANSKA	.	.	Lillah McCarthy.
GENERAL STRAMMFEST	.	.	Randle Ayrton.
SCHNEIDEKIND	.	.	Henry Miller.
FIRST SOLDIER	.	.	Drelincourt Odlum.

ARMS AND THE MAN

First performed April 21, 1894, the Avenue. Cast:

MAJOR PAUL PETKOFF	.	.	James Welch.
MAJOR SERGIUS SARANOFF	.	.	Bernard Gould.
CAPTAIN BLUNTSCHLI	.	.	Yorke Stephens.
MAJOR PLECHANOFF	.	.	A. E. W. Mason.
NICOLA	.	.	Orlando Barnett.
CATHERINE PETKOFF	.	.	Mrs. Charles Calvert.
RAINA PETKOFF	.	.	Alma Murray.
LOUKA	.	.	Florence Farr.

Revivals: 1895, March 30, Theatre Royal, South Shields— A. E. Drinkwater (Bluntschli), Ethel Verne (Raina); 1907, December 30, Savoy—Robert Loraine (Bluntschli), Granville Barker (Saranoff), Lillah McCarthy (Raina); 1911, May 18, Criterion—Arnold Daly (Bluntschli), Jean Sterling Mackinlay (Louka), Margaret Halstan (Raina); 1919, December 11, Duke of York's—Robert Loraine (Bluntschli), Stella Mervyn Campbell (Raina), Dorothy Holmes-Gore (Louka).

"Arms and the Man" was the first Shaw play produced in America—on September 17, 1894, at Herold Square Theatre. The cast was:

MAJOR PETKOFF	.	.	Harry Pitt.
NICOLA	.	.	Walden Remsey.
MAJOR SARANOFF	.	.	Henry Jewett.
CAPTAIN BLUNTSCHLI	.	.	Richard Mansfield.
CATHERINE PETKOFF	.	.	Mrs McKee Rankin.

213

| LOUKA | . | . | . | . | Amy Busby. |
| RAINA | . | . | . | . | Beatrice Cameron. |

Berlin, 1904, December 8, Deutsches.

The opera, "The Chocolate Soldier", was first produced at the Theater des Westens, Berlin, in 1909. The first London production was at the Lyric, September 10, 1910.

AUGUSTUS DOES HIS BIT

First production, January 21, 1917, Court (Stage Society). "Play in one Act by the author of 'The Inca of Perusalem'." Cast:

LORD AUGUSTUS	.	.	.	F. B.-J. Sharp.
HORATIO	.	.	.	Charles Rock.
A LADY	.	.	.	Lalla Vandervelde.

BACK TO METHUSELAH

First performed at Birmingham, October 9-13, 1923; in London, at the Court, February 18-22, 1924. Cast:

IN THE BEGINNING

ADAM	.	.	.	.	Colin Keith-Johnston.
EVE	.	.	.	.	Gwen ffrangçon-Davies.
SERPENT	.	.	.	.	Caroline Keith.
CAIN	.	.	.	.	Scott Sunderland.

GOSPEL OF BROTHERS BARNABAS

FRANKLYN BARNABAS	.	Wallace Evennett.
CONRAD BARNABAS	.	.	Frank Moore.
PARLOURMAID	.	.	.	Margaret Chatwind.
THE REV. WILLIAM HASLAM	.	Cedric Hardwicke.
SAVVY BARNABAS	.	.	Eileen Beldon.
JOYCE BURGE	.	.	.	Leo Carroll.
LUBIN	.	.	.	Osmund Willson.

THE THING HAPPENS

BURGE-LUBIN	.	.	.	Terence O'Brien.
VOICE OF TELEPHONE OPERA-		
TOR	.	.	.	.	Phyllis Shand.

BARNABAS	.	.	.	Frank Moore.
CONFUCIUS	.	.	.	Paul Smythe.
NEGRESS	.	.	.	Chris Castor.
ARCHBISHOP OF YORK	.	.	Cedric Hardwicke.
MRS LUTESTRING	.	.	Margaret Chatwind.

TRAGEDY OF AN ELDERLY GENTLEMAN

ELDERLY GENTLEMAN	.	.	Scott Sunderland.
FUSIMA	.	.	.	Caroline Keith.
ZOZIM	.	.	.	Albert Ingle.
ZOO	.	.	.	.	Eileen Beldon.
GENERAL AUFSTEIG (Napoleon)	Osmund Willson.
ORACLE	.	.	.	Evelyn Hope.
BADGER-BLUEBIN	.	.	Melville Cooper.
MRS BADGER-BLUEBIN	.	.	Louise de Lacy.
MISS BADGER-BLUEBIN	.	.	Phyllis Shand.

AS FAR AS THOUGHT CAN REACH

STREPHON	.	.	.	Osmund Willson.
CHLOE	.	.	.	Yvette Pienne.
HE-ANCIENT	.	.	Cedric Hardwicke.
ACIS	.	.	.	Raymond Huntley.
SHE-ANCIENT	.	.	Caroline Keith.
AMARYLLIS	.	.	Gwen ffrangçon-Davies.
ECRASIA	.	.	.	Frances Doble.
ARJILLAX	.	.	.	Albert Ingle.
MARTELLUS	.	.	Terence O'Brien.
PYGMALION	.	.	Colin Keith-Johnston.
OZYMANDIAS	.	.	Scott Sunderland.
CLEOPATRA-SEMIRAMIS	.	Evelyn Hope.
GHOST OF ADAM	.	.	Colin Keith-Johnston.
GHOST OF EVE	.	.	Gwen ffrangçon-Davies.
GHOST OF CAIN	.	.	Scott Sunderland.
GHOST OF SERPENT	.	.	Caroline Keith.
GHOST OF LILITH	.	.	Margaret Chatwind.

Producer—H. K. Ayliff.

New York: April 1922, Garrick Theatre.

CAESAR AND CLEOPATRA

First produced: Newcastle-on-Tyne, Theatre Royal, March 15, 1899, Mrs Patrick Campbell as Cleopatra. Revived: Leeds, September 16, 1907, and first produced in London, November 25, 1907, at the Savoy, with the same cast as at Leeds.

PERSIAN GUARDSMAN	S. A. Cookson.
BELZANOR	A. W. Tyrer.
NUBIAN SENTINEL	Frank Bickley.
BEL AFFRIS	C. D. Vaughan.
FTATATEETA	Elizabeth Watson.
JULIUS CAESAR	Forbes-Robertson.
CLEOPATRA	Gertrude Elliott.
POTHINUS	Charles Langley.
THEODOTUS	Sam T. Pearce.
PTOLEMY XIV	Master Philip Tonge.
ACHILLAS	John M. Troughton.
RUFIO	Percy Rhodes.
BRITTANUS	Ian Robertson.
LUCIUS SEPTIMIUS	Walter Ringham.
WOUNDED SOLDIER	William Pilling.
PROFESSOR OF MUSIC	Frank Ridley.
CHARMIAN	Dorothy Paget.
IRAS	Dora Harker.
MAJOR DOMO	A. Wheatman.
APOLLODORUS	Lewis Willoughby.

Revived: 1913, April 14, at Drury Lane, Forbes-Robertson's farewell performance—Gertrude Elliott (Cleopatra).

New York: 1906, October 30, New Amsterdam; 1913, October 20, Sir J. and Lady Forbes-Robertson; Shubert.

Berlin: 1906, March 31, Neues.

CANDIDA

First performed: South Shields, Theatre Royal, March 30, 1895—George Young (Morell), A. E. Drinkwater (Eugene), Ethel Verne (Proserpine), Lilian Revell (Candida). Revived: first provincial tour, by the Independent Theatre Company, at Her Majesty's, Aberdeen, July 30, 1897—Janet Achurch

(Candida), Charles Charrington (Morell). First London performance: Stage Society, Strand, July 1, 1900. First public performance in London: April 26, 1904, Court. Cast:

CANDIDA	Kate Rorke.
PROSERPINE GARNETT . .	Sydney Fairbrother.
THE REV. JAMES MAVOR MORELL	Norman McKinnel.
EUGENE MARCHBANKS . .	Granville Barker.
MR BURGESS . .	A. G. Poulton.
THE REV. ALEXANDER MILL .	Athol Stewart.

New York: 1903, December 9, Prince's—Arnold Daly as Eugene.

Dresden: 1903, November 19.

Brussels: 1907, February 7, Théâtre Royal du Parc—Shaw's first appearance in French.

Paris: 1908, May 7, Théâtre des Arts—first Shaw performance in France.

CAPTAIN BRASSBOUND'S CONVERSION

First produced: Stage Society, December 16, 1900, Strand; Manchester, Queen's, May 12, 1902—Harold V. Neilson (Brassbound), Janet Achurch (Lady Cicely); Court, March 20, 1906. Cast:

LADY CICELY WAYNFLETE .	Ellen Terry.
SIR HOWARD HALLAM .	J. H. Barnes.
CAPTAIN BRASSBOUND .	Frederick Kerr.
RANKIN . . .	F. Cremlin.
DRINKWATER . .	Edmund Gwenn.
REDBROOK . . .	C. L. Delph.
JOHNSON . . .	Edmund Gurney.
MARZO . . .	Michael Sherbrooke.
SIDI EL ASSIF . .	Lewis Casson.
THE CADI . . .	Trevor Lowe.
OSMAN . . .	Gordon Bailey.
HASSAN . . .	Jules Shaw.
CAPTAIN HAMLIN KEARNEY, U.S.N. . .	James Carew.
AMERICAN BLUEJACKET . .	Frederick Lloyd.

October 15, 1912, Little—Gerald Lawrence (Brassbound),

GEORGE BERNARD SHAW

Gertrude Kingston (Lady Cicely), Harry Nicholls (Drink-water).

New York: 1907, January 28, Empire—Ellen Terry (Lady Cicely).

DARK LADY OF THE SONNETS

First produced: Haymarket Theatre, November 24, 1910, at performance in aid of the Shakespeare Memorial Theatre. Cast:

WARDER	Hugh B. Tabberer.
WILLIAM SHAKESPEAR . .	Granville Barker.
QUEEN ELIZABETH . .	Suzanne Sheldon.
MARY FITTON . . .	Mona Limerick.

Revived: 1912, October 16, Dublin, United Arts Club.

THE DEVIL'S DISCIPLE

Copyright performance: Bayswater Bijou, April 17, 1897; September 26, 1899, Princess of Wales, Kennington—Murray Carson (Richard Dudgeon), Luigi Lablache (General Burgoyne), Grace Warner (Judith Anderson). Revived: Savoy, October 14, 1907. Cast:

DICK DUDGEON . . .	Matheson Lang.
CHRISTY DUDGEON . .	James Annand.
REV. A. ANDERSON . .	C. Rann Kennedy.
GENERAL BURGOYNE . .	H. Granville Barker.
MAJOR SWINDON . .	Arnold Lucy.
SERGEANT	Kenyon Musgrave.
LAWYER HAWKINS . .	Arthur Chesney.
UNCLE WILLIAM DUDGEON .	H. Williams.
UNCLE TITUS DUDGEON .	Jules Shaw.
CHAPLAIN MR BRUDENELL .	Lewis Casson.
MRS DUDGEON . . .	Miss Bateman.
JUDITH ANDERSON . .	E. Wynne Matthison.
AUNT WILLIAM DUDGEON .	Mrs Maltby.
AUNT TITUS DUDGEON . .	Ethel Harper.

First presented in America at Hermanus Bleecker Hall,

Albany, October 1, 1897, and the following Monday it was acted at the Fifth Avenue. Cast:

REV. A. ANDERSON	Benjamin Johnson.
JUDITH ANDERSON	Beatrice Cameron.
ANNE DUDGEON	Munda Monk.
RICHARD DUDGEON	Richard Mansfield.
CHRISTOPHER DUDGEON	A. G. Andrews.
UNCLE WILL	W. H. Griffith.
UNCLE TITUS	M. Le Fevre.
ETTIE	Lottie Briscoe.
LAWYER HAWKINS	Mr Hunter.
GENERAL BURGOYNE	Arthur Forrest.
MAJOR SWINDON	Joseph Weaver.
BRUDENELL	William Courtenay.
SERGEANT	Francis Kingdom.

Berlin: 1904, November 25, Berliner.

THE DOCTOR'S DILEMMA

First produced: Court, November 20, 1906. Cast:

SIR PATRICK CULLEN	William Farren (junr.).
SIR RALPH BLOOMFIELD BONINGTON	Eric Lewis.
SIR COLENSO RIDGEON	Ben Webster.
CUTLER WALPOLE	James Hearn.
LEO SCHUTZMACHER	Michael Sherbrooke.
DR BLENKINSOP	Edmund Gurney.
LOUIS DUBEDAT	Granville Barker.
REDPENNY	Norman Page.
THE NEWSPAPER MAN	Trevor Lowe.
MR DANBY	Lewis Casson.
A WAITER	Percy Marmont.
JENNIFER DUBEDAT	Lillah McCarthy.
EMMY	Clare Greet.
MINNIE TINWELL	Mary Hamilton.

Revived: St James', December 9, 1913—Nigel Playfair (Walpole), Leon Quartermaine (Blenkinsop), Dennis Neilson Terry (Dubedat), Lillah McCarthy (Jennifer).

New York: 1914, March 29—Granville Barker.

Berlin: 1908, November 20, Deutsches.

FANNY'S FIRST PLAY

First performed: Little Theatre, Adelphi, April 19, 1911.
Cast:

THE INTRODUCTION

SERVANT	A. E. Filmer.
CECIL SAVOYARD	Lewis Sealy.
COUNT O'DOWDA	Harcourt Williams.
FANNY O'DOWDA	Christine Silver.
MR TROTTER	Claude King.
MR VAUGHAN	S. Creagh Henry.
MR GUNN	Reginald Owen.
FLAWNER BANNAL	Nigel Playfair.

THE PLAY

ROBIN GILBEY	Fewlass Llewellyn.
MRS GILBEY	Gwynneth Galton.
JUGGINS	H. K. Ayliff.
DORA DELANEY	Dorothy Minto.
MRS KNOX	Cicely Hamilton.
JOSEPH KNOX	Arnold Lucy.
MARGARET KNOX	Lillah McCarthy.
LIEUTENANT DUVALLET	Raymond Lauzerte.
BOBBY	Shiel Barry.

Revived: Kingsway, February 13, 1915—Henry Ainley
(Juggins), Iva St Helier (Dora), Lena Ashwell (Margaret).
New York: 1912, September 16, Comedy; 1913, November
17, Coronet.
Berlin: 1911, October 20, Kleines.

GETTING MARRIED

First produced: May 12, 1908 (Matinee), Haymarket. Cast:

MRS BRIDGENORTH	Mary Rorke.
ALDERMAN COLLINS	E. Holman Clarke.
GENERAL BRIDGENORTH	Charles Fulton.
LESBIA GRANTHAM	Beryl Faber.
REGINALD BRIDGENORTH	William Farren (junr.).

MRS REGINALD BRIDGENORTH .		Marie Löhr.
BISHOP CHELSEA .	.	Henry Ainley.
JOHN HOTCHKISS .	.	Robert Loraine.
CECIL SYKES	.	Berte Thomas.
EDITH BRIDGENORTH	.	Auriol Lee.
REV. DE SOAMES .	.	James Hearn.
MRS GEORGE COLLINS	.	Fanny Brough.

New York: November 1916, Booth Theatre.

THE GLIMPSE OF REALITY

Produced: London, Arts Theatre, November 20, 1927.
Cast:

COUNT FERRUCCIO	.	Harcourt Williams.
GIULIA	.	Elissa Landi.
SQUARCIO	.	Harold B. Meade.
SANDRO	.	Terence O'Brien.

GREAT CATHERINE

First performed: Vaudeville, November 18, 1913. Cast:

VARINKA	.	Miriam Lewes.
PRINCE PATIOMKIN	.	Norman McKinnel.
COSSACK SERGEANT	.	J. Cooke Beresford.
CAPTAIN EDSTASTON	.	Edmond Breon.
NARYSHKIN	.	Eugene Mayeur.
EMPRESS CATHERINE II .		Gertrude Kingston.
PRINCESS DASHKOFF	.	Annie Hill.
CLAIRE	.	Dorothy Massingham.

HEARTBREAK HOUSE

First performed: October 18, 1921, Court. Cast:

ELLIE DUNN	.	Ellen O'Malley.
NURSE GUINNESS .	.	Lilian Talbot.
CAPTAIN SHOTOVER	.	Brember Wills.
LADY UTTERWORD	.	Edith Evans.
HESIONE HUSHABYE	.	Mary Grey.

MAZZINI DUNN	.	.	H. O. Nicholson.
HECTOR HUSHABYE	.	.	James Dale.
BOSS MANGAN	.	.	Alfred Clark.
RANDALL UTTERWORD	.	.	Eric Maturin.
BURGLAR	.	.	Charles Groves.

New York: November 1920, Garrick Theatre.

Berlin: 1926, Renaissance.

HOW HE LIED TO HER HUSBAND

First produced: New York, September 26, 1904, Berkeley Lyceum, as curtain raiser to "Man of Destiny". First London performance: February 28, 1905, Court. Cast:

HER LOVER	.	.	Granville Barker.
HER HUSBAND	.	.	A. G. Poulton.
HERSELF	.	.	Gertrude Kingston.

This was the first Shavian production to be staged at a music-hall—Palace, December 4, 1911. Cast:

SHE	.	.	Margaret Halstan.
HE	.	.	Harcourt Williams
HER HUSBAND	.	.	Dawson Millward.

Munich: 1913, November 5.

INCA OF PERUSALEM

First produced: Birmingham Repertory, October 9, 1916, as "An almost historical comedietta by a member of the Royal Society of Literature". Cast:

ARCHDEACON	.	.	Joseph A. Dodd.
ERMYNTRUDE	.	.	Gertrude Kingston.
PRINCESS	.	.	Cathleen Orford.
WAITER	.	.	William Armstrong.
HOTEL MANAGER	.	.	Noel Shammon.
INCA	.	.	Felix Aylmer.

Produced in London, December 16, 1917, Criterion—Gertrude Kingston, Nigel Playfair (Waiter), Randle Ayrton (Inca).

222

INTERLUDE

At the opening, on January 28, 1907, of the Playhouse, the new theatre of Cyril Maude, for whom it was written, at the production of "Toddles".

JOHN BULL'S OTHER ISLAND

Following rejection by the Irish Literary Theatre, for reasons both financial and intellectual, it was produced at the Court, November 1, 1904. Cast:

BROADBENT	Louis Calvert.
LARRY DOYLE	J. L. Shine.
TIM HAFFIGAN	Percival Stevens.
HODSON	Nigel Playfair.
KEEGAN	Granville Barker.
PATSEY FARRELL	Graham Browne.
FATHER DEMPSEY	Charles Daly
CORNEY DOYLE	F. Cremlin.
BARNEY DORAN	Wilfred Shine.
MATTHEW HAFFIGAN	A. E. George.
AUNTY JUDY	Agnes Thomas.
NORA	Ellen O'Malley.

Revivals: March 11, 1905, special performance for King Edward VII; September 11, 1905, Court—Lillah McCarthy (Nora); September 17, 1906, Court; December 26, 1912, Kingsway—Louis Calvert (Broadbent), Harcourt Williams (Larry), Ellen O'Malley (Nora).

New York: 1905, October 10, Garrick.

MAJOR BARBARA

First produced: November 28, 1905, Court. Cast:

LADY BRITOMART UNDERSHAFT	Rosina Filippi.
STEPHEN UNDERSHAFT	Hubert Harben.
MORRISON	C. L. Delph.
BARBARA UNDERSHAFT	Annie Russell.

SARAH UNDERSHAFT	. .	Hazel Thompson.
CHARLES LOMAX	. . .	Dawson Milward.
ADOLPHUS CUSINS	. .	Granville Barker.
ANDREW UNDERSHAFT	. .	Louis Calvert.
RUMMY MITCHENS	. .	Clare Greet.
SNOBBY PRICE	. . .	Arthur Laceby.
JENNY HILL	. . .	Dorothy Minto.
PETER SHIRLEY	. . .	F. Cremlin.
BILL WALKER	. . .	Oswald Yorke.
MRS BAINES	. . .	E. Wynne Matthison.
BILTON	. . .	Edmund Gwenn.

New York: May 1915, Playhouse—Miss Grace George.
Berlin: 1909, November 5, Deutsches.

MAN AND SUPERMAN

First produced: London, Stage Society, Court, May 23,
1905. Cast:

ROEBUCK RAMSDEN	. .	Charles Goodhart.
OCTAVIUS ROBINSON	. .	Lewis Casson.
JOHN TANNER	. . .	Granville Barker.
HENRY STRAKER	. . .	Edmund Gwenn.
HECTOR MALONE	. . .	Hubert Harben.
MR MALONE	. . .	J. D. Beveridge.
ANN WHITEFIELD	. . .	Lillah McCarthy.
MRS WHITEFIELD	. . .	Florence Haydon.
MISS RAMSDEN	. . .	Agnes Thomas.
VIOLET ROBINSON	. . .	Sarah Brooke.
PARLOURMAID	. . .	Hazel Thompson.

Revivals: October 23, 1905, Court; October 29, 1906,
Court; May 27, 1907, Court—Robert Loraine (Tanner),
Dennis Eadie (Hector); October 12, 1908, the Coronet—
Granville Barker (Tanner), Frances Dillon (Ann); September
28, 1911, Criterion—E. Ion Swinley (Octavius), Robert
Loraine (Tanner), Pauline Chase (Ann); April 8, 1912,
Criterion—Robert Loraine (Tanner), Hilda Bruce Potter
(Ann), Frederick Sargent (Octavius).

New York: 1905, September 4, Hudson—Robert Loraine.

DON JUAN IN HELL

June 4, 1907, Court (followed by "Man of Destiny"). Cast:

DON JUAN	Robert Loraine.
DONA ANA DE ULLOA . .	Lillah McCarthy.
THE STATUE . . .	Michael Sherbrooke.
THE DEVIL	Norman McKinnel.

MAN OF DESTINY

First produced: July 1, 1897, Grand, Croydon. Cast:

NAPOLEON BONAPARTE . .	Murray Carson.
SUB-LIEUTENANT . . .	E. H. Kelly.
GIUSEPPE	Horace Hodges.
STRANGE LADY . . .	Florence West.

Revived: March 29, 1901, Comedy—Granville Barker (Napoleon), Margaret Halstan (Lady); June 4, 1907, Court (preceded by "Don Juan in Hell")—Dion Boucicault (Bonaparte), Irene Vanbrugh (Lady).

New York: 1899, February 16, Empire—American Academy Dramatic Art.

1904, September 26, Berkeley Lyceum.

Berlin: 1904, February 10, Neues.

MISALLIANCE

First produced: Duke of York's (Repertory Theatre), February 23, 1910. Cast:

JOHN TARLETON, JUNR. . .	Frederick Lloyd.
BENTLEY SUMMERHAYS . .	Donald Calthrop.
HYPATIA TARLETON .	Miriam Lewes.
MRS TARLETON . . .	Florence Haydon.
LORD SUMMERHAYS .	Hubert Harben.
JOHN TARLETON . . .	C. M. Lowne.
JOSEPH PERCIVAL . . .	Charles Bryant.
LINA SZCZEPANOWSKA .	Lena Ashwell.
JULIUS BAKER . . .	O. P. Heggie.

New York: November 1917, Broadhurst Theatre.

MRS WARREN'S PROFESSION

Privately produced: Stage Society, January 5, 1902, New Lyric. Cast:

PRAED	. . .	Julius Knight.
SIR GEORGE CROFTS	. .	Charles Goodheart.
REV. SAMUEL GARDNER	. .	Cosmo Stuart
FRANK	. . .	H. Granville Barker.
VIVIE	. . .	Madge McIntosh.
MRS WARREN	. .	Fanny Brough.

Glasgow: Royalty Theatre, April 10, 1913—Frederick Sargent (Frank), Ruth Mackay (Mrs Warren), Richard Fielding (Crofts), Helen Brown (Vivie).

First public performance in England: Birmingham, Prince of Wales, July 27, 1925; in London, at the Regent, September 28, 1925. Revived: March 3, 1926, Strand—A. Bourchier and Charles Macdona (86 performances).

America: 1902, October 27, Hyperion, The New Haven; 1905, October 30, Garrick—R. Mansfield.

Berlin: 1907, November 16, Central.

MUSIC CURE

First performed as curtain raiser to G. K. Chesterton's "Magic", Little, January 28, 1914. Cast:

LORD REGINALD FITZAMBEY	.	William Armstrong.
DR DAWKINS	. .	Frank Randell.
STREGA THUNDRIDGE	. .	Madge McIntosh.

OVERRULED

First produced: Duke of York's, October 14, 1912, with plays by Barrie and Pinero. Cast:

GREGORY LUNN	. .	Claude King.
SIBTHORPE JUNO	. .	Adolphus Vane Tempest.
MRS JUNO	. .	Miriam Lewes.
MRS LUNN	. .	Geraldine Olliffe.

New York: February 1917; Maxine Elliott Theatre.

PASSION, POISON AND PETRIFACTION

First produced in aid of the funds of the Actors' Orphanage in a booth in Regent's Park, July 14, 1905. Cast:

LADY MAGNESIA FITZTOLLEMACHE	Irene Vanbrugh.
PHYLLIS (her maid) . .	Nancy Price.
GEORGE FITZTOLLEMACHE (her husband) . . .	Eric Lewis.
ADOLPHUS BASTABLE (a leader of fashion) . . .	Cyril Maude.
LANDLORD	Lennox Pawle.
POLICE CONSTABLE . .	Arthur Williams.
DOCTOR	G. P. Huntley.
CHOIR OF INVISIBLE ANGELS .	Messrs. Mason, Tucker, Mancy and Humphreys.

THE PHILANDERER

First performed: February 20, 1905, at the Cripplegate Institute. First West End performance: February 5, 1907, Court. Cast:

LEONARD CHARTERIS . .	Ben Webster.
MRS GRACE TRANFIELD . .	E. Wynne Matthison.
JULIA CRAVEN . . .	Mary Barton.
COLONEL DANIEL CRAVEN, V.C.	Eric Lewis.
MR JOSEPH CUTHBERTSON .	Luigi Lablache
SYLVIA CRAVEN . . .	Dorothy Minto
DR PARAMORE . . .	Hubert Harben.
THE CLUB PAGE . . .	Cyril Bruce.

New York: first given 1913.
Berlin: 1908, September 4, Hebbel; 1909, January 3, Hebbel.

PRESS CUTTINGS

First performed: July 9, 1909, Court—Civic and Dramatic Guild. Cast:

GENERAL MITCHENER . .	Robert Loraine.
BALSQUITH	Leon Quartermaine.

MRS FARRELL	.	.	.	Agnes Thomas.
ORDERLY .		.	.	Ernest Cosham.
MRS BANGER	.	.	.	Alice Beet.
LADY CORINTHIA FANSHAWE		.		Ethelwyn Jones.

First public performance: Gaiety, Manchester, September 27, 1909. Cast:

GENERAL BONES	.	.	.	Ian MacLaren.
AN ORDERLY	.	.	.	B. Iden Payne.
JOHNSON (Prime Minister)		.		Charles Bibby.
MRS FARRELL	.	.	.	Ada King.
MRS BANGER	.	.	.	Emily Patterson.
LADY CORINTHIA	.	.	.	Edith Goodall.

Produced in America in 1912, at a Woman's Suffrage Party benefit, by Oswald Yorke and Co.

PYGMALION

First performed: Berlin Lessing Theatre, November 1, 1913. First English performance: April 11, 1914, His Majesty's. Cast:

HENRY HIGGINS	.	.	.	Sir Herbert Tree.
COLONEL PICKERING	.	.		Philip Merivale.
FREDDY EYNSFORD-HILL		.		Algernon Grieg.
ALFRED DOOLITTLE	.	.		Edmund Gurney.
BYSTANDER .	.	.		Roy Byford.
ANOTHER ONE	.	.	.	Alexander Sarner.
ELIZA DOOLITTLE .		.	.	Mrs Patrick Campbell.
MRS EYNSFORD-HILL	.	.		Carlotta Addison.
MISS EYNSFORD-HILL	.	.		Margaret Bussé.
MRS HIGGINS	.	.	.	Rosamond Mayne-Young.
MRS PEARCE	.	.	.	Geraldine Oliffe.
PARLOURMAID	.	.	.	Irene Delisse.

Revived: February 10, 1920, Aldwych — Mrs Patrick Campbell (Eliza).

New York: October 20, 1914, Park Theatre; December 1914, Liberty Theatre; March 24, 1915, Irving Palace — Mrs Patrick Campbell as Eliza.

ST JOAN

First performed: New York, December 28, 1923, by the Theatre Guild (Winifred Lenihan in the title part). First London performance: New, March 26, 1924. Cast:

ROBERT DE BAUDRICOURT	Shayle Gardner.
STEWARD	Francis Hope.
JOAN	Sybil Thorndike.
BERTRAND DE POULENGY	Victor Lewisohn.
ARCHBISHOP OF RHEIMS	Robert Cunningham.
MGR DE LA TRÉMOUILLE (Constable of France)	Bruce Winston.
COURT PAGE	Sam Pickles.
GILLES DE RAIS (Bluebeard)	Milton Rosmer.
CAPTAIN LA HIRE	Raymond Massey.
THE DAUPHIN (later Charles VII)	Ernest Thesiger.
DUCHESS DE LA TRÉMOUILLE	Beatrice Smith.
DUNOIS, BASTARD OF ORLEANS	Robert Horton.
DUNOIS' PAGE	Jack Hawkins.
RICHARD DE BEAUCHAMP (Earl of Warwick)	E. Lyall Swete.
CHAPLAIN DE STOGUMBER	Lewis T. Casson.
PETER CAUCHON (Bishop of Beauvais)	Eugene Leahy.
WARWICK'S PAGE	Sidney Bromley.
THE INQUISITOR	O. B. Clarence.
D'ESTIVET (Canon of Bayeaux)	Raymond Massey.
DE COURCELLES (Canon of Paris)	Francis Hope.
BROTHER MARTIN LADVENU	Lawrence Anderson.
EXECUTIONER	Victor Lewishon.
ENGLISH SOLDIER	Kenneth Kent.
GENTLEMAN	Matthew Forsyth.

SHOWING UP OF BLANCO POSNET

First performed: Abbey Theatre, Dublin, August 25, 1909, by the Irish National Theatre Society's Company, and repeated by them at a production under the auspices of the

Incorporated Stage Society, at the Aldwych, December 5 and 6, 1909. Cast:

BABSY	.	.	Eileen O'Doherty.
LOTTIE	.	.	Daisy Reddy.
HANNAH	.	.	Sheila O'Sullivan.
JESSIE	.	.	Mary Nairn.
EMMA	.	.	Eithne Magee.
ELDER DANIELS	.	.	Arthur Sinclair.
BLANCO POSNET	.	.	Fred. O'Donovan.
STRAPPER KEMP	.	.	J. M. Kerrigan.
FEEMY EVANS	.	.	Sara Allgood.
SHERIFF KEMP	.	.	Sydney J. Morgan.
FOREMAN OF JURY	.	.	J. A. O'Rourke.
NESTOR	.	.	John Carrick.
WAGGONER JOE	.	.	Eric Gorman.
THE WOMAN	.	.	Maire O'Neill.

WIDOWERS' HOUSES

First produced: Independent Theatre Society, Royalty, December 9, 1892. Cast:

HARRY TRENCH	.	.	W. J. Robertson.
COKANE	.	.	Arthur Whittaker.
SARTORIUS	.	.	T. Wigney Percival.
LICKCHEESE	.	.	James Welch.
WAITER	.	.	E. P. Donne.
PORTER	.	.	W. Alison.
BLANCHE	.	.	Florence Farr.
ANNIE	.	.	N. de Silva.

Revival: June 7, 1909, Coronet—Basil Dean (Waiter), Lewis Casson (Trench), Mona Limerick (Blanche); Matinee, Coronet, March 8, 1912.

New York: 1907, March 7, Herold Square.

YOU NEVER CAN TELL

First produced: Royalty, by Stage Society, November 26, 1899; May 2, 1900, Strand. Cast:

FERGUS CRAMPTON	.	.	Herman Vezin.
MR BOHUN, Q.C.	.	.	Charles Charrington.

PLAY PRODUCTIONS

FINCH M'COMUS . . .	George Raimond.
MR VALENTINE . . .	Yorke Stephens.
PHILIP CLANDON . . .	W. Graham Browne.
JO	Leopold Profeit.
WAITER	James Welch.
PARLOURMAID . . .	Alice Powell.
MRS CLANDON . . .	Elsie Chester.
DOLLY CLANDON . . .	Audrey Ford.
GLORIA CLANDON . . .	Mabel Terry Lewis.

Revived: May 2, 1905, Court—Granville Barker (Valentine), Louis Calvert (Waiter), Nigel Playfair (Bohun), Miss Sydney Fairbrother (Dolly), Tita Brand (Gloria); July 9, 1906, Court—Henry Ainley (Valentine), James Hearn (Bohun), Lillah McCarthy (Gloria), Dorothy Minto (Dolly), Henrietta Watson (Mrs Clandon); September 16, 1907, Savoy—Harcourt Williams (Valentine), Ellen O'Malley (Gloria).

New York: 1905, Garrick.

Berlin: 1906, September 24, Kleines.

Paris: 1913, January 28, Théâtre des Arts.